*

*

*

COMING REVOLUTIONS
IN
BLACK AFRICA

By

S.Adebanji Akintoye, Ph.D.

Former Director of African Studies, Obafemi Awolowo
University, Nigeria
and
Former Nigerian Senator

Published by Pathfinder Media LLC.
3331 Toledo Terrace, Suite D 108
Hyattsville, Maryland 20782. USA
Printed in the United States of America.

ISBN:978-0615843971

C O N T E N T S

DEDICATION

THIS BOOK IS DEDICATED TO THE YOUTH OF
BLACK AFRICA
AT HOME AND ABROAD

This is a new moment of great promise. Only this time - - - it will not be giants like Nkrumah and Kenyatta who will determine Africa's future. Instead, it will be you – the men and women - - - the young people brimming with talent and energy and hope, who can claim the future that so many in previous generations never realized.

~ President Barack Obama at the Ghana Parliament,
Accra, July 11, 2009.

Our answer is the world's hope; it is to rely on youth...the qualities of youth, not a time of life but a state of mind, a temper of the will, a quality of the imagination, a preponderance of courage over timidity, of the appetite for adventure over the love of ease.

~ Robert F. Kennedy at the University of Cape Town,
Union of South Africa, June 6, 1966

Political Map of Africa, 2013

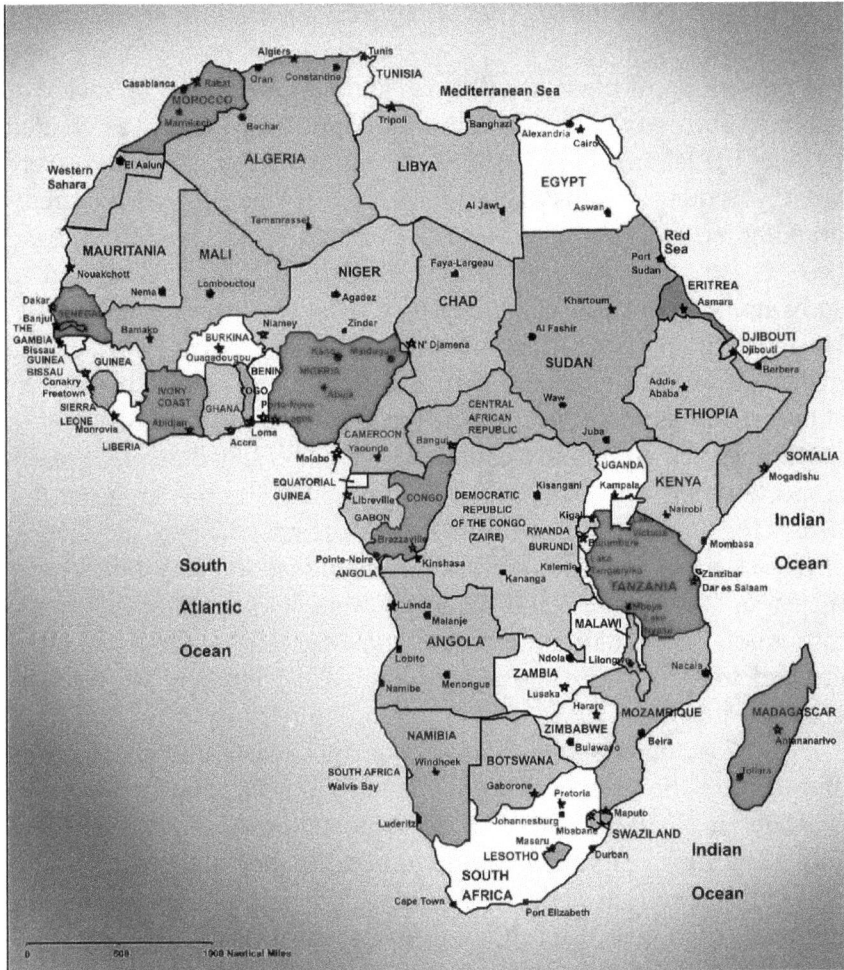

Prologue: *Subcontinent Trapped on a Path to Ruin*

My perception of the Black African situation is from deep inside of it. I was born only 21 years after my country, Nigeria, was created by the British in 1914. By 1914, my father and mother were already young adults getting ready to marry. My great-grandfather, who had ruled our small kingdom for over fifty years, had passed away just as the first British officials had started to show up, in about 1899, in our part of what was to become Nigeria. His cousin, the new king, was the ruler who gave most of the missionaries, as well as the British officials, the land to build their stations. My grandfather, whom the first local British officials in our hometown commonly called "Great Chief", had been a greatly respected member of the group of high chiefs in our kingdom for nearly ten years before the first British officials visited. He died in 1929, six years before I was born. His oldest son (my father) and many of my uncles and cousins were chiefs of our people throughout the colonial era and experienced at first hand the cultural transformations, and the cultural disruptions, wrought by colonial rule.

Most of my schooling was in the years after the Second World War, the years made unbelievably intoxicating by the noise of Nigerian "nationalism" and the expectation of "independence". In the last four years before Nigeria became independent in 1960, I was a student in Nigeria's only university institution, the University College, Ibadan, an overseas college of the University of London. I became one of the leaders in the politics of the student community, was president or secretary of a number of student organizations, and very proudly represented my country in many international student conferences in various parts of the world. Representing Nigeria abroad, in those magical years, was a thing out of this world. Among other things, it created the circumstance that I came to know, at fairly close range, some of Africa's "nationalist" leaders of the time (later rulers of independent African countries), as I skipped around Africa in meetings and conferences of the excitable crowd of us who, on the fringes of the nationalist whirlwind preceding independence, presumed ourselves to be "Africa's youth leaders" – or, more ambitiously, "Africa's future leaders".

On graduating from university, and while teaching high school, I became one of the national youth leaders of one of Nigeria's leading political parties. Soon after I started graduate school, I was nominated (I usually say 'drafted') by the people of my home constituency, in Nigeria's first post-independence Federal election (1964), as candidate for a seat in the Nigerian Federal House of Representatives. According to some in the news media, I was, Nigeria-wide, the youngest candidate in that historic election. The fraudulent manipulation and rigging of that election started the newly independent Nigeria on the path to disorder, conflicts, mass killings, military coups, a sanguinary civil war, and a political culture of fraud, corruption and confusion.

During the decades of military rule, I completed graduate school in African History and then taught and wrote on that subject – and became the Director of African Studies in one of Nigeria's leading universities. Then I took part in founding, and serving on the leadership of, a major political party, and was elected to the Nigerian Senate in 1979. From the opposition benches in the Nigerian Senate, I witnessed at very close range, for four years, a civilian chapter in the brutalization and wrecking of Nigeria under a vicious weight of lawlessness, fraud and corruption. To our cries of alarm from the opposition benches about the disaster that was being compounded, the government countered that we were mere prophets of doom.

The predictable economic collapse came. Another predictable military coup and military dictatorship followed. The new military dictators, posturing at first as non-partisan, in the end threw the powers of state more against us former members of the opposition who had relentlessly fought against the corruption in the civilian government.

I found myself, in the company of tens like me, in detention in prison without charge or trial for months. As I walked away from prison after my release, I had become convinced that those of us who thought we could promote open democratic politics and accountable leadership in Nigeria and turn Nigeria around need to rethink. And what was true of Nigeria was roughly true of most countries of Black Africa.

In the months after my release from detention, it became obvious that our military rulers were very edgy about well informed and politically influential persons like me. After I was re-arrested and interrogated – on suspicion, I learnt later, of joining with some other college professors to plot against the military rulers – I knew I needed to move my family out of their way and beyond their reach. And indeed, not long after we left, one military regime did unleash a murderous reign of terror against the elite of some of the nationalities of Nigeria, particularly mine.

In the two decades that followed, the Nigerian military regimes and their civilian cronies virtually went on and wrecked Nigeria. By 2005, many informed people in the world, including researchers close to United States policy-making agencies, were predicting that Nigeria could soon break up. By 2010, Nigeria's National Bureau of Statistics announced that 60.9% of Nigerians were living in "absolute poverty" and that more and more Nigerians were falling into the same condition. Violent crimes, inter-ethnic and religious conflicts, and organized terrorism, were spewing steams of blood across the face of Nigeria.

My Hopes for Africa

Africa is my love. As college student, professor and elected public official, I traveled and interacted extensively in Africa, intent on understanding its life and its affairs. For me, the euphoria of Africa remains strong. The duty that goes with the privileges of ancestry, education and elevation remains compelling also. Hence this little book, this personal statement – this blending of insight, love, outrage and hope. Leading ones among men should not fear to look even the ugliest facts squarely in the face.

Black Africa has suffered abominably, even as its leading citizens refuse to recognize the facts and handle the truth. Since 2002, a very major effort has been on to restructure and re-energize the Pan-African muscle for better effect on Africa's affairs. But, for this to succeed in reconstructing Africa and setting it on the path of political peace, sanity and progress, it must strive beyond merely seeking continental security. African governments, African leaders, African peoples, in our various countries, cannot afford to continue to operate as they have done since independence – cannot afford to continue to live on assumptions, claims, and expectations that have no basis in reality, that negate the basic rights and dignity of man, and that generate political storms and human suffering. For the rest of the world too to help meaningfully and effectually, they need to understand.

Obviously because I am a product of Black Africa, I rate the political devastations, and the consequent poverty, the seriously inhibited progress, and the suffering, in my Black African subcontinent as the world's most troubling challenge of our time. What we have here is a whole subcontinent of some 500 million people trapped in a path to more and more suffering. The rest of the world is duty-bound to help, and the rest of the world can help in very many ways. It is my humble hope that the pages that follow offer some useful understanding of the Sub-Saharan African political disaster of our time, as well as some pointers to how it can be helped.

Dark clouds of upheavals and revolutions hang over the countries of Sub-Saharan (or Black) Africa. Strangely, exactly two weeks after I completed writing my first draft of this book in December 2010 and sent it to colleagues and friends for their comments, the massive upheavals in the countries of the other region of Africa, Mediterranean Africa, began in Tunisia, and quickly spilled over into Egypt and then Libya. I had to hold back further action on the draft and wait to watch the events in Mediterranean Africa unfold.

Countries of Black Africa, like those of Mediterranean Africa, are heading for revolutions too. However, between the "revolutionary dynamics" in the Mediterranean African countries and those in the Sub-Saharan African countries, there are very significant differences. The similarities consist of mass rejections of dictatorship, lack of freedom, corruption, and deepening, grinding, poverty. The big difference is that in Sub-Saharan Africa, the upheavals against the same evils are sure to be set against the background of serious ethnic complexities and are therefore likely to be more confusing and probably more destructive.

The root of the complexity is deep inside Black Africa's political history and consciousness. First, Black Africa arrived in the modern world as a sub-continent of mostly very small nationalities. Secondly, the problems inherent in that reality was further confused and compounded by the European imperialist creators of today's Black African countries – countries that should never have been created or that should never have been structured in their present forms. And thirdly, since independence, Black Africa's characteristic pattern of politics and leadership has relentlessly advanced its difficulties into the making of very complex poverty and conflicts, producing almost continual explosions of inter-ethnic violence, pogroms and acts of genocide. If any of the coming revolutions in Black Africa go violent, their violence in many countries is almost certain to be something radically, and shockingly, different from what the world has seen in the streets of Tunis or Cairo or Tripoli.

Thus, since Africa's "Independence Decade", the 1960's, Sub-Saharan Africa has been continually devastated by political storms. From the valley of the Senegal on the westernmost coasts of West Africa to Somalia's Horn of Africa, and from the valley of the Upper Nile in Sudan to the valleys of the Limpopo and Zambezi in Southern Africa, the trends are the same. Relentlessly, the lives of the peoples of these countries are being buffeted by virtually intractable political disorder, mind-boggling public corruption, rigged and violently disputed elections, military *coups d'état*, military regimes marked by crude power and graft, civil wars, blood-curdling inter-ethnic conflicts, pogroms, ethnic cleansing, genocide, and more.

The world greeted the independence of these Black African countries in the 1960's with hope and optimism. By the last years of the century, the hope had turned mostly to shock and dismay. And as the 21st century advances, the rest of the world appears to stand at a bewildered arm's length from the Black African political nightmare, uncertain how to relate to it.

Why? Why have Black African governments and political parties tended to fracture into passionately, irreconcilably, hostile factions? Why have Black African elections been so often marred by rigging and violence? Why are political violence, mass murders, civil wars, and massive displacements of people so rampant in Black Africa? Why have men trained in the same army in so many Black African countries tended to break up into hostile bands that seek nothing less than the extermination of one another?

Why have neighbors who have raised their children together on the same streets and worshipped together in the same churches or mosques been known to turn against one another in orgies of the grossest human carnage in so many Black African countries? Why have Black African men and women educated at the expense of their countries and then vested with power to lead their countries turned, almost invariably, into autocrats and glorified robbers. Why are so many African rulers intent only on accumulating limitless power and wealth for themselves, in callous indifference to sharply deteriorating economic and social conditions among their countrymen?

Far much more importantly, what is the way out of this morass? Can the Africans themselves find such a way? And how can the rest of the world help? This is the over-arching challenge of Black Africa in our times. But it is not a challenge for Africans alone; it is a challenge for the whole of mankind. And it is a very desperate challenge indeed.

In this era of great, profound and rapid changes in the world, Sub-Saharan Africa is not marching in tandem with the rest of the world. This three-fourths of Africa is falling dangerously behind the rest of the world. Poverty, disease, starvation, destitution – all continue to be more visible in Black Africa than in other continents, and their scope and severity seem to be escalating in many of its countries.

Of the causes of this sad state of affairs, political instability takes the lead. In terms of natural resources, the African continent is one of the richest parts of the earth. But the political storms are causing serious distractions and disruptions and destroying incalculable assets. They are also forcing out of the continent large numbers of educated young people and thus bleeding the sub-continent of major parts of its most productive human capital.

Much of the returns on investments in education in many Black African countries are wasted through unemployment and under-employment. Much of the rest are lost as the young educated flee out to feed the skilled labor needs of other lands in the world. And the outcome is that these emigrants' homelands are left with a low, and even declining, capacity to take advantage of the development tools being generated by the contemporary world.

The gap between Africa and the developed world widens relentlessly. Other regions of the Third World increasingly outpace Black Africa in development. United Nations and other international agencies often tell the world that the 21st century might be Africa's century. And here and there on the sub-continent, the statistics have been showing some increases in gross domestic products. However, if this sub-continent's political devastations persist, it is difficult to see how it can come to turn the corner significantly any time soon. Moreover, even if significant economic growth does materialize, how can the masses of the people of a country benefit much from it since the political elite arrogate virtually all the gains to themselves and keep alive the curse of political instability and conflicts?

What many observers saw as some ray of hope in the situation arose, as would be remembered, in 2002, when the Pan-African concert took the promising step of replacing the Organization of African Unity with the African Union. Under this new umbrella, Africa embarked on crafting ambitious measures for security on the continent. The structures and institutions being established under the new initiative, their general thrust, and the apparent commitment and seriousness of their creators, should raise hopes in the world that Africans themselves have arisen to recreate the life and destiny of their continent.

However, even if this promising Pan-African initiative comes to perform at maximum efficiency, while the present patterns of political reality and behavior in country after country in Black Africa remain substantially unchanged, Black Africa would still not overcome its terrible political debacle. Ultimately, the center of truly transformational change has to be in the political life of every country. Without a major shift to a clearly more realistic perception of their countries by the leading citizens of Sub-Saharan African countries, and without a consequent change of approach to the issues of politics, human rights, ethnic national rights, and nation building in each country, even the most ambitious Pan-African construct will change nothing. In short, irrespective of the African Union, violent revolutions seem inevitable – and even imminent – in most of Black Africa.

The central proposition and hope of this book is that the needed change, the revolution, can, and should, be peacefully accomplished. I see the founding and the structural details of the African Union as evidence of sincere desires among African leaders to engineer peaceful change on our continent. But the African Union is insufficient, because it commands no means of changing the ways in which the rulers of individual Black African countries perceive and run the affairs of their countries. If change does not begin manifestly to materialize inside the political lives of our many countries, then Black Africa may become the scene of a new rash of violent upheavals and conflicts much more devastating than the world has seen so far even in that region of the world.

One of the reasons why the Black African political situation has been so tenacious and so difficult to tackle is that it is so little understood. Most people outside of Africa hear of Black Africa's political explosions and see on their television screens the pictures of the horrendous carnage, the massive human displacements, and the barbarism of terrorist movements and of refugee camps, without understanding why those things are happening there. Even inside Black Africa itself, probably most people do not really understand what is wrong with their countries and societies. Even among some of the most educated Africans, clear knowledge and understanding are quite often replaced by woolly patriotic hope. Where, in all reality, what is called a country is no more than a fragile bubble or a badly disjointed contraption, it is common to meet well educated Africans exuberating about their country – when they should be seriously engaged in asking the question how their so-called country can be made to become a proper country.

This short book hopes to provoke Africans, and the rest of the world, to ask questions about, in order to understand, the Black African political troubles, and thereby save Black Africa from further, and more damaging, political disasters.

Including Ethiopia and Liberia

Among the countries of Black Africa, Liberia in West Africa and Ethiopia in Northeastern Africa are different in one significant respect – namely, that they were neither created nor ruled by European imperialists. The ancient Empire of Ethiopia crushed an Italian attempt at conquest in 1896. Some decades later, in the 1930's to the 1940s, it managed again to get rid of another Italian imposture. Liberia was created in the 1820's by a group of African Americans from the United States who (returning to their homeland) came to the West African coast, staked a claim to a large expanse of territory, and proclaimed a country. Later in the century, when European states began the scramble for African territorial possessions, Liberia lost big slices of its territory to them, but it did survive as an independent country. Nevertheless, the developments in Ethiopia and Liberia find a place in this book because they both share the same realities as the other countries of the sub-region and came to be swept along in the turmoil wracking the countries around them.

Political Map of Africa, 2013

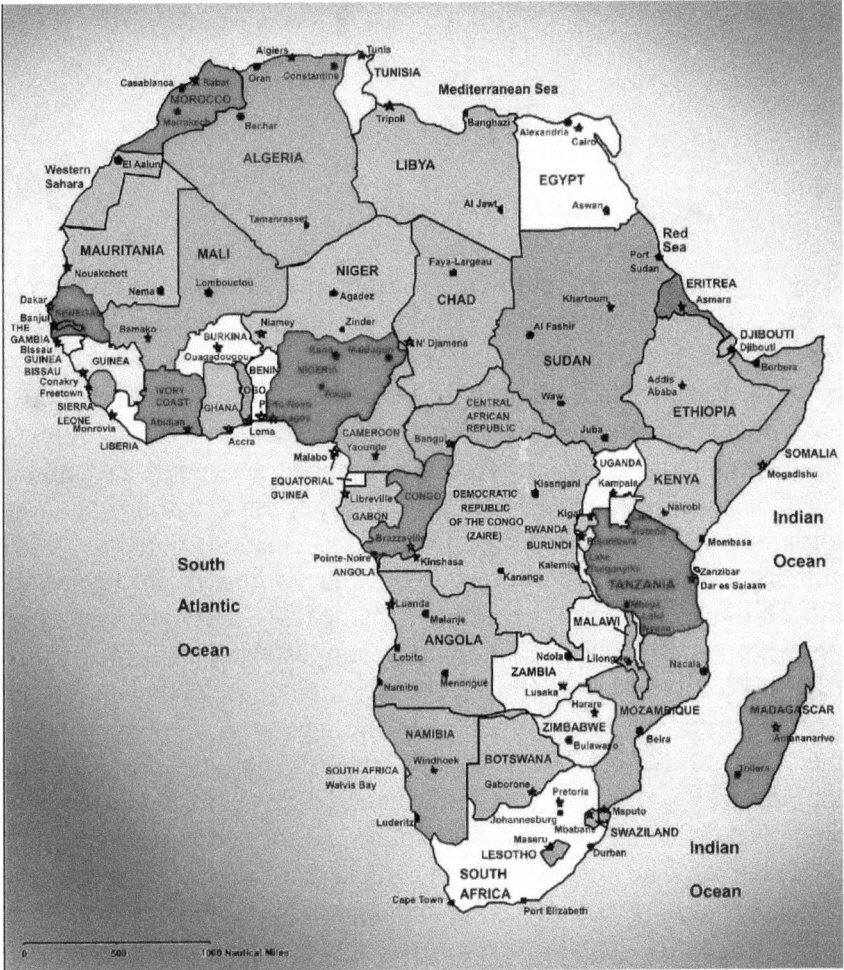

CHAPTER ONE

A Plague on all our Houses?

The drums of political disaster and failure began to roll over Africa as soon as various African countries achieved independence from European rule in the 1960's. They have continued to roll more than fifty years later: in   rigged elections, horrendous communal violence, military coups d'état, counter-coups and more coups, inter-ethnic carnage and pogroms, ethnic cleansing and genocide, well-armed rebel movements and war lords out of control, states gripped in the chaos of collapse of all authority and order, the horrors of displaced hordes on the move, the chilling barbarism of refugee camps — a whole continent pock-marked by zones of unrelenting tempests and turmoil.

Political troubles in Black Africa since independence have developed in two broad phases, the first spanning the period from the 1960s to the late 1970s; the second from roughly the 1980s to the present – the one dovetailing imperceptibly into the other. The first phase is dealt with in this chapter, and the second phase in the next chapter. The general difference between the two phases is that the latter has been much more destructive, and much more tortuous. Most of the crises of the earlier phase featured overthrows of governments, but in the latter phase, most of the crises have featured horrific inter-ethnic clashes, resulting in mass killings, massive displacements of people, and some of the largest and most dehumanizing refugee camps in the world.[1]

Following upon these two phases, there has followed some lull in some of our countries in Sub-Saharan Africa. In the light of such a lull, many observers have, in recent times, been breathing a sigh of relief and voicing optimistic predictions about the political future of Sub-Saharan Africa. Naturally, out of love and duty, any African would wish that these optimistic predictions should come to be fulfilled. But, also out of love and duty, no African should engage in self-deception about the true character and direction of the powerful political undercurrents that are shaping Sub-Saharan Africa's political future – powerful political forces that are preparing the ground for a third, most complex, most transformational, and probably most violent phase of the sub-region's political turmoil.

The four-year period between June 1965 and May 1969 alone witnessed the staggering number of fourteen military coups on the Black Africa sub-continent — Congo (Kinshasa) in November 1965, Dahomey (later Benin Republic) in December 1965, Central African Republic in January 1966, Nigeria in January 1966, Upper Volta (later Burkina-Faso) in January 1966, Ghana in February 1966, Nigeria again in July 1966, Burundi in November 1966, Togo in January 1967, Sierra Leone in March 1967, Sierra Leone again in April 1968, Congo Brazzaville in August 1968, Mali in November 1968, Sudan in May 1969. After 1970, the annual averages of coups eased off somewhat. But the storm of coups has continued, so that, as these words are being written, of about forty-five Sub-Saharan African countries, almost all have experienced military coups.[2]

Either in the act or in the aftermath, the turmoil and the power seizures of the sixties and seventies resulted in the violent deaths of hundreds of high public officials. The first Prime Minister of the Congo Democratic Republic (later Zaire, and now Congo again), was killed violently, within months of the country's independence, by people of parts of his country that were hostile to him.

In Nigeria, the Prime Minister and one of his senior ministers as well as two of three Regional Premiers were killed in the January 1966 coup; a military Head of State and a Regional Governor were killed in another coup six months later, and yet another military Head of State in 1975.

In Ethiopia in 1974, the revolutionaries who had seized the government executed 59 former ministers and senior functionaries of the ousted imperial government, including two former Prime Ministers, and are widely believed to have strangled the deposed emperor. And in Ghana, after one of the coups in 1979, all three surviving former Heads of State and five senior military officers who had taken part in government met their ends facing firing squads.

Even worse than these political assassinations and executions, accounts of some inter-ethnic clashes, pogroms and genocide in Africa shocked the world in the sixties and seventies. In late 1966, tens of thousands of ethnic Igbo of Eastern Nigeria lost their lives in the streets of Northern Nigerian cities and towns, in days of sordid, unrestrained slaughter by their Northern Nigerian countrymen.

In Uganda, under the Idi Amin regime in the seventies, deliberate slaughter of members of certain ethnic groups and destruction of their villages seemed to form part of government policy. Accounts of genocide from the Republic of Sudan were even more shocking, being more persistent. The Sudanese government, controlled by the Muslim Arab people of Northern Sudan, pursued policies of slaughter and destruction of the non-Muslim Black peoples of southern Sudan. The Sudanese army and air-force were sent in to wipe out villages, hospitals and schools. Southern Sudan became the scene of some of the worst refugee and humanitarian disasters in the world.

Usually a concomitant of the inter-ethnic conflicts, civil wars were also a common event in tropical African countries in the sixties and seventies. Congo (Kinshasa), Nigeria, Chad and Sudan were scenes of destructive civil wars.

In presenting all this turmoil in this first chapter and the next, we shall adopt a country-by country approach, focusing on selected countries. This is to drive home the profundity of the disarray of the countries of Black Africa, and the virtual incapability of their ruling classes to change their ways and effect change for the better for their countries. The same trends have been going on, and even worsening, in nearly every country, from decade to decade, and from regime to regime (civilian and military), and, for some countries, no change seems to be in sight even as this is being written in the fifth decade after the "independence decade".

Congo (Kinshasa)

The Congo Democratic Republic, Africa's second largest country in territory at independence, became independent of Belgian rule on January 30, 1960. Six days later, the collapse of the country began. Congolese soldiers in the country's army, angry that their own government did not immediately replace their Belgian officers with Congolese indigenes, mutinied against their Belgian officers and committed acts of violence against resident Belgians in some parts of the country. Belgium responded by flying troops into the country to protect Belgian citizens. Following an incident involving a Belgian naval force in the coastal city of Matadi, an incident in which some Congolese were killed, the Congolese soldiers intensified attacks on Belgian residents.

But, in essence, the trouble with the Belgians was no more than the surface of a much deeper problem. The government of the country simply did not have the capacity or strength to maintain order and hold together this huge country of great ethnic and geographic diversity. On July 11, mineral-rich Katanga Province announced its secession from the Congo Republic. On August 8, South Kasai Province followed suit and announced secession.

Then the collapse attained utmost heights as the government itself began to disintegrate. The two leaders of the government, President Joseph Kasavubu and Prime Minister Patrice Lumumba, who belonged to different parts of the country and had never really known each other well, fell out. On September 5, Kasavubu announced the removal of Lumumba as Prime-minister, and Lumumba responded by announcing the removal of Kasavubu as President. The chaos that thus ensued reached its climax with the arrest and assassination of Lumumba by some elements of the Congolese army in January 1961. The termination of this first-generation of conflicts and civil war in the Congo Democratic Republic can be dated to November 25, 1965, the date on which Joseph Mobutu (better known to history by his chosen name of Mobutu Sese Seko), by then Commander-in-Chief of the Congolese army, seized control of the government of the country.[3]

Fig. 1: *Patrice Lumumba, first Prime Minister of Congo Democratic Republic.*

Republic of Sudan

The Republic of Sudan, the country with the largest territorial size in Africa at independence, was almost continuously engulfed in civil war for over fifty years from the date of its independence in 1956. In fact, its civil war had commenced some months before its day of independence. In 1955, as the country prepared for independence, soldiers from the seriously marginalized southern provinces of Sudan mutinied against their northern commanders and formed a guerrilla army with the name of Anya Nya. The semi-independent northern-led government of the country ordered the invasion of the southern provinces. In the midst of this, the British granted independence to the country in 1956, and the hostilities escalated, with the northern army pursuing a policy of totally destroying orderly life in the south – destroying schools and hospitals, wiping out countless villages, killing countless women and children, and forcing millions to flee their homes into the forests – very many perishing in destitution and starvation, and the rest ending up in desperately poor and savage refugee camps and displaced peoples' camps. The massive human flights quickly brought distress into the territories of Sudan's neighbors – Central African Republic, Congo Republic, Ethiopia, Chad, Uganda and Kenya.

A Northern military officer, Gaafar Mohamed al-Nimeiri, seized the government of Sudan in 1969, and decided that the way to end division and conflict in the country (that is, to achieve national unity), was to pursue a vigorous policy of culturally assimilating the south to the north. He therefore embarked on a policy of employing the powers of the government to force the peoples of the South, who were mostly Christians or followers of various indigenous religions, to accept the Islamic religion of the northerners. While the Northern army continued to rampage and destroy, the government ordered the building of mosques and koranic schools, the teaching of the Arabic language of the north, and the establishment of Islamic law. Although politics in the North resulted in the ouster of this general in 1964, the Northern rulers who followed after him all continued the policy of forcible assimilation of the South.

As the conflicts in the South increased in ferocity, neighboring countries became restless, and worried voices were raised in the world. These, combined with sharp problems in the politics of northern Sudan itself, compelled the Sudan government to seek peace in 1971. The outcome was a peace meeting in Addis Ababa, in Ethiopia, in 1972, between the leaders of the North and South of Sudan, and the making of an agreement bringing the war to an end, the dissolution of Anya Nya and its integration into Sudan's National Army, and the agreement to grant some internal autonomy to the southern provinces. The first generation of Sudan's civil wars thus came to an end.[4]

Nigeria

Nigeria, Africa's most populous country (the home of about one-fourth of the population of Black Africa), became independent of British rule on October 1, 1960 – as a federation of three states called Regions (Eastern, Northern, and Western Regions). Less than two years later, the country stumbled into serious political problems. Under a pre-independence constitution which had come into effect in 1951-2, the three Regions had enjoyed some limited autonomy and self-government, allowing indigenous politicians to govern their Regions under British supervision. During those years, the three Regions had seen commendable progress in many directions of development. One of the Regions, the Western, had done considerably better than the other two – had, in fact, become the development pace-setter in education and many other facets of modernization in the Nigerian federation.

Nigeria's First Prime Minister
Rh.Sir Abubakar Tafawa Balewa

Fig.2: *The four rulers of the Nigerian Federation at Independence [Tafawa Balewa, Obafemi Awolowo, Nnamdi Azikiwe, Ahmadu Bello]*

At independence in 1960, the Western Region's mainstream leadership was not included in the executive arm of the Federal Government but constituted the official opposition in the federal parliament. Suddenly in 1962, the parties in alliance in the Federal Government, citing a political disagreement in the party ruling the Western Region, declared a state of emergency over the Western Region, suspended its elected government, arrested and detained its mainstream political leaders, and clamped an appointed emergency administrator on the Region.

These actions brought the Federal Government into conflict with the majority of the Western Region's citizens. The confrontation continued to deepen until late 1965, when massive federal-backed electoral fraud in the Western Region's election of a new Regional Government finally ignited a huge political conflagration which destroyed countless homes and lives, virtually shut down the authority of the Federal Government and the fraudulently elected Regional Government in many parts of the Western Region, and shook the whole Federation to its foundations. Overwhelmed by the enormity and stubbornness of the rebellion, the Federal authorities unwittingly, but gradually, abdicated control to the Police and the Armed Forces. Early in the morning of January 16, 1966, some elements of the Nigerian army took action, abducted and killed the federal Prime Minister and the federal Minister of Finance and, beyond the federal capital city, killed the Premiers of the Western Region and the Northern Region. The coup makers were a handful of middle-level officers from the army; the army itself and its top command were not involved and were totally surprised. It was not clear what, in the hands of the coup makers, was going to become of the country. However, the leadership of the army then stepped forth and seized the Federal and Regional governments, abrogated the Constitution, and proceeded to rule the country by their own decrees.

But all of these were still no more than the prologue to a very big drama of national fragmentation, horrendous blood-letting, and years of bitter, sanguinary, civil war. The military government, led by an officer from the Igbo nationality of the Eastern Region, embarked on policies that appeared to be aimed at eliminating the Regions and drawing all power to the federal centre, thereby provoking anger widely, especially in the Northern Region. In May 1966, masses of citizens of the Northern Region exploded and, for days, went around in their towns killing Igbo residents. In July 1966, a faction of the army (led by officers of Northern Region origin) struck, killed the Head of the Federal Military Government and the Military Governor of the Western Region, and proclaimed itself the government of the country. There then followed a resumption of the killings of Igbo residents

23

in the north. For the next three months, this pogrom crested in wave after wave. By the time it finally subsided, it had taken (according to most popular estimates) the lives of more than 40,000 Igbo men, women and children. From all over the country, Igbo nationals fled to their own Eastern Region.

After months of deadlock and futile negotiations, the Igbo people finally, in May 1967, announced the secession of their Region from Nigeria and the creation of their own new country with the name of Biafra. The Federal Military Government responded by ordering the army to stamp out the secession, and a civil war ensued. The bitter civil war was to go on until 1970, after taking more than one million lives, many of those through starvation and massive displacement of people in the Eastern Region. With the end of this destructive war, the first generation of Nigeria's political storms ended.[5]

Benin Republic

Nigeria's immediate neighbor to the west, Benin Republic, is a small country of about 70,000 square miles and a population of about eight million at independence in 1960. But it contains about forty ethnic groups. This country bore the name Dahomey under the French, but a few years after independence it changed its name to Benin.

Happily, in this country, inter-ethnic conflict has never played out in violence or bloodletting, but it has been very real indeed – in fact, according to Denis Amoussou-Yeye, it is "omnipresent" in all of the socio-economic and socio-political life of the country. In the years of French colonial rule, responses to colonial rule varied from ethnic group to ethnic group. Then, from the moment in the late 1950s when the French allowed Constitutional changes that introduced elective politics, ethnic confrontations became the major defining factor in the ensuing politics – in the evolution of the political groupings, the choice of election candidates, the daily maneuvers and deals. The fact that the country was very poor at independence, and very poor in natural resources, has served as a sad backdrop to all its affairs. A broad political division between the South and the North roughly crystallized, but each of the South and North nevertheless had internal ethnic fragmentations of its own.

In the midst of this tortuous ethnic web, the country became independent in1960. In the years after independence, the impact of ethnic rivalries in Benin politics became one of the most intense in Africa. In particular, the struggle for the country's highest political position, the position of Head of State, became so frenetic as to rule out any political stability. Soon after independence, ostensibly for the purpose of fostering national unity, the party of the incumbent Head of State maneuvered the country into a one-party state.

In thus opting for a one-party state, the rulers of Benin were merely doing something that was quite common in Africa at the time. In most countries of Africa, the strongest political groupings advocated the one-party state as the surest cure for the centrifugal forces of "sectionalism" and "tribalism". But, as in all other African countries where it was opted for, the one-party state quickly failed in Benin. More than in any other African country, the so-called party of national unity in Benin was a huge self-deception. The mostly ethnic-based groupings in it more or less openly preserved their independent existence. The persistent failure of this country to find some generally acceptable mode for managing its ethnic fragmentation was subsequently to result in various kinds of constitutional and political experimentation – including a short stint with a three-man Presidential Commission or Provisional Government (essentially a three-man presidency). Almost inevitably, as in almost all other Black African countries, there came military intervention in Benin's political life, and the emergence of military dictatorships. Between 1963 and 1972, Benin experienced six military coups.

The military officer who seized power in 1972, Matthew Kerekou, was to have the longest military regime of all – he held power until 1989. Searching frantically for some formula that would unify and stabilize the country under him, Kerekou first declared a "populist" revolution of youths, workers and women, and established a political party to promote the revolution; then he moved on to what he called a socialist revolution based on Marxist-Leninist principles; and, ultimately, he returned to what his regime had really been from the beginning – namely, a nebulous and corrupt military dictatorship. When by 1989 his regime was no longer able to pay even the basic salaries of public employees, Kerekou's time as dictator was up. The return that was then made to civilian politics has seen considerably less turmoil, but the basic problems of fragmentation and economic poverty have remained.[6]

Fig. 3: *Matthew Kerekou, Military ruler of Benin Republic, 1972-89*

Ghana

The British colony of the Gold Coast became independent in 1957 and immediately changed its name to Ghana. This was the first Black African country to achieve independence, and it and the man who guided it to independence, Dr. Kwame Nkrumah, have a special place in the heart of Black African peoples. In both land area and population Ghana is a small country. Its population by 2006, after fifty years of rapid population growth, was estimated at 22 million. However, like almost all Black African countries created by European colonialism, Ghana is a country of many nations – a total of some forty-one. Of these nationalities, the largest are the Akan who occupy most of the southern provinces of Ghana. In many ways similar to the Yoruba of Nigeria, the Akan lived in a number of small kingdoms before the coming of British rule. Of these, the largest and most powerful was the Ashanti kingdom, about which more will be said in subsequent chapters. Another large people, the Ewe (Ghana's second largest nationality) inhabit Ghana's southeastern coastlands. Many small nationalities inhabit the northern provinces.

The political problems springing from Ghana's multi-nation composition were already very much alive even before the independence of the country. As soon as some measure of elective politics was introduced in the early 1950s, some of the different nations (the Ashanti and the Ewe, and some of the northern peoples) began to advocate some system of local autonomy that would enable them to manage some of their own affairs. Political parties arose to champion these demands. The Ashanti and the Ewe emerged as the leading voices in the movement. Ashanti and Ewe farmers produced almost all of Ghana's cocoa crop, Ghana's largest export crop and foreign exchange earner. Among other considerations, these two peoples wanted constitutional arrangements that would enable them to derive some more benefit from their own cocoa farming enterprise than the other peoples of Ghana would.

With the Ewe, there was a further complication. The colonial border split the Ewe between Ghana and the neighboring French territory of Togo. As the excitement of coming independence grew generally in Africa, Ewe nationalism stirred, the objective being to reunite the Ewe nation. Moreover, by some arrangement with France, the Ewe of Togo earned better prices for their cocoa exports than their Ghana kinsmen did for theirs. A movement arose among the Ewe of Ghana for separation from Ghana and unification with their kinsmen in Togo. Kwame Nkrumah's political party stood up as the true nationalist party to confront all these agitators, and in the pre-independence elections, some violent conflicts between it and their sectional parties flared in some parts of the country.

Fig. 4: *Dr. Kwame Nkrumah, first President of Ghana.*

None of the sectional demands were granted by the British before independence, and independent Ghana therefore plunged immediately into the agitations and troubles generated by them. As head of the new government, Nkrumah resolved that what the situation demanded of him was strength – strength to defeat all the sectional pressures and preserve the new country intact and strong. The conflicts were destined to impact Ghana's political history disastrously.

However, economic problems also arose to add to, and further complicate, the troubles facing the government. Structured by the colonial government to depend almost entirely on the export of one crop, cocoa, the economy began to weaken as a result of declines in the world market price of cocoa. That spelt havoc to Dr. Nkrumah's ambitious development plans, caused an intimidating build-up of foreign debts, and led to distress among Ghana's people.

Dr. Nkrumah only made things worse by shifting massively into a new socialist direction of economic planning and development. As the new measures further weakened the economy, made enemies for Nkrumah in the context of the worldwide Cold War, and intensified distress among the people, support for the government weakened rapidly, even at the highest levels of Dr. Nkrumah's party. Dr. Nkrumah responded with ever escalating strong-arm measures for dealing with the opposition, ultimately reaching a peak with a Preventive Detention Act which authorized the government to detain any citizen for as long as five years without any trial – even without any formal indictment. Some prominent politicians were so detained, and some others fled into exile abroad, including even some of the leading men in Dr. Nkrumah's original team. Allegations by the government that some prominent persons were plotting to assassinate the president added new venom to the politics of the country. Fervently supported by a rising crop of radical young politicians, Nkrumah turned the country, by law, into a one-party state, and withdrew more and more from the public. While he was away abroad on some state duty in June 1966, the Ghanaian military seized power. He was never able to return to the country.

Ghana thus entered into an era of military dictatorships, with short interludes of civilian politics and government. The new dispensation was to witness the rise of intense inter-ethnic rivalries. In particular, the Akan and the Ewe, who were initially happy to work together after the fall of Nkrumah, soon became bitter rivals. This came to draw the ethnic lines very sharply, sometimes so sharply as to make it risky, during some interludes of civilian politics, for people to support parties that were not led by their own ethnic kinsmen. Persistent accusations by the Ewe (Ghana's second largest nationality) that the Akan (the largest nationality) aspired to hegemony over Ghana kept the politics of Ghana confused and tense. Inevitably, such trends penetrated the military and the civil service and compromised their cohesion and efficiency. In the process, instability became intense, the country plunged into deeper and deeper economic distress, inviting repeated military interventions, and forcing large numbers of Ghana's people to migrate abroad, most of them to Nigeria where millions of them quickly accumulated. When Nigeria forcibly deported over one million of these, Ghana's problems became a great deal worse. In the midst of all the distress, accusations of corruption against all post-Nkrumah rulers of the county became popular. In that political frenzy, after one of the coups led by a young military officer named Jerry Rawlings in 1979, the three living former military rulers were arrested and summarily executed. Rawlings was to lead another coup later, and then, when yet another civilian constitution was instituted in 1992, he offered himself for election and was elected president of Ghana for a four-year term – and then reelected for another term in 1996.

How Ghana would manage its ethnic problems remained to be seen even as the country seemed, in the final years of the 20th century, to be making some beginning in settling down politically. It is significant that, even in the course of the election campaigns of 1992, ethnic rivalries were still so intense in the politics of the country that a troubled citizen wrote in a letter to the press:

"If it can be helped, no native Ashanti or Ewe should be considered for president. The truth is that these tribes have since independence been bitter rivals for political power. We do not want to carry this rivalry into the Fourth Republic".[7]

Chad

Nigeria's neighbor to the north-east, the Republic of Chad, the fifth largest country in land area in Africa at independence, became independent on August 11, 1960. Almost from the first day, the government of this country was confronted by hostilities and rebellions in various provinces, especially in the northern provinces. To survive, the government sprang to a viciously repressive response, and sought international military help – first from Chad's former colonial ruler, France, and then from Chad's northern neighbor, Libya. Even with the help of French troops, the government found it impossible to suppress the rebels. Meanwhile, Libya, rather than help the Chadian government, sent troops into the northernmost province of Chad – the desert area known as the Aczou strip (which Libya claimed to be part of Libyan territory). From then on, Libya became a major player in the Chadian turmoil, at various times supporting this or that Chadian government, attempting to seize more land in northern Chad, or even proposing a merger of Chad and Libya.

The embattled first Prime Minister of Chad was finally assassinated in 1975, only to be replaced by a vastly more repressive and more violent government. More rebellion and more rebel groups surfaced – as the pattern established at independence continued, more or less, with alternating episodes of armed conflicts, violent seizures of government, conflicts, negotiations, agreements, brief fragile peace, and more conflicts. The Libyan connection finally came to an end, with Libya withdrawing from Chadian affairs after being granted the Aczou strip by an international arbitration. The regime which seized power in 1990 and held power into the next century may be said to mark the end of Chad's first phase of political troubles, but even it continued to strive against rebellions and attempted seizures of power.

Central African Republic

Central African Republic became independent of French rule on August 13, 1960, and plunged almost immediately into serious political troubles and official corruption. On January 1, 1966, Col. Jean-Bedel Bokassa of the army seized power, abolished the constitution, dissolved the National Assembly, and vested all legislative and executive authority in himself. After ten years of repressive and corrupt leadership of his country, Bokassa abolished the republic and, on December 4, 1976, promulgated a monarchy instead – with the country becoming Central African Empire, with Bokassa as emperor. Bokassa and his corrupt empire became a laughing stock worldwide, and faced increasing confrontations at home. In late 1979, riots shook the capital city of Bangui, and violent response by the government resulted in the killing of about 200 students. On September 20, 1979, opposition elements (with some French military help) overthrew Bokassa and restored the republic. But that did not end the troubles of this country. Only two years later, the government was toppled by another coup.

Uganda

Of the new countries of Africa, Uganda acquired perhaps the greatest notoriety in the world during the 1970's for erratic and brutal government. This country arrived at independence on October 9, 1962, with a very pronounced problem of cohesion and stability. Treaties and agreements with the British dating to the nineteenth century provided certain constitutional guarantees for the kingdom of Buganda, the largest of the many small kingdoms in Uganda. Buganda is also the kingdom of the Baganda people, the largest single nationality in Uganda. Therefore, at independence, a troublesome question hanged over the future of Uganda: how to reconcile the quasi-autonomy of the kingdom of Buganda with the demands of Uganda's unity and statehood.

In 1963, an accommodation was assayed with a republican constitution under which the Bugandan king, the Kabaka Mutesa ll, was appointed President and the elected leader of government, Milton Obote, was appointed Prime Minister. It did not work. Confrontation between the central government and the kingdom of Buganda steadily grew. In 1966, the Prime Minister introduced another constitution which terminated the special constitutional status of Buganda. The Baganda rose in mighty protest, and civil war seemed imminent. The Prime Minister moved fast, ordered troops to seize the palace of the Kabaka, thus forcing the Kabaka to flee into exile abroad, and preempting a Bagandan armed resistance.

Fig. 5: *Milton Obote, First Prime Minister of Uganda*

Another constitution in 1967 was aimed at strengthening the unification of Uganda by abolishing the Buganda kingdom and all other kingdoms in the country, by breaking Buganda into four districts, and by generally increasing the powers of the central government. While all these measures were greeted in some African quarters as acts of statesmanship, they did not much advance the spirit of unity in Uganda. In particular, most of the Baganda rejected them. In his continued quest for solutions, Prime Minister Obote opted for a socialist direction for his country, in the hope of advancing a common ideology for the literate elite of all the various peoples of his country to rally around. This too did not only fail to produce the desired effect, it came to label Obote as a socialist and earn for him very influential enemies in the world, in the context of the worldwide Cold War. Obote's position thus grew markedly weaker in general. In January 1971, he was ousted by a military coup led by the most senior Ugandan military officer, Maj. Gen. Idi Amin.

Though immediately popular with the Baganda, Idi Amin faced opposition from other significant elements, especially Obote's loyalists in the army, and his move against such opposition initiated the reign of terror that was to characterize the government of Uganda under him. In the years that followed, Idi Amin became the world's most hated tyrant. For ethnic groups known or suspected by him to be opposed to him, his answer was to try and exterminate them. Orgies of mass killings in the army, raids and destruction of villages, killings of prominent citizens in high public positions, pursuit of fleeing refugees into neighboring countries – all these regularly emblazoned Uganda's name on news media all over the world. As these insane acts battered the economy of Uganda, Amin rose to the challenge by printing more and more paper money (thus unleashing a run-away inflation), by expelling the substantial Indian population which owned a significant part of Uganda's commerce, and by allocating the businesses and properties of the expelled Indians to his cronies.

Uganda plunged deeper and deeper into poverty. Repeated attempts by elements of the army to remove or assassinate Amin only intensified the ferocity of his brutalities. Declaring himself life president in 1976, he laid claim to territories of some of Uganda's neighbors, and thereby provoked border incidents. His cup finally overfilled when, in 1978, he invaded the borders of Tanzania. This provoked a counter-invasion of Uganda by Tanzania in 1979, the unification of some of the anti-Amin forces in Uganda, the rapid disintegration of the Amin regime, and Amin's flight into exile (for the rest of his life).[8]

Rwanda and Burundi

The two countries that are southwestern neighbors of Uganda – Rwanda and Burundi – became centers of intractable political conflicts as soon as both became independent in July 1962. In each of the two countries, Belgian colonial policies had resulted in the circumstance that a Tutsi minority (roughly 15% of the population in each country) had a firm hold on the government and the military establishment at independence. With the literate elite of Burundi's Hutu majority (about 85% of the population) mounting a resistance against this political imbalance, Burundi plunged immediately into violent conflicts. Armed Hutu challenges provoked massive killings of Hutu civilians in 1965 and again in 1972, when some 100,000 to 200,000 Hutu (including almost all the Hutu literate elite) were massacred by the country's armed forces. A culture of personal insecurity gradually came to hold sway, as each side lived in the conviction that, to survive, it must retaliate for the wrongs done to it by the other side, or even mount pre-emptive attacks. A large Hutu exile population built up in the Kivu Province of eastern Congo (Kinshasa), and from there sent insurgent militias into Burundi from time to time.

The political situation in Rwanda was identical, with cyclical political explosions and vicious blood-letting – as in the 1950's (the last years of Belgian rule), and then 1963 and 1972. The only difference was that in Rwanda, the Tutsi were mostly the victims of the killings. A substantial number of Rwandan Tutsi (mostly educated elements) gradually accumulated as refugees in neighboring Uganda. Convinced that the only way they could ever return home was by the use of force, these Tutsi refugees in Uganda forged themselves into a liberation army. The grounds were thus being prepared for some of the greatest human disasters of modern times.[9]

Revolution in Ethiopia

The Ethiopian Revolution, beginning quietly in 1974 and then escalating to horrid levels of violence and destructiveness, may be said to have rounded off the Black African storms of the 1960s and 1970s, and also to have set the stage for the more violent and more tortuous kinds of turmoil beginning from the 1980s. As political order stumbled in country after country in Sub-Saharan Africa in the course of the 1960s, the ancient empire of Ethiopia seemed immune from such weaknesses. Ethiopia's ancient imperial government, the solid image of its emperor, Emperor Haile Selassie, and its record of victorious defiance of European colonizers, all were widely celebrated in Africa in the independence years as pillar of strength on the continent.

In reality, however, Ethiopia experienced weaknesses not dissimilar from those of other countries of Black Africa. Like them, it was a country comprising many different nationalities insensitively held together. It was also a country whose rulers would not respond to the wishes of the people for change – a country where change could only come through military interventions or violent upheavals.

The empire's main strength had historically rested on its two ancient peoples, the Amharas and Tigrayans of the central plateau of Ethiopia, united by their long history of ancient aristocratic culture and Coptic Christian civilization, one of the oldest Christian civilizations in the world. But since the late 19th century, the rulers of the empire had expanded its boundaries to include many other peoples. Most of the late 19th century expansions had been towards the south – over the Oromo territory in the south and Somali territory to the southeast (especially the Ogaden Plateau), all of which resulted in doubling the size of the empire. In the course of the 1950s also, Ethiopia succeeded in influencing the United Nations to agree to the federating of former Italian possession of Eritrea in the north with Ethiopia. Then in the years that followed, Ethiopia gradually whittled down the autonomy of Eritrea, until Eritrea ultimately (in 1962) became simply one of the provinces of Ethiopia. By the independence decade, therefore,

Ethiopia was a typical Black African multi-nation state – with all the weaknesses characteristic of such a country.

It was in these modern territorial additions to the empire that Ethiopia's troubles of the late 20th century commenced. Oromo and Somali restiveness in the southern provinces finally crystallized into well-organized insurgencies in the 1960s, as well as direct conflicts between the armies of Ethiopia and of newly-independent Somalia. Though Ethiopia managed to deal with these insurgencies and to repulse the armies of Somalia, the difficulties in these provinces continued to exert heavy burdens on the empire's resources. Then trouble arose from Eritrea in the north. Here, guerrilla forces launched a war to free their country from Ethiopian rule, and Ethiopia had to put up a major military effort to contain them. Ethiopia was thus confronted by troubles from many directions.

All these troubles gradually showed up the weaknesses of the imperial government. Traditionally and as designed by the modern Ethiopian constitution, the emperor was the government of the empire, powerfully upheld by the ancient Amharic and Tigrayan provincial nobility and the powerful institutions of Ethiopia's Coptic church. The monarchy, nobility and the church owned all the land, and the peasants farming the land were tenants on the land, rendering most of their harvests, and obliged to supply other kinds of services, to their landlords. Emperor Haile Selassie did take steps to modernize his country – granting a parliament, establishing a modern army, and building educational institutions, etc. But as the growing class of literate Ethiopians demanded modernization of their country's system of government itself, the emperor did not seem to understand. Rather, his understanding was that the ancient system of government, with the emperor as controller of all power and maker of all decisions, was unchangeable. Even as age gradually robbed him of his naturally formidable capabilities of mind, he held on to the minutest details of governing. As a result, the quality of governance deteriorated steadily, and disaffection brewed in countless directions, especially notably among the rising literate classes and the lower ranks of the army. In such circumstances, the unrest in the various provinces was hard on the system, and when a huge natural disaster befell the country, the system of government went into rapid collapse.

Fig. 6: *Emperor Haile Selassie*

Historically, Ethiopia has long suffered from droughts and famines. In 1973, one such disastrous famine came, and particularly ravaged the province of Wollo where it is estimated to have taken the lives of more than 100,000 peasants. While this devastation raged, the imperial government did nothing to help. Even worse, the government hid the situation from the rest of the world and did not seek help from international agencies that could have helped – all out of a desire to protect the image of the emperor and his government in the eyes of the world. But the awful story of death in Wollo could not but spread in the country, and as it did, the emperor and his government lost a lot of support and prestige, especially among the literate classes.

The outcome of all these was that a small mutiny over food in a military outpost in southern Ethiopia in January 1974 quickly spread rebellion to all units of the army, and set a full-scale revolution in motion. A select group of junior military officers from various military outposts, forming themselves into a group named the Derg (Amharic for 'committee'), took control and, with the enthusiastic support of the educated youths and students, as well as protesting groups like teachers and workers, demolished the old system of government step by step. The climax was reached in September-November of the year when the Derg deposed the emperor and locked him up in custody, and ordered the summary execution of fifty-nine high-ranking former officials of the imperial government, including two former Prime Ministers. Adjudged guilty of various crimes against Ethiopia (including responsibility for the mass deaths in the Wollo famine), the emperor lived the last months of his life in prison – until August 1975 when, according to popular belief, he was murdered by the leaders of the Derg..

With the Derg government in full control, the revolution became more and more radical, and more and more violent. Splits in the ranks of the members of the Derg itself were resolved with gun fights and assassinations, until one young soldier, Major Mengitsu Haile Mariam and his supporters, became the undisputed rulers of Ethiopia. In 1974, a socialist revolution was embarked upon, resulting in a rush of changes. In 1976, Mengitsu at last announced Marxism-Leninism as the official ideology of Ethiopia. Banks and other businesses were nationalized. Sweeping land reforms nationalized all land, abolished all private land ownership, and gave control of all farmland to the peasants who farmed it. But the peasants were immediately robbed of the fruits of their new gains by the government's agricultural policies which compelled peasants to sell their harvests at officially low prices, and which set quotas of grains that each peasant must deliver to the government. To growing discontent among the peasant population over these policies, the government responded by flooding the provinces with officials who were instructed to enforce the laws with brutality.

Soon, this whole violent system of government began to provoke resistance in various quarters. Former land owners and landlords organized revolts in some provinces. In Tigray province in the north, a well-organized rebellion arose, and in Afar in the northeast, an Afar Liberation Front arose. In Eritrea, neighbor to Tigray, a powerful liberation movement for secession from Ethiopia arose. Among some former fanatical allies of the revolution – students' and teacher' organizations and other groups – a strong move arose to put an end to military control of the revolution and to replace it with civilian control. Some of these youths, having no other way to make their voices heard, began to use violence against the revolutionary government – attacking government offices and assassinating some public officials.

Mengitsu rose to the occasion by personally launching what he called a "Red Terror" against the youths and intellectuals. Armed squads hunted down students, teachers and intellectuals in the streets and slaughtered many thousands of them. Many more were imprisoned and mercilessly beaten. Those youths groups that had excitedly supported the revolution at its beginning were wiped out. To subdue the revolts in the provinces, especially in Tigray and Eritrea, Mengitsu raised up an enormous army.

But the revolutionary government stumbled in the provincial wars. By mid-1977, it had lost most of Eritrea. At that point, Somalia decided to launch a full-scale attempt to take back the Ogaden, and quickly succeeded in taking most of that province. It looked as if the revolutionary government was heading for defeat on all fronts.

However, at that point the Soviet Union and Cuba stepped in to save the socialist government of Ethiopia. Large quantities of Soviet weaponry, and many Soviet advisers, poured into Ethiopia. Communist Cuba sent an army. By early 1978, the counter-offensive, led mostly by the Cubans, had crushed the Somali invasion, and most of the revolutionary government's military effort was then shifted to Eritrea and Tigray.

While these wars were going on, another round of drought and famine, even more devastating than the 1973 famine, descended on Ethiopia in 1984. Mengitsu, who had held the late emperor guilty for the ravages of the 1973 famine, now ignored, and tried to hide from the outside world, the ravages of this famine, so as to be able to concentrate on his plans for a mammoth celebration of the tenth anniversary of his revolution, as well as on his wars in the provinces. When he found that he could not continue to do nothing about the famine, he decided on a policy of resettling the peasants from the worst famine areas to areas that were less prone to droughts, employing force to relocate many reluctant families. By the time the enormity of the famine's devastations finally forced him to alert the world and to allow international aid, many more tens of thousands of peasants had died than had died in 1973. International aid workers and observers who saw the horror that was unfolding in the provinces of Ethiopia cried out to the world, and caused the whole world to respond with the largest movement of Third-world aid in the history of the modern world. But even this did not persuade Mengitsu to put off his provincial wars or to modify his agricultural policies.

Mengitsu's end finally came in 1991. The collapse of the Soviet Union itself in that year resulted in the collapse of Soviet and Cuban military support to Ethiopia. Unable to continue to resist a joint army of Eritrean and Tigrayan rebels, Mengitsu fled Ethiopia and sought refuge in Zimbabwe. His revolution quickly disintegrated. Some months later, a national conference of Ethiopian leaders decided to let Eritrea hold a referendum to decide its future. Two years later, Eritrea became independent.

Overview of First Phase

As is common experience in situations of serious societal disorder, the common people—the weak, the poor, the illiterate masses — bore the brunt of all the political turmoil in these African countries. As the modern literate leadership of each country remained almost perpetually embroiled in conflict in the years after independence, orderly attention to the demands of economic and social development flagged. Even in naturally rich countries of the continent, poverty and unemployment grew steadily among the masses, and so did crime of all shapes and colors. Members of the political elite gradually grew into the tendency of grabbing and engrossing for themselves whatever their official positions gave them access to in their country's resources, thus instituting a vicious and powerful culture of public corruption and high-class crime. In that way, they deepened the poverty among their people—especially because the large amounts of funds which the powerful stole never became productive in their countries' economies but were mostly consumed in ostentatious life styles or spirited out and stashed away in foreign bank accounts. In the countries going through civil war, the desperate poverty among the masses fed the political turmoil, by making available large numbers of poor youths and children for forced recruitment into the contending armies of warlords. In the latter way, especially, the grounds were being prepared in Africa for the next generation of very tortuous and very complex devastations.

The political crises in most African countries in the years immediately after independence usually started, as they still often do, at the point of constitutional procedures for the change of leadership—that is, at elections. Of the first Presidents or Prime Ministers of independent African countries, the persons who emerged from the anti-imperialist independence struggles as rulers of their countries, hardly any saw his position as anything other than a life-long appointment. The ruling politician's ambition to stay forever in power was usually reinforced by the ambition of the political elite of his ethnic group to stay forever in control of the affairs of their country (that is, to exercise dominance forever over the other ethnic groups of their country). In the context of such tenacious sectional ambitions, free, fair, democratic elections were unacceptable to the persons and groups in power after independence, since free and fair elections posited the possibility of sudden loss of power to other persons and other groups. Hence the pervasive efforts by Africa's first rulers to employ governmental power to suppress and control incurably democratic elements like labor unions, students organizations, the news media, etc., to repress certain ethnic groups, and to prevent or disrupt alliances of dissenting ethnic groups. Not infrequently, actions against dissenting and suspect ethnic groups involved actual violence against them — like murders of members of their elite and destruction of their villages, employing the apparatuses of government.

The coercion sometimes succeeded so well that elections tended to become mere docile affirmations of the ruler by an intimidated citizenry, affirmations usually further secured with criminal falsifications of the electoral process. When all the coercion seemed insufficiently effective, the rulers usually resorted to full-scale, unabashed, falsifications of the electoral process. At its most successful, the combination of coercion and election rigging took the ruler, in many a country, to such apparent heights of political success and dominance that he and his henchmen became emboldened to say that there was no good reason to let the laws continue to provide for the existence of more than one political party. In such situations, many African rulers in the years soon after independence made, or attempted to make, laws converting their countries to one-party states. The usual argument for the one-party state was that it would facilitate national unity.

And in the one-party state, the ruler's own party became the only party recognized by the law and all other parties became illegal.

But the illusion of unassailable dominance always proved short-lived. Sooner or later, the self-deception became obvious, as was to be seen in the rash of military coups d'état in the sixties and seventies. Dissent, forced underground and denied legitimate outlets, forced itself out through other outlets. The military coups were invariably welcomed with wild jubilations by erstwhile apparently quiescent masses of people. In many cases, military personnel from suppressed or marginalized ethnic groups emerged as coup leaders and military rulers. Reaction and counter-action by the displaced dominant ethnic groups then tended to produce counter-coups — thus continuing the cycle of instability and violence.

Some of the election-time gymnastics of some of Africa's rulers in the sixties and seventies were weird in the extreme. For instance, in the Nigerian federal elections of 1964 (four years after that country's independence), the allied political parties controlling the federal and two of the four regional governments of the Nigerian Federation employed the powers of government to prevent the candidates of other parties from filing their nominations with the Electoral Commission. This was done by having the candidates of the opposing parties arrested and detained, or by seizing the electoral officer and hiding him (sometimes hiding him beyond the borders of Nigeria), after he had legally received the nomination of the ruling parties' candidate. The ruling parties' candidate would then be declared "elected unopposed". One year later, when the regional election in one of the Regions became due, the regional government there, with the support of the federal government, proceeded to employ the same fraud on a huge and blatant scale – and thus, as would be remembered, provoked the people of the Region to explode in a revolt of destruction and carnage that took countless lives and burnt countless homes throughout the Region, and led to the first military coup in Nigeria. In Sierra Leone in 1967, Prime Minister Albert Margai lost the election to Siaka Stevens, leader of the opposition party. The Governor-General invited Siaka Stevens for swearing in as new Prime Minister. When the swearing-in ceremony was about to begin, the head of the army, Brigadier David Lansana, apparently acting in support of Margai, moved in and surrounded the State House with troops (on the pretext that some parts of the elections were not yet decided) - thereby incarcerating both the Governor-General and Siaka Stevens. Some days later, some lower military officers took action, pushed Lansana aside, suspended the constitution, and took over the government. But the political disorder thus initiated only escalated. Another group in the military soon overthrew the military rulers and had Siaka Stevens sworn in as Prime Minister in April 1968. Then Siaka Stevens too embarked on making himself and his party permanent rulers. In 1978, all political parties, with the exception of Siaka Stevens' party, were abolished – and resentment in the country began to rise dangerously. In a 1970 election in Lesotho, Prime Minister Lebua Jonathan, finding in the final hours of the election day that he had lost at the polls, announced suspension of the constitution, ordered the arrest and detention of the leaders of the winning party, the Basuto Congress Party (BCP), and continued to rule. The leader of the BCP, Ntsu Mokhehle, fled into exile, and organized a futile series of guerrilla attacks against the Jonathan government from there.

After every military coup d'état, the military rulers came forth promising law and order, war on corruption, fairness to all sections, respect for the law — in short, a brief corrective regime, to be followed by a return to elective civilian government. All these usually turned out, in virtually every country, to be empty promises. Basically, most of these military men lacked the education or skill or character for the job of governing. Moreover, the successful coup maker who became ruler knew quite well that his footing was fragile and, therefore, he tended to engage in making himself rich quickly, and in using the powers of government to strike down his suspected enemies – and such conduct was usually certain to frighten and embolden his enemies into striking back at him.

Thus in the hands of the military in many countries, governance deteriorated abysmally in honesty, fairness, respect for law, and in dignity. The military coups of the 1960's and 1970's gave Africa most of its most grotesque regimes. Many military regimes turned unabashedly into agents of particular ethnic groups in their countries and inflicted deep wounds on other ethnic groups. Shielded behind the threat constituted by their guns, the military rulers took corruption to great depths, many of them retiring, if they were lucky to be able to retire, into great wealth and opulence. Nigerian military men who held public offices in the military regimes of petroleum-rich Nigeria became, overnight, a super-rich elite, some of whom could be counted among the richest people in the world. The military ruler of the Congo Democratic Republic (or Zaire), Mobutu Sese Seko, by stealing the wealth of his mineral-rich country, became, according to some reports, one of the highest of the world's richest. At some point, there were even reports that he was lending money to his country! The examples are legion.

Even worse, usually when pressure for return to popular, participatory, politics became irresistible in a country under military dictatorship, many a military dictator would sit over the writing of a new constitution creating a civilian government, and then offer himself as candidate for election to the presidency. Employing the powers of his current position, as well as his enormous wealth (to buy and rig election), he would succeed himself as civilian ruler, and thus continue the era of brazen corruption and crude power. In Nigeria, the rich retired military brass came to hold an unshakeable lien on Nigeria's civilian political life, becoming the agency for deeply and irreversibly clamping on the country a culture of the most sordid public corruption.

CHAPTER TWO

Deepening Plague

The second phase of Black Africa's political turmoil was generated from the womb of the situations created during the first phase, and only a few countries will be selected to illustrate it. Generally, in the second phase, the basic traits of the first phase continued. The rigging of elections, and loss of faith in the political system, continued – as the world has seen in, among others, Nigeria in 1983, 2003 and 2007, Kenya in 2008 and Zimbabwe in 2008. The rash of military coups continued also, although with decreased frequency. In Angola, Chad, Somalia and Sudan, civil wars, started in the sixties, continued. In Congo (Kinshasa), a second civil war erupted in the nineties.

But the defining character of the crises of this second phase has been their profound confusion and tortuousness. In many countries where civil wars had been going on for decades, warring bands that had fought against other bands broke up into fragments and turned on one another – creating in some countries a situation almost akin to a war of all against all, and conditions of mind-boggling savagery.

Somalia

Among Africans, Somalia on the Horn of Africa in eastern Africa, is generally spoken of as the symbol of the era of total collapse of order in Black African countries. All orderly governance collapsed in this country in 1991. In the course of the early nineties, the collapse of authority and order became so profound that even international peacekeeping troops became targets of the opposing Somali warlords, and the whole world watched on television as corpses of peacekeepers were dragged through the streets of Mogadishu by armed youths out of control. All government and orderly authority have continued to elude this sad country even as this is being written over twenty years later. Estimates by 2008 put the number of dead from this war in

Somalia at hundreds of thousands, of internally displaced persons at over one million, and of Somali refugees in refugee camps at over 800,000. In spite of continual efforts to negotiate peace, the Somali debacle explodes into a new round of fighting from time to time, occasioning further civilian casualties and massive displacements of people. The war has also drawn in neighboring countries like Ethiopia and Eritrea. The forces of the African Union succeeded in restoring some order to the capital city of Mogadishu by late 2011; but even so, no final end seems to be in sight.[1]

Liberia

Before Somalia, some countries of West Africa had started on the path of total disintegration of government and all order. In the Republic of Liberia, a very unfortunate political tradition had developed since the founding of the country. The African-American immigrant founders of this country (better known as Americo-Liberians) early held themselves separate from the country's indigenous peoples (usually referred to as up-country people), and proceeded to develop political, economic and social policies not too dissimilar from the apartheid system of the Union of South Africa. On 12th April 1980, a group of young non-commissioned military officers (all from various parts of the up-country), led by a Sergeant Samuel Doe, stormed the state house, slaughtered and mutilated the president, and seized the government of Liberia. The victorious soldiers arrested and executed thirteen of the leading members of the deposed government, and more than 200 citizens lost their lives in the turbulence of the take-over.

But the new government was not able to hold the country together in order for any length of time. Within months, some members of the group were accused of plotting to assassinate their head of state and were executed. Some others escaped and fled into hiding. The government was melting down. When, in November 1985, one of the escapees returned secretly, attempted a coup, failed and was executed, the troops loyal to the government burst into a frenzy of destruction and killings against his ethnic group and other ethnic groups suspected of sympathy for him. In the midst of this whirlwind, Samuel Doe organized and massively

47

rigged an election in 1985, thereby, as he believed, establishing his legitimacy as president.

At last, in December 1989, civil war finally erupted in Liberia. A former functionary of the government, Charles Taylor, who had been accused of stealing large amounts of public money and had escaped and fled, returned to the country after he had received some military training in Libya. Joined by recruits from among ethnic groups that had suffered the most in the 1985 killings, and assisted by troops and financing from some neighboring countries (Burkina Faso, Ivory Coast, and Sierra Leone) whose rulers had their own grouses against Doe and their own interests in Liberia, Taylor embarked on an attempt to conquer the country. As his rebel force marched through the country, it plunged into indiscriminate destruction and mass murders among those ethnic groups who would not offer support. But it was not long before hostile factions broke off from this rebel army – resulting in a tangled war of many combatants bent on exterminating one another, and a mad orgy of destruction, looting, raping, maiming, and killing. Even within each of the rebel forces, there were frequent reports of mass executions occasioned by internal conflicts and ethnic differences. Every rebel force abducted and trained – and drugged – large numbers of children to bear arms and kill. The troops loyal to the government defended the government by engaging in similar orgies against suspect ethnic groups. The rebel forces were only narrowly stopped from taking the capital city, Monrovia, by peace-keeping forces of the Economic Council of West African States (ECOWAS) comprising mostly Nigerian troops. In September1990, Samuel Doe, who had continued to claim to be president of the country on the strength of his 1985 election, was captured by one of the factions and viciously mutilated. From then on, the collapse of all semblance of authority and order became real – with blood-chilling consequences of massive inter-ethnic brutalities, murders, and rampage.

In August 1995, the factions reached some sort of agreement brokered by Nigeria and others, making a government of national unity possible. Under it, Taylor was allowed to return to Monrovia as president, but all he then did was to favor the country with indescribable corruption, rapacity, and murders – and to give help to some rebel forces in neighboring countries like Sierra Leone. From the Sierra Leonean rebels, he was alleged to have taken substantial amounts of diamonds pillaged from that country's diamond mines. How many Liberians died in this sickening war before international intervention brought it to an end in 2003, and how many scattered into various destinations worldwide, will probably never be known for sure. The war left everything of value in Liberia shattered and ruined – schools, churches, water and electric installations, government offices, homes, villages, etc. – and robbed one whole generation of Liberian children of the benefits of schooling and education.[2]

Sierra Leone, Ivory Coast & Guinea

Since the peoples of Liberia's border areas have close ethnic affinities with peoples in the neighboring countries, there quickly mushroomed huge, sprawling, refugee camps of displaced Liberians within the borders of Ivory Coast, Sierra Leone and Guinea. The disaster in Liberia quickly spilled over into these countries.

As would be remembered, political order had steadily become fragile in Sierra Leone since the military coups of 1967-8. The growing political weakness of the country had escalated with the establishment of a one-party state in 1978. In the Ivory Coast, the mostly Muslim peoples of the northern provinces had fretted since independence, complaining that the government, controlled almost exclusively by the southern and mostly Christian peoples, treated them as if they did not belong to the country. Under the shadow of the huge troubles going on in Liberia, attacks on governments, and then civil wars, erupted in Sierra Leone, Guinea (Conakry), and Ivory Coast, producing in some cases conditions of wanton carnage and orgies of destruction very similar to those in Liberia. Because of the ethnic complexity of the borders of these countries with Liberia, help flowed freely between their rebel forces and the rebel forces of Liberia. In Sierra Leone, where the civil war began in 1991, the main rebel force (the Revolutionary United Front, RUF), widely believed to be receiving substantial financial and material help from the Taylor regime in Liberia, came to earn a notoriety for extreme brutalities. The RUF would attack a village, decapitate the village head and display his head on a stake, and then kill most of the villagers. Its particular signature brutality was amputations of hands, arms, legs, lips and ears of its victims. After the RUF captured some of the richest diamond mines of Sierra Leone, it became a lot more formidable, and that earned it a brief participation in one of the short-lived regimes of the civil war. Hundreds of thousands of Sierra Leoneans died in the civil war; hundreds of thousands others fled into neighboring countries; and about two million (representing roughly one-third of the total population) were displaced from their homes. In 2000, the RUF exported its brutalities into neighboring Guinea (Conakry), where economic and ethnic animosities had simmered below the surface since independence in 1958, and where an estimated 200,000 Liberian and Sierra Leonean refugees had accumulated. The guerrilla activities destroyed some Guinean towns and villages, displaced tens of thousands of people, forced cancellation of legislative elections scheduled for 2000, and the relocation of many of the foreign refugees. Furthermore, taking advantage of the crisis which broke out in the Ivory Coast in September 2002, Taylor extended the guerrilla war into the western provinces of the Ivory Coast – as a means of fighting Liberian guerrilla forces bent on toppling his regime. As the Ivorian civil war assumed great confusion and savagery, both sides in it were soon using Liberian guerrilla forces.

Meanwhile in the same sub-region, a war of secession which the Biola people of the Casamance province of Senegal had started in 1982, had dragged on into the mid-1990's, resulting in many refugees and displaced persons. This war in the Casamance inevitably fed into the other wars in the sub-region in the 1990s, especially with the secessionists establishing shelter and operational bases in neighboring Guinea.[3]

Sudan

In the Republic of Sudan, systematic violations of the Addis Ababa agreement of 1972 by the Northern-led government, and the government's push to control the areas of the south in which petroleum was discovered in the 1970's, ultimately led to the outbreak of the second generation of Sudan's civil wars in 1983. In that year, the government abrogated the Addis Ababa

Agreement, cancelled the constitutional guarantees that had been granted to the South, declared Arabic the official language of Sudan anew, and Islamic sharia law the law of the country. The southerners formed a unified army to defend their interests – the Southern Peoples Liberation Army (SPLA). But rather than remain simply a war between the north and the south, Sudan's second-generation civil war soon acquired a very confusing complexity. While terrible fighting and negotiations alternated in the face-off between the government and the SPLA in the south, new fronts to the war came to develop in the eastern and western parts of the south, where various armed rebel groups emerged.

Of these, the war in the western provinces, the area known as Darfur, gripped the horrified attention of the world from 2003 on. Darfur lies in a critical part of the general northern African demographic divide belt where Arab groups and Black African peoples are interspersed. The Arabs here are pastoralists (raising camels in some parts and cattle in others), while the Black African peoples (the Fur, Zagawa, Masalit, and others) are mixed farming and pastoralist peoples. Droughts and environmental deterioration in this part of northern Africa in modern times have created the circumstance that the land, water and grazing resources have gradually become insufficient for supporting the peoples who live there, and the consequence has been growing conflicts, largely along the line of Arabs against the Black Africans. In this whirlwind of conflicts, the actions of the Arab-led government of the Sudan generally worked in favor of the Arabs against the Black African peoples. A 1994 reorganization by the government divided the province into three regions, with Arabs in strong positions of power in each. In 2003, the African peoples rose in rebellion, and two strong rebel forces crystallized and launched attacks on government targets. Though the national army won victory after victory against the two, it soon became obvious that it did not command the ability to bring Darfur under full control. A negotiated agreement in 2006, though it was accepted by one of the rebel groups, was rejected by the other, and the fighting continued – with tens of small rebel groups emerging.

Meanwhile, a totally new kind of atrocity appeared on the scene in Darfur – a weird version of inhumanity not seen before or elsewhere in the modern world, and probably never seen before in the history of the world. From among the Arab pastoralists of the province, the government of Sudan raised, trained and armed large numbers of independent Arab militia groups known as Janjaweed and unleashed them on the African population. The task of the Janjaweed militias was to rampage freely and independently throughout this unhappy land, surprise defenseless villages of Black African peoples, destroy and burn the villages, obliterate all assets of village life (water wells, farms, livestock, etc.), kill all the inhabitants that they could lay their hands upon, in particular rape the women and then slaughter them and their children. After some six years of this unbelievable crime against humanity, the destruction of villages and their inhabitants was observed to slow down, for the obvious reason that there were fewer and fewer villages left to destroy. Even then, the government of Sudan was widely reported to be still supporting and maintaining the Janjaweed squads.

By many estimates, the Janjaweed crimes had taken as many as 400,000 lives in Darfur by 2010, and seriously disrupted the lives of at least 4.7 million, representing 75% of Darfur's total pre-2003 population. An estimated three million Darfuris, roughly 50% of Darfur's prewar population, lost their homes; of these, over 300,000 found their way to refugee camps in Chad and about 2.7 million to displaced persons' camps in Darfur itself. Crowded into these crude and subhuman camps, the people could not make farms to feed themselves, and depended on the meager supplies that international humanitarian organizations could get to them. And even such supplies were, according to complaints by the humanitarian and relief agencies, obstructed from time to time by the Sudan government. Therefore, the camps regularly held some of the world's harshest scenes of poverty and starvation.

Meanwhile, in spite of the Comprehensive Peace Agreement it made with the peoples of Southern Sudan in 2005, the government of Sudan made real peace impossible there – by refusing to carry out important provisions of the Peace Agreement, such as border demarcation and the sharing of the oil revenue. Therefore, tension in the region continued to hover close to resumption of violent conflicts.

In December 2009, the International Crisis Group (ICG), the authoritative think-tank based in Brussels, issued a report and urgent warning on the seriously deteriorating situation in Sudan. The report titled "Sudan: Preventing Implosion", warned that unless the international community (especially the United States, the United Nations, the African Union Peace and Security Council, and the Horn of Africa Inter-Government Authority on Development (IGAD) immediately joined hands and moved to support peace moves in Sudan, a full-scale return of the North-South war in that country, and an escalation of the Darfur disaster, were likely. It alerted the world to the fact that, due to the lack of implementation of peace deals earlier concluded between Khartoum and the South, East and West of Sudan, Sudan was sliding towards "violent breakup". It added, "The main mechanisms to end conflicts between the central government and the peripheries – the Comprehensive Peace Agreement (with the South), the Darfur Peace Agreement, and the East Sudan Peace Agreement – all suffered from lack of implementation, largely due to the intransigence of the National Congress Party of President Omar al-Bashir and the government in Khartoum".[4]

Crisis Peak In Burundi & Rwanda

In the early 1990's, the history of political conflicts in Burundi and Rwanda finally reached a horrific climax. At first, from 1990, some hope emerged that these countries could fashion out a peaceful democratic new path. Under massive international pressure, the Tutsi president of Burundi, Pierre Buyoya, agreed to negotiations with the Hutu opposition, and the negotiations produced agreement on a system of multi-party democracy. However, Buyoya's hopes that some of the Hutu elite would join his party did not materialize. In the election that came in June 1993, the Hutu party swept the polls, and a Hutu-led government arose, led by President Melchior Ndadaye. Four months later, Tutsi extremists in the army assassinated Ndadaye and his cabinet – and another round of massacres ensued, bringing the total of massacred citizens of Burundi by the Tutsi-led army and insurgent Hutu militias to about 150,000, mostly Hutu.

The 1993 developments in Burundi immediately cast a dark shadow over the affairs of Rwanda. Here, a 1973 coup had brought to power as president a moderate Hutu, Juvenal Habyarimana, who promised to promote national unity. But he had gone on to establish an authoritarian one-party state as his means of achieving national unity. However, he had also carried out some generally welcome economic and social reforms, as well as political reforms including the appointment of a Tutsi Prime Minister. His was a difficult position, however, since most leading Hutu actually preferred that the Tutsi be severely marginalized – or perhaps even eliminated. By 1990, there were reports of killings of Tutsi in some parts of the country by the government's military forces, and such activities agitated the Tutsi exile forces in Uganda and increased their pressure on the county's borders.

This was the situation when the news of the massive killings of Hutu in Burundi came. Influential Rwandan Hutu (including many who were in the government) openly increased the forming of death squads. Reports of killings of Tutsis (and of retaliatory killings of Hutus by elements of the Tutsi exile troops) increased. This turn of events was by no means secret, but the international community did nothing to arrest it. The flashpoint finally came when the aircraft conveying President Habyarimana, who was in the midst of negotiations for further political reforms, crashed in very suspicious circumstances, killing him.

The evening following his death, Hutu death squads began to massacre any Tutsi that they could find, as well as any Hutu moderates. In the gory record of political brutalities in modern Africa, the grand prize for evil belongs to these Rwandan massacres of 1994. A small United Nations peace-keeping force on the spot, lacking the authority or resources to intervene effectually, watched helplessly as hundreds of thousands of men, women and children were hacked to death. One reporter on the spot exclaimed, "There are no devils left in hell; all of them are on duty in Rwanda". As these killings continued, the Tutsi liberation army entered the country in full force, and reprisals against the Hutu began. An estimated three-fourths of a million people (Tutsi and Hutu, but mostly Tutsi) perished. Millions (almost all Hutu) fled their homes and headed for neighboring countries, mostly to Congo (Kinshasa), large numbers of them dying of starvation and hardship on the march. The huge refugee camps that sprang up in eastern Congo became scenes of extreme deprivation and insecurity and death.[5]

Second Congo War

The complications generated by the Rwandan disaster compounded the rapidly deteriorating political conditions of the Congo Democratic Republic. In 1996, the greatest and most confusing war in modern African history, the Second Congo War, began. Now commonly referred to as Africa's World War, or the Great War of Africa, this war came to involve some eight countries of central Africa and at least 25 heavily armed groups.

Decades of massively bad government and corruption under President Mobutu Sese Seko had gradually dragged the country's economy down and generated conflicts. Various opposition groups had developed into insurgent groups in parts of the country. The best organized of these insurgent groups, entrenched in the distant eastern provinces, was led by a long-time opponent of Mobutu, Laurent-Desire Kabila. The massive flight of Rwandan Hutu into these eastern provinces, consequent on the Hutu-Tutsi genocide in Rwanda in 1994, added enormously to the deterioration of order and security. So did the presence of Ugandan rebel forces using the Congo as base for attacks on the government of Uganda. From among the great stream of Rwandan Hutu refugees, militia groups organized attacks across the border into Rwanda (intent on destroying the Tutsi-controlled government of Rwanda) and into Burundi (to assist the Hutu rebel groups fighting the Tutsi-controlled government of Burundi). The Rwandan government protested to the Mobutu government, but the latter was too weak to do much. Thereupon, the Rwandan government took action to arm the ethnic Tutsi people of eastern Congo (the people known as the Banyamulenge), even as the Mobutu government protested helplessly. Taking advantage of the situation, Laurent Kabila, his rebel forces swollen by forces of the Rwandan Tutsi, the Banyamulenge, and some Ugandan rebel forces, launched an offensive westwards towards Kinshasa in December 1996. Encountering only weak resistance on the long march, Kabila entered and seized Kinshasa in May 1997, and took control of the government as president. Mobutu fled the county into exile abroad (where he died soon after).

But all these were only a prelude to this war's most vicious and most destructive phase, which began in 1998. Kabila expected that, as soon as power was secured by him, his Tutsi (and Ugandan) allies would leave and return to their own countries; but the Tutsi, worried about the huge Hutu refugee hordes in the Congo and the threat they posed to Rwanda, were reluctant to leave. Tension developed between Kabila and his allies, and trouble started when, in July 1998, Kabila replaced his Rwandan chief of staff with an indigenous Congolese, and ordered the Rwandan and Ugandan forces to get out of his country.

Events soon showed, however, that the Kabila government did not command enough strength to keep the situation under control. On being sworn in as president, he had promised democratic reforms. But he had soon banned all political parties, and had turned more and more to repression against his political opponents. He also failed to revive the economy – with the result that economic hardship and tensions grew in the country. Moreover, revelations that his Tutsi-supported insurgent forces, during their long march to Kinshasa, had slaughtered thousands among the Rwandan Hutu refugees fleeing across the Congo, seriously damaged his image, in spite of his denials. Within weeks of his order to his foreign allies to leave, his government was confronted by massive rebellions. A formidable Banyamulenge force emerged, greatly strengthening the Rwandan and Uganda forces. As this coalition of forces marched ominously nearer and nearer to Kinshasa, it seemed as if the Kabila government would be crushed by it. However, Kabila managed to throw them back just before they reached Kinshasa, but then the rebellion spread.

Various insurgent groups emerged, holding various provinces of the country, led by opposition politicians, Mobutu sympathizers, and disenchanted former allies of Kabila. As the Kabila government reeled under these pressures, some countries of the region (Sudan, Angola, Namibia, Zimbabwe) sent forces to Kabila's support. The regional war was on.

The governments sending assistance to the Kabila government did so in order to prevent the confusion in the Congo from spreading and engulfing the whole region. Some of them had interlocking ethnic interests in their borders with the Congo; some were confronted by civil wars of their own and were anxious to prevent linkages between rebel or dissident groups in their countries and militia groups operating in the Congo. Meanwhile, various independent Tutsi militia groups emerged, intent on defending the Tutsi populations of eastern Congo as well as the security of Rwanda and Burundi. Of the various Hutu militia groups that emerged, the objectives were to overthrow the Tutsi-led governments of Rwanda and Burundi, to effect ethnic cleansing of Tutsi in the Hutu populated provinces of eastern Congo, and to protect the Hutu hordes that had fled from Rwanda to the Congo, large numbers of whom were still on the move and seeking security. Uganda's national army entered into the war for the stated objective of protecting the borders of Uganda against Ugandan groups operating against the Ugandan government from inside the Congo. However, there arose widespread allegations that Uganda was exploiting the confused situation to enter into the Congo for the purpose of illegally seizing mineral resources from there. Of the various indigenous Congolese militia groups that arose, many were against the government, but some were in support of the government's efforts to drive the foreign armies and militias out of their country. By 1999, in spite of peace-making interventions by the United Nations and by Africa, the country was firmly fragmented between the Kabila government and the rebels. The situation threatened to become even further confused when President Laurent Kabila was assassinated in 2001.

However, Joseph Kabila, Laurent's son, succeeding him as president, prosecuted the war somewhat more successfully than his father had done, and was also more inclined to cooperate with United Nations peace efforts. As a result, negotiations made it possible for the foreign armies to agree to leave the Congo in 2002, for the various Congolese parties to reach a main agreement in 2003 to share power in the government, and for the United Nations to send in a large peace-keeping force. In spite of all these, hostilities continued to flare from time to time, different armed groups continued to hold some parts of the country, and the recognized Provisional Government was reasonably effective in only a part, albeit a large part, of the country.

Moreover, allegations continued to be heard that Rwanda and Uganda were still keeping troops in the country. In fact, by November 2008, a Tutsi militia group, led by a Tutsi warlord named Laurent Nkunda, had firmly established its control over an eastern province of the Congo – which it seemed to be determined to hold as a sort of independent buffer state designed for the permanent protection of the Rwanda and Burundi states and of the Congolese Banyamulenge.

In January 2009, a sudden and totally unexpected truce between the Congolese official forces and the Rwandan army led to the capture of Nkunda and the collapse of his terrorist empire in eastern Congo. But that was only one of the common shifts and turns in this strange and complex war, which found ways to keep dragging on even after Nkunda's removal from the scene.

By the time of the 2003 peace settlement, an estimated 5.4 million people had died in the Second Congo War (mostly from starvation and diseases) – the largest human casualties of any one war since the Second World War of 1939-45. Even until as late as at the time of this writing, the toll in human life has continued, and scattered terrorist gangs are still reported in parts of the Kivu Province of Eastern Congo.[6]

The Mozambique Civil War

Unlike most of the countries emerging into independent statehood from European colonialism in the 1960's, the Portuguese possessions – Angola, Mozambique and Guinea (Bissau) – had the misfortune of having to fight vicious wars of liberation before they could achieve their independence. In the years after the Second World War, while other European powers had gradually, though reluctantly, advanced their African possessions towards ultimate independence, Portugal had insisted that its own African territories were not colonies but actual provinces of Portugal, and that therefore the concept of independence from Portugal was inapplicable to them. As African counties attained independence in the years from about 1960, the peoples of the Portuguese possessions found that they would need to use force to wrench their own independence from Portugal. For about fifteen years, wars of liberation against Portugal (assisted by Western powers) wreaked serious havoc on these countries and divided their citizens into hostile factions. This unfortunate prelude to independence preconditioned these countries (especially the large countries of Angola and Mozambique) for some of the most destructive civil wars that Africa was to experience in the last decades of the 20th century.

Mozambique, the large country on the east coast of southern Africa, emerged from its war of liberation from Portugal a badly shattered country. Moreover, its leading nationalist movement (Mozambique Liberation Front – FRELIMO) had lost its experienced leaders in the liberation war. Though it had control over most of the country, its hold was weak in many provinces. Its orientation and image had also been shaped by the events of the liberation war. It had received military and other types of assistance from the Eastern (communist) Powers in the worldwide Cold War, and therefore embarked, as Mozambique's ruling party, on communist plans and strategies for national development. This earned it the continued hostility of the Western Powers (America and Western Europe), of the apartheid government of the Union of South Africa, and the white minority dictatorship of Zimbabwe. In the Union of South Africa, the African National Congress, ANC, was waging a resistance war against the apartheid government, and in Zimbabwe, the Zimbabwe African National Union, ZANU, was waging a resistance war against the white minority government. FRELIMO allowed both the ANC and ZANU to establish bases in Mozambique, and the governments of South Africa and Zimbabwe immediately became active enemies of Mozambique.

Meanwhile, the early socialist policies of the FRELIMO-led government were making many enemies in many parts of the country. In particular, the white Portuguese settlers, many of whom were fleeing from the country, were assisted by the white minority government of Zimbabwe to form a resistance movement called RENAMO, for the purpose of frustrating and destroying the FRELIMO-led government. The apartheid government of South Africa soon entered into the situation, with substantial military and financial assistance to RENAMO. In fact, after Zimbabwe won its independence from the white minority dictatorship, South Africa became the main sponsor of RENAMO. With large numbers of disenchanted African citizens of Mozambique joining the RENAMO forces, RENAMO became a formidable enemy to the FRELIMO-led government.

Mozambique's civil war was a very complex conflict. It was a proxy war of the worldwide Cold War, pitching the Western powers, with South Africa as front, against the Eastern Powers, supporters of FRELIMO. It was a part of the wars of survival by the white minority governments of South Africa and Zimbabwe. It was a war by white settlers of Mozambique, partly to hold some ground in the country - and, since that seemed to become increasingly impossible, to wreck and destroy as much of the country as possible. It was also a war against FRELIMO by those ethnic groups that were not represented in FRELIMO. RENAMO's activities were almost regularly productive of destruction and ruin, resulting in the total wiping out of villages, the killing of countless people, and the displacement of many more. But FRELIMO's engagements against RENAMO, marked by intense bitterness, were often equally destructive. All this destruction went on until the United Nations stepped in in 1992 to arrange a settlement. The peace settlement, concluded in 1994, brought the fighting to an end. Some of RENAMO's fighting men were integrated into the Mozambique national army. RENAMO as a movement converted peacefully into a regular political party under the laws of Mozambique.

The Mozambique civil war was one of the most brutal wars in its time in Africa. In its sixteen years, it took over one million lives, through violence, starvation and disease. It displaced over four million people from their homes, and sent over two million fleeing into refuge in neighboring countries. Even for years after the cessation of hostilities, the death toll continued, as unexploded land mines kept on killing or maiming thousands throughout the country.

Angolan Civil War

In the other large Portuguese dependency of Angola, a country of many fairly large ethnic nationalities, the war of independence that began in 1961 soon spawned different guerrilla forces located in different provinces – of which the strongest came to be MPLA (Popular Movement for the Liberation of Angola) based in the capital town of Luanda and the neighboring coastal provinces, FLNA (National Front for the Liberation of Angola) in the northern provinces, and UNITA (National Union for the Total Independence of Angola) in the southern provinces. Although each of these guerrilla movements claimed to be national, each was, in reality, strong mostly in its own native area, and there was no coordination among them. The size and geography of the country, and the savagery of Portuguese reprisals, had made contact and coordination impossible among these nationalist movements. At last in 1975, Portugal reluctantly admitted failure, and each of the freedom-fighting groups declared independence in its own locale – independence for Angola. Moreover, the small province called Cabinda, the location of most of the petroleum reserves belonging to Angola, but separated from the rest of Angola by a narrow strip of Congolese territory, insisted on not being a part of Angola. Cabinda based its secessionist claims on treaties with the Portuguese, treaties which did not expressly make Cabinda part of Angola.

Unfortunately too, Angola thus became independent at a very inauspicious time in world politics. The Cold War between the world's Western and Eastern power blocks was at its peak, and each block was eager to draw the new countries of Africa into its camp. When the MPLA became clearly a client of the Soviet Union, the United States offered help to UNITA and FLNA, and any possibility of peaceful unification of Angola was destroyed. Twenty-seven years of one of the most savage civil wars in the modern history of the world ensued. The MPLA, supported by the Soviet Union with money and weapons and by communist Cuba with troops (which ultimately came to number as many as 50,000), gradually became the strongest force and therefore the group with the best claim to being the government of Angola. But the FLNA and UNITA continued to enjoy various kinds of support from the United Sates. Moreover the Union of South Africa had strategic interests that attracted South African forces to the support of UNITA in southeastern Angola. South Africa was locked in conflict with an armed liberation movement (the South-west African Peoples Organization – SWAPO) fighting to free Namibia from South African control. Ethnic affinities along the borders of Namibia and Angola made it easy for SWAPO to establish bases in southern Angola. In response, South Africa began to give support to UNITA against MPLA in southeastern Angola. Eventually,

South African forces became fully involved in the Angolan civil war. Also, for reasons of close ethnic affinities between the Bakongo people of Congo (Kinshasa) and the Bakongo of northern Angola, the Mobutu government of Congo (Kinshasa) gave strong support to FLNA. Consequently, the MPLA government forces (known as the FPLA) did not command enough power to take over the areas controlled by UNITA and FLNA, and the bitter conflicts continued from year to year. In the process, millions of Angolans were displaced from their homes and villages, many becoming refugees in refugee camps in Angola itself or in neighboring countries (especially Congo), while the rest simply fled into the forests – where they lived in barbarous conditions and died in countless thousands. Many provinces of Angola, one of the naturally richest countries of the world, sank into very desperate poverty.

Following a major battle in the southeast in 1988 in which FPLA, UNITA, Cuban forces and South African forces fought to a long stalemate, an agreement was brokered by the United Nations for the departure of Cuban and South African troops from Angola. Outside Angola, that agreement led to the independence of Namibia. But the fighting in Angola continued. After four more years of intense clashes, a treaty was signed by MPLA and UNITA in 1992 to end hostilities and to hold elections. An election was held, but UNITA rejected its outcome because the magnitude of MPLA's electoral victory appeared suspicious. Greatly intensified fighting then resumed – resulting in, according to some estimates, at least 30,000 civilian casualties and the displacement of many tens of thousands of people.

At last, in 2002, the death of the leader of UNITA, Jonas Savimbi, brought this terrible civil war to some sort of end. The cessation of fighting thus opened the door for effective unification of Angola under an MPLA-led government. However, it remained obvious that the road to harmonious unification of the many peoples of this country into one country was still far, and that the attitudes and policies of the government, and the tone of national politics, would be crucial in the quest for unification. For most of the following decade, the commonest assessment by informed observers was that the MPLA-led government appeared to assume that victory in the civil war had solved all problems of Angolan national unity – an assumption that could come to prove disastrous in the future.

Moreover, the issue of Cabinda's secessionist posture remained to be resolved. The enormous petroleum wealth of Cabinda makes this small enclave crucial to Angola's economy. In late 2002, forces of the MPLA-led government of Angola entered Cabinda and were confronted by a coalition of Cabindan freedom fighters, the Front for the Liberation of the Enclave of Cabinda (FLEC). The latter commanded only a few thousand troops and was no match for the larger, better armed and more experienced Angolan FPLA forces. Cabindan secessionism remains a threat, though a weakening threat, in Angola's side – especially a threat to the petroleum industry (the source of almost all of Angola's revenue and foreign exchange).[10]

The Zimbabwe Crisis

Zimbabwe's political history is somewhat similar to Angola's. British rule in this country which the British first named Southern Rhodesia, began in the 1890's, and developed essentially as rule by a small minority of white farmers who were given incentives by British authority to come and settle, and who never numbered more than 4% of the total population. The excessive claims of the white settlers to land and to political power early united the indigenous African peoples in a resistance struggle that ultimately became an armed struggle. In 1965, the white minority, in defiance of British authority and the Black majority, declared Zimbabwe independent – under unrestrained white minority rule. But this over-ambitious venture was doomed to fail. Opposed by Britain, by the countries of Africa, and by the international community in general, and confronted by a greatly escalated war of liberation by the Black majority, white minority rule fizzled out, and Zimbabwe became legally an independent country in 1980, with a democratic constitution providing for elective majority rule.

In its final years, Zimbabwe's liberation war had spawned two major guerrilla forces, based roughly in the homelands of the two main peoples of the country – Zimbabwe African Peoples Union (ZAPU) based among the Ndebele, and Zimbabwe African National Union-Patriotic Front (ZANU) based among the larger

Shona. The leaders of the two movements, Robert Mugabe of ZANU and Joshua Nkomo of ZAPU, served together on the first independence government, and everything seemed to point upwards for their country. Moreover, the utterances and disposition of Mugabe, who was enormously popular as liberation war hero, seemed to promise for this country a conciliatory and unifying leadership. Zimbabwe began immediately to make impressive economic and social progress, and seemed to have one of the rosiest futures among the countries of Africa.

But all of that happy prospect was soon to crash. Tension gradually built between the Shona and the Ndebele political elites, especially over Mugabe's desire to make the country a one-party state. Early in 1982, Mugabe fired Nkomo from the cabinet. Then a few weeks later, the government claimed to have discovered some secret arms caches, and alleged that these were weapons being secretly assembled by ZAPU for a violent overthrow of the government. Nkomo fled into exile; but he returned soon after, and the country plunged into violence. Terrorism spread in Matabeleland, homeland of the Ndebele, and the government forces sent there to quell the trouble committed, according to most reports, serious human rights violations. These brutalities reached a peak in 1987 and resulted in the killing of countless men, women and children. Matabeleland plunged into distress and serious food shortages.

In these circumstances, ZAPU agreed in December 1987 to merge with ZANU, and thereafter, Mugabe and Nkomo worked together again. But the divisions already engendered between the two peoples of the country would not go away. Worse still, Mugabe leaned more and more on his Shona ethnic support for political strength – and, whenever he found himself facing any serious political challenge, he developed the propensity to launch into erratic policies and into repression against his opponents. Thus, as his popularity waned in the 1990's, he (who had once spoken eloquently of accommodation and tolerance) embarked on the policy of seizing the white farmers' lands for distribution to the indigenous peasants. Land seizure and distribution revived Mogabe's popularity immediately, but it did serious havoc to the economy by destroying much of the white farmers' very significant contribution to the economy. And most of the farms seized ended up in the possession of Mugabe's cronies rather than of any peasants.

As Zimbabwe's economy declined, Mugabe's popularity plummeted. These developments reached a sort of climax in 2008. Defeated in an election in early 2008, Mugabe refused to accept the results of the election, launched a reign of terror against his opponents, and forced the country to go through another election. With his leading opponents in detention, in flight, or frightened into withdrawing from the contest, Mugabe claimed victory – but had to agree, reluctantly, to a power-sharing arrangement with his opponents. All this disruption dragged the already ailing Zimbabwean economy sharply down, resulting in uncontrollable inflation, drastic shortages of goods, intense distress all over the country, the emergence of civic disturbances and riots – and, inevitably, rising doubts about the country's future. A cholera epidemic came soon to compound Zimbabwe's disaster. But Mugabe held on to power, even as significant voices in the world called on him to step down, and even as the drastic sufferings of his people made his position untenable.[11]

Nigeria's Gradual Meltdown

It is absolutely easy for the foreign observer to miss or misunderstand one other manifestation of this second generation of Africa's political disasters. In Nigeria, Africa's largest country in population, some semblance of peace has reigned since the end of the Biafran war of secession. But in reality, there rages persistently below the surface an insidious war, and openly an almost unbroken series of local wars and vicious blood-letting, all of which combine to make this country one of the most disjointed and insecure countries on the African continent.

As will be seen in subsequent pages, the pattern of relentlessly hostile relationships among most of the nearly three-hundred nationalities of this country was established under British colonial rule. This was Britain's most valuable possession in Africa, and the British, before leaving, took very deliberate and detailed steps to install in firm control the favored elite of one of the nations – the Muslim Hausa-Fulani people of the North whom the British rulers believed they could count on to protect British interests after independence. Hence, the dominant theme in the politics of Nigeria consists of a perpetual war - between the relentless efforts by the Hausa-Fulani, not merely to hold on to power, but to keep expanding on it, and the efforts of the other peoples to resist, even though they have never managed to unite to do so. In the circumstance, Nigeria does not practice politics as politics is known in the rest of the world. Most of what goes for politics in Nigeria is a truculent rivalry among the larger ones of Nigeria's nearly 300 nationalities, a contest in mutually hostile intrigues, crookedness and falsifications, all wrapped in mutual accusations, insults and undermining. Nigeria's political parties are, in all essence, cabals of the elite of these larger nationalities, made to look Nigeria-wide through a uniquely Nigerian brand of interwoven intrigues, sordid and shrouded dealings, bribery and corruption. Employing the unequalled influence that flows from the control of the federal apparatus from the day of independence, the British-favored Hausa-Fulani has invariably succeeded in holding on to federal power, in using the federal power and resources to concoct the most dominant "party" in Nigeria, in recruiting subordinate "allies" from among the elite of the other nationalities into that party, and in enriching those allies and rigging elections for them all over the country. Since the 1970's Nigeria has not fought another civil war like the Biafran war, but it has continually fought a less visible war that is a lot more destructive of good relations, societal values, and economic wellbeing.

Countless observers in the international community have written about this Nigerian enigma - the monumental and defiant culture of official corruption, the perpetual election rigging and election conflicts, the political assassinations, the almost sub-human propensity of Nigerian public officials to lie and cheat, the barbarism and sadism of the crimes on Nigerian highways and in Nigerian cities, the casual impunity in the slaughter of ethnic and religious opponents, etc. The response of Nigeria's rulers to all the writings and warnings is that they are merely part of a Western conspiracy to give Nigeria and Africa a bad image in the world.

Since the end of the 1970's, Islamic fundamentalism has loomed larger and larger as a factor in the contorted political life of Nigeria, contributing one of the most devastating inputs yet. It started with efforts to impose Sharia law on the country, even though the country is roughly 40% Muslim, 40% Christian and 20% devotees of various traditional religions. In particular, Christian culture among the large Igbo nation of the Southeast (estimated at about 40 million), and the smaller peoples of the Southeast and the Middle Belt, resistance arose powerfully to the Islamizing agenda. Among the large Yoruba nation of the Southwest – a people over 40 million in population, with equal millions of Christians and Muslims, and with strong ancient traditions of religious tolerance – the tradition of religious tolerance and accommodation held firm and the Muslims resisted all enticement into radical or fundamentalist Islam. Northern Muslim frustration with all the resistance gradually bred hostility towards non-Muslims, with Muslin mobs suddenly arising to destroy churches and massacre Christians in northern towns. Then, there emerged organized radical Islamic youth groups burning and destroying churches and slaughtering Christians and moderate Muslims, rampaging through towns and villages and leaving scenes of devastation, death and ruin in their path. More and more, southerners (mostly Christians) resident in northern cities have had to live in fear for their lives. In some retaliation, some southern cities occasionally become dangerous for resident citizens of northern origin.

In the Middle Belt region of Nigeria where the smallest and most marginalized nationalities live, neighboring Muslim and Christian nationalities are more and more at war with one another, resulting in unspeakable viciousness, blood-letting, and ethnic cleansing. The relentless expansion of the Sahara Desert southwards in some farthest northern parts of Nigeria, and the loss of grazing land to Fulani nomadic pastoralists there, have been adding a murderous element to the Nigerian mix. Those Fulani who have lost their cattle make a practice of forming armed gangs that violently seize cattle from the others. Forced to bring their cattle further to the south, the pastoralists have increasingly had, out of desperation, to fight and kill farming folks in order to grab some grazing space for their cattle, a development that is generating horrific danger for the pastoralists and the farming populations in many parts of the country – even as far as the southernmost states. In the Niger Delta provinces of Nigeria, where all of Nigeria's mineral oil is produced, neglect and marginalization has provoked an armed rebellion more or less since independence; in recent times, that rebellion has grown very mature in strategy, in tactics, and in weaponry, and attracts increasing worldwide attention.

In the course of the first decade of the 21st century, the tradition of organized Islamic fundamentalist youth groups finally produced a very major group named Boko Haram. As of this writing, Boko Haram ranks as the most violent Islamic fundamentalist group in Africa, and the most notorious worldwide. Defying Nigeria's military forces, it has killed about 13,000 people (according to some official sources), and virtually subdued the three states of the Nigerian Northeast (Bornu, Yobe and Adamawa), over which it claims to have established a caliphate.

In Nigerian politics, there is no calling to high ideals like loyalty to the people, patriotism, or dedication to the improvement of the people's quality of life. From the persons holding public office in the Federal Government, to those holding public office in the State Governments and the Local Governments, the culture of public service is the same: on a regular basis, share among the members of the power elite much, sometimes even most, of the revenue accruing to the government. One visitor to Nigeria joked that in other countries, public corruption means that the public official steals some of his country's resources that are put under his command, but that in Nigeria it can often mean that the public official steals all. This culture of graft, corruption and violence holds Nigeria in its grip, rigging its favorites into positions of power in elections at all three levels of government (federal, state, and local), and not hesitating to assassinate those who appear to stand in its way. Even among the favorites, assassinations and brutalities are common – occasioned by internal rivalries over access to public money. The system perpetuates itself and renders itself unassailable by employing public money to corrupt persons employed in all agencies of government – the judiciary, the police, the security establishments, regulatory bodies like the electoral commission, etc. No matter what direction its opponents turn for redress or justice, its immovable rock awaits them. No matter how much electoral support the opponents may have among their own people in their home bases, the heavily corrupted electoral apparatus is there to crook up the election results against them and give victory to the favorites. And, if the robbed candidate petitions the courts, the heavily corrupted election tribunals await him. Started under British rule, the edifice of corruption became systematized into an avowed instrument of governance in the 1970's and 1980's, as Nigeria's oil revenues ballooned. The credo of governance in the late 1980' was "every person has a price"; and the practice was to identify particular citizens or citizen groups and 'settle' them – that is, heavily bribe them into keeping quiet or into joining the corruption mainstream. The enormous revenue accruing to Nigeria from Nigeria's huge petroleum resources provides the abundant funds for this style of government.

Nigeria is one of the world's leading producers of mineral oil, and the fifth largest supplier of oil to the United States. In spite of such enormous wealth, the weaker and more vulnerable of Nigeria's citizens live in ever deepening poverty, and the smallest and easily marginalized nationalities live in ever deepening neglect. In Nigeria, contracts for the building or maintenance of public facilities (roads, electricity, water installations, etc.) are usually tools for stealing and sharing public money, with the result that the country has steadily grown poorer in infrastructures. Denied resources, Nigeria's public educational institutions suffer unrestrained decay and degeneration, as well as frequent strikes by teachers and professors and frequent rioting by students. Quite commonly in Nigeria's public universities, undergraduate courses that are supposed to be completed in four academic years drag on for six or more years – as a result of the strikes and riots, and consequent closures. Unemployment among Nigeria's school and college graduates is rated among the worst in the world.

For most self-respecting educated youths, the best option is to flee abroad, resulting in a large Nigerian diaspora in most countries of the world, and the unhappy outcome that, in more and more countries, even in Africa, Nigerian immigrants are increasingly being rejected. Thousands of Nigerian youths have been reported every year trying to reach southern Europe by walking across the Sahara Desert to North Africa, many dying in the desert, and probably most of the rest ending up in prisons in countries of the North African coast or on islands in the Mediterranean. Crimes – some staggeringly unbelievable crimes –

grow exponentially, making life generally insecure, even in the remotest rural communities. Destitution, street begging, prostitution (including prostitution for export) are the lot of increasing numbers of Nigerian citizens. Stories of parents selling their young children, many into an export slave trade, are on the increase.

With all of Nigeria's oil revenue and other resources, the country should be a land of great business opportunities for its business-inclined citizens, the greatest land of business in Africa. On the surface, it is, and many Nigerians do manage to do well in business. But too much of what goes for business in Nigeria consists of pieces in the Nigerian culture of corruption – contraptions put together for sharing stolen public resources, huge public contracts that are not meant to build or supply anything but to pull out public money for sharing between the contractors and the public officials, public constructions for which contracts are awarded over and over and over, fraudulently over-priced public contracts, sophisticated bribery and money laundering schemes, etc. The fact that Nigeria is always awash with such fraudulent deals and practices tends to cast a shadow of distrust on Nigerian business people in general both at home and abroad, and to attract the most fraudulent people in international business into Nigeria. That creates very serious problems for Nigeria's genuine business people, both at home and abroad. Also, as sharing of stolen public money has become the dominant means of personal enrichment in the Nigerian economy, Nigeria has become increasingly a country in which the ambitious and enterprising tend to avoid genuinely productive enterprises and veer into political or quasi-political wheeling and dealing where access to the sharing of stolen public money is the easy road to wealth.

Moreover, the very strong ethnic dominance factor in Nigeria's affairs has usually produced the tendency to appoint the persons in control of the commanding heights of the Nigerian economy (the Minister of Finance, the Minister for Economic Planning, the Governor of the Nigerian Central Bank, the key persons controlling the Nigerian Customs, the Nigerian National Ports Authority, etc.) on considerations of dominant ethnicity only, often with little or no regard for qualification or experience. Worse still, the mode of management of Nigerian affairs (with elected legislators earning remunerations reportedly larger than that of the President of America) has gradually nurtured the outcome of depressing the business and middle class while emphasizing and boosting a rich political class – an outcome which diverts resources away from productive capital formation into huge unproductive wealth in the hands of politicians, and that accounts for the fact that Nigerians own some of the largest accumulations of the Third World's stolen public money hidden in foreign banks. Nigeria lacks the will, and the desire to nurture the will, and even the awareness of the need, to develop in openness and order, and to prosper together as one country. The management of its economic life, like that of its political life, is governed by caprice, conflict and confusion, with consequently deepening poverty for the masses of its people. In the richness and variety of natural resources, Nigeria stands among the highest in the world. Sadly, from that rich resource base, Nigeria is somehow managing to produce great poverty for most of its people. According to national information published by the Nigerian National Bureau of Statistics, close to 70% of Nigerians lived in "absolute poverty" by the year 2011, and the condition was growing worse.

Some of the bitter fruits of the Nigerian situation are already coming in. As would be remembered, one region of Nigeria, the oil-producing Niger Delta, has been up in arms against the federal government for decades. In the course of the first years of the 21st century, the spirit of Biafran secessionism, repressed by force in the civil war of 1967-70, has arisen strongly again. A group of highly educated youths of the Igbo nation (one of the three largest of Nigeria's nationalities) founded a militant organization with the deliberately defiant name of MASSOB – Movement for the Actualization of the Sovereign State of Biafra. In spite of official Nigerian efforts to suppress MASSOB with the police and the armed forces, MASSOB has continued to grow in organization and in strategic and tactical sophistication – and in popularity among its people. Among the Yoruba too (another one of the three largest Nigerian peoples) a militant youth organization with the name of Odua Peoples Congress (OPC) has existed since the late 1990's. Founded for the purpose of forcefully defending Yoruba interests against the violent military regime of the 1990's, OPC has continued to exist – a potentially formidable source of

71

strength for the defense and promotion of Yoruba interests. The emergence and existence of these movements and others mark a very significant phase in the political history of Nigeria. More and more, rumblings of secessionist agitation intensify. In fact, by the year 2010, Nigeria's spate of inter-ethnic and religious conflicts and mass killings, and the pace of disintegration, began to rise to new heights, leading to worldwide fears that the final stumbling of this country towards its ultimate implosion had started.

CHAPTER THREE

Distorting Africa's Future

The Black Africa of the previous chapters is the Black Africa of today – the Black Africa that emerged from the crucible of the European imperialism of the 20th century. Before European imperialism, there had been the Africa that had long been ordered by indigenous African governments and political systems, all of which had been evolved over millennia by African peoples and nations themselves. Most of these pre-colonial Black African peoples and states were small or even very small but, in spite of that, and in spite of three centuries of ravages by the trans-Atlantic slave trade, none was, in the late 19th century, the home of mass violence, pogroms and genocide, of masses of displaced persons and refugees, or of massive refugee camps.

We will now deal with the genesis of how this earlier Black Africa has come to turn to the troubled and tormented Black Africa of today. As Black Africa stood by the last years of the 19th century, there were strong possibilities of state formations with which the subcontinent could have entered into the 20th century's world of changes in a considerably more orderly and more sustainable manner. Unfortunately for Africans, those possibilities were forcibly preempted by European imperialist intrusions and disruptions, producing convoluted problems that now seem intractable. It is not being contended that this is the only cause of the instability and disorder plaguing Black Africa in our times; but it is the foundational root.

Preliminary Considerations

Before delving into the subject, however, it is important to give a brief attention to certain preliminary considerations. The first concerns the manner in which African troubles are perceived in the world. The root causes of Black Africa's political conflicts are, certainly, very complex. For that reason – among the consequences of the complexity – reports of the African conflicts in the world's news media tend to be both paltry and superficial. For instance, according to Wadim Schreiner[1], in the period from

January 1, 2002 to June 30, 2003, less than 0.2% of all British, German and United States TV news and reports on conflicts in the world focused on conflicts and wars in Africa – even though some of the world's biggest and most destructive wars and conflicts were raging in Africa. Because African conflicts and wars often do not appear to affect obvious interests of Western powers, and involve less and less of Western intervention, they are treated as if they do not deserve attention. Even the few news and reports tend commonly to focus only on the brutalities of the conflicts and wars, and to suggest very simplistic, and even racist, explanations about Black Africans and their conflicts. Black Africans tend to be represented as peculiar – different from all other humans, too primitive and too intellectually immature to understand and manage modern states, modern businesses, and modern institutions. Black Africans are also represented as being so conditioned by the political oppression of their long pre-colonial history as to be unable to reject oppression decisively in modern times. All of these are echoes from pseudo-scientific and ethno-centric beliefs that were very popularly held in the Western World for centuries into the era of European imperialism in Africa. Though explicitly avowing them may have become universally unacceptable today, they still tend to taint much of Western views and attitudes concerning Africans and African issues. To get into grips with the roots of Black Africa's political conflicts and political problems in our time, the world needs to abandon these backward prejudices.

The other special consideration is closely related to the above. This author is aware that his use of the words 'nations' and 'nationalities' for the peoples of Black Africa will provoke objections in some quarters. A very significant feature of the heritage of European colonialism in Africa is the categorization of the ethno-linguistic groups of Africa – that is African peoples each of which has its distinct culture, language, and homeland territory of its own, and whose members regard themselves as one distinct group – as "tribes". Similar entities in Europe are 'nations' or 'nationalities'. European imperialist agents and administrators in Africa, and European scholars working for or with European imperialist establishments, drummed up and popularized such categorizations of African peoples in order to trivialize the complexity of African societies. Literate Africans themselves then accepted it from their European rulers and teachers, and entrenched it in their serious writings about their peoples as well as in their general political vocabulary – with the result that 'tribe' has come to be universally perceived as a more or less unique tropical African category, an African primitive human-group type, hardly to be found in other parts of the world

To be sure, most of the ethno-linguistic groups of Black Africa are small or very small, and that, undoubtedly, is a very major and fundamental reality in the political difficulties of Africa in modern times – as will be seen further on. But such smallness does not detract from the status of these African peoples as nations or nationalities – just as the smallness of the small peoples of the Balkans, the Caucasus, parts of the Alps, and parts of the Low Countries in Europe does not detract from their status as nations or nationalities.

This point is crucial to a clear understanding of the African situation. It is not merely academic – or merely a product of African nationalism. Perception directs much of human choices. Because the agents of European imperialism, as they came scrambling for territorial possessions in Africa in the last decades of the 19th century, regarded the national groups of tropical Africa as inferior entities in comparison to the nationalities of their own Europe, they went on to conceive of the political geography of Africa in ways that generated actions that seriously disrupted and distorted the lives of African peoples – thereby creating a problem that now haunts Africa. For Africans to understand what has happened to them as peoples and cultures, and to be able to re-orientate themselves towards reordering their affairs towards orderliness, peace and progress in the modern world, Africans themselves need to look a lot more perceptively, more carefully and more correctly at their continent. And to understand the predicament of modern Africa, and be correctly intellectually ready to help the African situation, the rest of the world – especially the peoples of the Western World – need to get rid of encrusted perceptions born of the eras of the Slave Trade and of European imperialism in Africa; and need a clear understanding of Africa and what is wrong with Africa today.

Roots Deep in African Political Structure

Black Africa is peculiarly a land of mostly very small ethnic groups or nationalities. Even at today's population levels (after a century of rapid population growths), almost all of the sub-continent is still home to very small nationalities. Its largest nationalities are the three that live in the West Africa sub-region, namely the three giants of Nigeria (Yoruba, Hausa-Fulani and Igbo, each of which is estimated at about between 35 and 45 million). After these three, the few that are next in population size are much smaller, ranging roughly between 11 million and 18 million. These include the Nguni of the Union of South Africa (consisting of many small loosely related linguistic groups), the Ijaw of the Nigerian Niger Delta (also consisting of many small loosely related linguistic groups), the Bakongo of the Congo basin (now split between Congo Kinshasa, Angola, and Congo Brazzaville), the Akhan (in the Republic of Ghana), the Fula spread thinly over much of the West African Sudan and Sahel, the Shona of Zimbabwe, the Somali of the Horn of Africa, and the Amhara and Oromo of Ethiopia. The next ones below these are also few and much smaller. Each of them is estimated at between five and nine million in population. They include the Sotho of the Union of South Africa, the Kikuyu of Kenya, the Ewe of Ghana, the Kanuri and related peoples, as well as the Edo and related peoples, of Nigeria.

The rest of the sub-continent is shared among thousands of nationalities. Some have populations in the range of a couple of millions. Of the overwhelming majority, each has much less than that – many having populations of only a few tens of thousands.

With this minute ethno-linguistic fragmentation of the Black African sub-continent, every Black African country of our times, including the two (Liberia and Ethiopia) that are not creations of modern European colonialism, comprises tens of nationalities. Nigeria, the largest in population, with some 170 million people, has over 300 nationalities – of which the three largest share about 130 million. Clearly over one-hundred of Nigerian nationalities have populations of only a few hundred thousand or less each. Nigeria's immediate western neighbor, the small Republic of Benin with a population of about eight million, is home to about 40 nationalities – a condition about typical of most Black African countries. Tanzania, with a population of about 38 million, has about 120 ethnic groups.

Of the two neighboring continents – Asia and Africa – subjected to European imperialism in modern times, Asia is considerably different from Black Africa in this. Larger nationalities share most of the land mass of Asia. Besides the largest two (the Han Chinese and the Hindu, the largest and second largest nationalities in the world), Asia boasts of many other fairly large nationalities – the Koreans, Vietnamese, Japanese, Javanese – as well as smaller but still considerably large ones like the Burmese, Malays, Laotians, etc. Asia does have many small nationalities too, but she does not approach the minutely fragmented condition characteristic of most of Black Africa.

The British scholar, Margery Perham, wrote in the 1950s that the dealings of European imperialists with Africa had to be different from their dealings with Asia.

"The dealings between tropical Africa and the West must be different. Here, in place of the larger unities of Asia, was the multi-cellular tissue of tribalism".[2]

Her language here is typical language of European colonial attitudes in Africa – language meant more to denigrate and trivialize African subjects than to describe. Nevertheless, the facts are easy to separate from her verbiage. Asia presented many more of "larger unities" of nationality and culture than Black Africa did at the advent of European colonialism.

Therefore, no matter whatever form Black Africa's entry into the world of the 20th century (the world of the second Industrial Revolution, of exploding technology, of fast growing modern world economy, etc.) would have taken, this fundamental problem would have been indeed a difficult reality to handle. But, unfortunately, Black Africa's entry into the world of the 20th century actually took perhaps the worst form imaginable in the circumstance – namely, through conquest, control and direction by a people who were operating from deep reserves of disrespect and even spite for Black African peoples. In the process, European imperialism came to compound and confound the sub-continent's fundamental problem – and made of it a massive and tenacious nightmare for all its peoples. Approaching Africa with the typical attitudes of the Europe of the time, the makers of various European "possessions" trampled down their parts of the sub-continent, conceding no respect or consideration to any people, cutting boundaries through even obviously solid peoples, and creating territorial agglomerations in such ways as to make room for little or no likelihood of cohesion immediately or in any future.

Distinctive Pre-colonial Features

These makers of European colonialism in tropical Africa were absolutely not disposed to see or recognize any distinctive entities anywhere in Black Africa. But there were indeed many distinctive states and peoples. Within its national homeland territory, each people had been evolving its own unique political structure and traditions for many centuries or perhaps even millennia before the 19th century, and the general tropical African situation was by no means, politically, a featureless medley or a static or immobile landscape. It was a product of on-going political evolutions. Among the features of the long history of evolution and change was, as in Europe and other continents, the emergence here and there of centralized states, of expansionist kingdoms, and of empires ruling over large territories and, sometimes, over many different nationalities. All this meant, at bottom, successful farming, trade, long-distance trade routes, development of art in various mediums, and the making of wars, conquests, alliances, etc., resulting in expanding or shrinking command of wealth, as well as expanding or shrinking states, etc. It also meant adjustment to changing conditions and changing opportunities, and the production of significant leaderships in political, religious and other areas of life.

The West African region (today the home of a majority of Black Africans) was home to the largest nationalities of Africa (but also to many small nationalities), and of some of the most memorable African kingdoms, even before the earliest European explorations of the African coasts in the 15th century. A generally suitable land for farming, watered by many river systems (of which the River Niger is the most important) led in Late Stone Age times to fairly large and growing human populations in this region of Africa. As the spread of population gradually became

78

differentiated into ethno-linguistic or national groups, some of the national groups developed into the largest nationalities in Black Africa. Migrations in various directions were a part of this picture. The beginning and spread of the use of iron from about the 7th century BC made agriculture more prosperous and further enhanced the growth of population. Trade developed, resulting in a copious network of trade routes linking most of the sub-continent. From about the beginning of the Christian era, various types of state formation began. About the same time, a major development entered the scene – namely the growth of long trade routes linking the Mediterranean coast of Africa to parts of West Africa through the Sahara Desert, bringing new opportunities for trade and wealth – and, some centuries later, bringing the religion of Islam. In the long period from the first century to the 16th century, the basin of the Upper Niger and the grasslands around it spawned a series of West Africa's first large empires – Ghana, Mali, and Songhai. By the 13th century, eye-witness accounts testified to widespread existence of cities and urban civilization in these lands – in an age when such did not exist in much of Europe. Further eastwards and southeastwards, in the countries of the Hausa, Kanuri, Akan, Nupe, Tiv, Yoruba, Igbo, and Edo, many small rich kingdoms were born, many of them homes of cultural and artistic flowering, and, in the more northern regions, some pockets of Islamic faith.

This was the situation when Europeans came to the western coasts of Africa in the last years of the 15th century, leading to the beginning of the Atlantic Slave Trade in the early 16th century. The smallest, and the least politically organized nations, (but also some of the larger ones) lost large numbers of people to the Slave Trade in the course of the next three centuries, and suffered various kinds and degrees of disruption. Some of the larger and better organized peoples fared better. In the forests of the coasts of the Bight of Benin, the Edo kingdom of Benin became a rich middle-man trader on the coast and mostly prevented the sale of its citizens into the Slave Trade. Many of the neighboring Yoruba kingdoms were hardly touched by the devastations of the slave trade, and during the period continued to grow as a great farming, manufacturing and trading people, with a sophisticated monarchical system and highly advanced art traditions. In fact, one Yoruba kingdom of the far northern Yoruba country, close to the southern banks of the

Middle Niger, prospering from the advantages of the trans-Saharan trade, expanded and built the largest empire in the West African forest country south of the Niger, unifying substantial numbers of Yoruba kingdoms, as well as some non-Yoruba peoples, into one polity. In the territory of the Niger Delta on the coast, a number of trading city states arose. In the country of the Akan (in territory that would later become the modern Republic of Ghana), one of the many Akan kingdoms became rich and powerful and absorbed a number of other Akan kingdoms, to become one of the most notable states of West Africa.

The Accelerated Transformations of the 19ᵗʰ Century

From the opening of the 19ᵗʰ century (in some cases from the last decades of the 18ᵗʰ), the pace of change markedly accelerated in most parts of Black Africa. Historians are yet to identify many of the indigenous elements in the causation of these developmental jumps beginning from about 1800. In the expansive grasslands of the West African interior, some empire-building movements arose, each having Islam as part of its motivating force – and each succeeded in forging political unity for a large expanse of territory and many peoples. South of the Middle Niger, the large and prosperous country of the Yoruba people, home of many rich small kingdoms, was swept by a revolution that shook the Yoruba traditional order, generated a series of internal wars, and engineered big demographic, economic and political transformations. This ultimately produced, among other major changes, a strong armed effort initiated by the large Yoruba city of Ibadan (Yorubaland's, and tropical Africa's, largest town in the century) to end the political division of Yorubaland into many kingdoms, and to unify the Yoruba country into one all-encompassing Yoruba state. In the far end of southern Africa, a sudden rush of political change wiped out most of the small Bantu chiefdoms and generated much larger kingdoms. About the same happened in the Great Lakes region of east-central Africa-resulting in stronger kingdoms in Buganda and, to some extent, in Burundi.

In short, though most of the Black African sub-continent was still home to countless thousands of mostly small nationalities by the second half of the 19th century, fairly large and distinctive polities had emerged and were emerging in all regions of the sub-continent. In terms of political formation, the picture of tropical Africa was being transformed by its own peoples, with its own indigenous means, and in its own indigenous ways.

Meanwhile, a series of worldwide forces began to come during the 19th century to reinforce and add new color to this process of faster transformations. The trans-Atlantic Slave Trade and Black African slavery in the Americas and other Atlantic lands waned gradually as various European and American countries gave them up during the century. Trade in African products with the outside world grew. Responding to the new trade and benefiting from it, Black African farmers in most parts of the sub-continent, as well as craftsmen and artisans, expanded production, and indigenous merchant champions of the new trade emerged in commercially strategic places in the sub-continent.

At the same time, many persons liberated from slavery in the Americas trickled back home, mostly to West Africa, bringing new skills, new cultural assets, new perspectives on life, new crops, and the new religion of Christianity . Those of them who were Muslims before being taken to the Americas or who were converted to Islam by fellow slaves in the Americas, arrived to reinforce Islam, especially in West Africa's coastal countries. On the heels of the swelling stream of repatriates (also known as the emigrants) came Christian missions of various denominations and various European nationalities. And with the Christian missions, assisted by the growing crowd of returnees from the Americas and other parts of the Atlantic world, came Western education and literacy.

In an increasing number of places on the coast and in the interior, the impacts of the emigrants, Christian evangelism, Western education, the new trade and its merchants, the indigenous political and social systems, all were combining to produce new patterns of political, economic and social order. All of these held forth enormous possibilities and potentialities for all peoples of Black Africa.

In short, Black Africa, taking advantage of a whole array of native and worldwide influences, was already charting its own path, in its own way, to the modern world and the modern world's economy that were gradually evolving in the late 19th century. The possibilities were limitless for every people on the African continent.

European Intrusions and Disruption

But then, the massive European military and political intrusions began, stopping, redirecting, distorting, and massively disrupting the on-going transformations. Every Black African people, large or small, was forced into directions that it neither chose nor contributed to – especially into political formations that, in independent and realistic consideration of their interests, they might not have chosen.

The following, then, are brief descriptions of a selection of some of the most significant Black African peoples and polities that came to be impacted in this way by the European imperialist intrusion and onslaught at the end of the century. The objective here is not a general or comprehensive account of the European scramble for African territorial possessions in the last decades of the 19th century; it is only to make the point that there were indeed notable and significant peoples and states in most parts of Black Africa, peoples and states many of whom put up creditable resistance to the European intrusion. Every region of Africa had some of such peoples and states. What is common to them all is that they were all responding (each in its own unique way) to the formative influences impacting their world in the course of the 19th century, but were suddenly forcibly diverted to totally different, and often disruptive, paths by the coming of European imperialism. The cumulative consequence of all their experiences is that Africa was denied the freedom to choose, chart, and pursue its own kinds of entry into the emerging modern world of the 20th century.

The Yoruba Nation[3]

We start with the Yoruba of West Africa – the people now numbering about 50 million in the south of the middle Niger, and split between Nigeria, Benin Republic and Togo Republic. The Yoruba had, long before the 19th century, built the most advanced urban civilization in Black Africa – with very many fairly large walled towns only a few miles apart in their large homeland, sophisticated monarchical states (much like Germany and its many states before German unification in1871), a vibrant economy, and the richest art culture in Black Africa.

The political framework of the culture had a significantly democratic character. Kings and chiefs of the Yoruba kingdoms were not automatically succeeded by their biological sons. When a king died, his subjects selected a successor from among the pool of eligible princes of the royal lineage. And when any of the quarter or neighborhood chiefs died, his usually large lineage held meetings to select one of themselves (one that was adjudged most acceptable to themselves, to the other chiefs of the kingdom, to the king, and to the whole community), and handed him to the king and the chiefs and priests to install as chief. The culture regarded every individual as a chip of the ancestors (the progenitors of the nation and of the lineages) – and therefore as someone worthy of respect in his person, and worthy to be respectfully heard in the affairs of his lineage, societal associations, and the whole community. In the circumstance, protection of the freedom of speech became essentially a religious duty of agencies of leadership in all aspects of community's life. The culture also developed a uniquely strong kind of respect for its women. According to Yoruba mythology, the world was put together in such a way at its beginning that, for anything to succeed in it, the place of the women must be conscientiously guaranteed. Part of the inclusion of women in economic life was that Yoruba women became, almost exclusively, the managers of the group's commercial life, and enjoyed the freedom to take trade to distant parts of the Yoruba homeland – and even to distant parts of their continent. As a result, rich Yoruba women traders were regularly among the richest people in the community, and among the most influential - and, as long-distance traders, among the most knowledgeable about other lands and peoples. And every Yoruba kingdom had special cadres of women chiefs.

The first European foreigners who saw the interior of Yorubaland (the English explorer Hugh Clapperton and his team in 1825)[4] recorded that the roads through Yorubaland were good (were in many parts *"a long broad and beautiful avenue"*) and well protected ("*carefully watched by overseers*"); the country everywhere was richly farmed (with "*fields of Indian corn*", "*plantations of cotton*", "*extensive plantations of corn and plantains*", "*rich plantations of yams*"), the highways were busy day and night with traders and their merchandise porters, as well as other general travelers. The people lived under very respectable government (and "*pay the greatest respect to the laws*") and were happy and wonderfully hospitable. "*We experienced as much civility from them as our own countrymen would have bestowed upon us in our own native land.*" In every town or village, the explorers were thronged by inquisitive crowds who "were, generally speaking, neatly dressed - - - and very cleanly in their personal appearance", and "pleasing in their manners" and self-respecting. The explorers wanted to pay money to young men to carry their leader (Clapperton) in a hammock, but found that no Yoruba youth would do such a thing; it was a task which, they all responded, was "*fit only for horses*". In one village a group of strong boys, after a lot of entreaties, reluctantly agreed to do it, and lifted the hammock to their shoulders – but, wrote the explorers, "*the bearers had proceeded only a few paces when it was, for some uncountable reason, suddenly let down, and the fellows scampered away as fast as their legs would carry them*". No Yoruba boy would do that kind of job for anybody. However, the explorers were regularly able to recruit porters for their loads and borrow horses from some rulers and rich citizens.

The whole country was dotted throughout with large walled towns at short distances from one another, and the towns were "densely inhabited" and remarkable for their cleanliness, their music and their art. Even the small villages in between the towns were "cleanly habitations". Most towns were "*delightfully situated*", and were approached "*through a beautiful walk of trees*" or "through a spacious avenue of noble trees". In every town, large and crowded market places sold innumerable kinds of merchandise. On a busy market day, the collective swell of bargaining in any of these market places could be heard like a roaring of the sea from many miles away. Some market places specialized in night-time trading, with every trader using an oil lamp to illuminate her merchandise. When one approached one of such marketplaces in session, it was as if one was heading towards a sea of stars.

The rulers and subordinate chiefs in every town or village were dignified and very professional and respectable. They generally welcomed the explorers with kindness, and were always ready to help. About king after king they wrote of a monarch "richly dressed", with ornaments. One king was in a meeting with his chiefs when the explorers arrived. The explorers were kept waiting until the king was ready to see them. They wrote of him, *"We found him in earnest conversation with his elders - - - altogether forming the most venerable-looking group of human beings I ever saw"*. The king was *"a tall thin man, well stricken in years, and respectably dressed in a silk tobe and trousers of country cloth. On his head he wore a cap thickly studded with various colored glass beads - - and small gold-colored tassels of beads hung from it to the shoulders."*

After seeing Yoruba sculptural art in all the towns and villages, the explorers wrote that the Yoruba people *"appear to have a genius for the art of sculpture, which is in great repute with them; and some of their productions rival, in point of delicacy, any of a similar kind that I have seen in Europe"*. Many pieces of sculpture decorated most buildings, especially public buildings like palaces and shrines. About a century later, a European ethnologist (the German, Leo Frobenius who visited Ife in the heart of Yorubaland in1910), wrote of Yoruba naturalistic sculptural art that it is *"eloquent of a symmetry, a vitality, a delicacy of form directly reminiscent of ancient Greece"*, and a late 20th century British art historian (Frank Willet) wrote that they *"stand comparison with anything which ancient Egypt, classical Greece and Rome, or Renaissance Europe, had to offer"*.

By the late 1840's in the Yoruba coastal town of Lagos, a rich indigenous merchant class, (men and women) already existed. In the ensuing competition for the trade of the large Yoruba interior, these indigenous Yoruba merchants commanded many advantages over the foreign companies – Portuguese, British, Brazilian, German, and French. As a result, the foreign companies generally left all of the trade of the interior (distribution of imported goods, procurement and movement of export goods to the coast) in their hands. Many owned large mercantile businesses in

Lagos and in the interior as early as the 1850's; one of the most famous was a woman, Madam Tinubu; at least one even had a shipping line of his own by the 1870's. And much of the wealth was being invested in the establishment of schools as well as in sending children to Europe for higher education. An indigenous class of professionals (lawyers, accountants, journalists, doctors, etc.) was growing rapidly, and the earliest local newspapers made their appearance as early as 1859. In the Yoruba interior, the ancient Yoruba institution of trade caravan (made up of many traders and their merchandise porters traveling together) blossomed enormously. One British Anglican missionary estimated that a caravan that he traveled with in the vicinity of Ibadan in 1854 consisted of *"not less than 4000 persons"*, and an American Baptist missionary, after extensive travels through Yorubaland about the same time, described Yorubaland as a land of caravans. The American missionary, William H. Clarke, wrote:

"The trade in native produce and art keeps up continual intercommunication between the several adjacent towns, the one interchanging its abundance of one article for that of another. Thus on those smaller routes may be seen caravans of fifties passing almost daily from one town to another, acting as the great reservoirs of trade. (On the longer routes) a network of trade is carried to a distance of hundreds of miles, and with an energy and perseverance scarcely compatible with a tropical people. Hundreds and thousands of people are thus engaged in the carrying trade. Not infrequently, the articles from the Mediterranean and Western (European) coast may be seen in close proximity, and productions of the four quarters of the globe within a circumference whose diameter may be measured by a few yards".[5]

Clarke added that in certain circumstances when several caravans were thrown together, *"a correct idea of the extent of trade may be found in the imposing numbers that stretch over several miles in length"* across the countryside. Even if there was war in a particular locality, a lot of trade kept going in all directions there, because the Yoruba laws of war accorded special protection to the trader and the peaceful traveler.

A class of big local merchants and small retailers grew up in the towns of the Yoruba interior. One of the best known of the former, a woman chief in the town of Ibadan about one hundred miles north of Lagos, owned not only one of the largest commercial businesses in the country but also a large farming enterprise which, in the 1870's, employed more than 2000 workers. Travelers in the country observed that large-scale food-crop farming, and the production of export crops (like palm oil, cotton, kola-nuts, etc.) were widespread and increasing very noticeably in all parts.

While the roots of a potentially dynamic modern economy were thus crystallizing in the country of the Yoruba, political and other developments also pointed to a future of great possibilities for the Yoruba nation. By 1865, the Ibadan-based drive to unify all of the Yoruba country through the force of arms had achieved much outstanding successes, but it was to encounter significant resistance in some parts of the country in the years that followed, and its chances in some of those parts were doubtful. However, other potentially unifying forces were entering onto the scene. Growing literacy was creating a literate Yoruba elite that increasingly promoted pride in Yoruba culture and traditions. This movement gradually generated a very virile movement of Yoruba Cultural Nationalism featuring, among other things, researches into and writings on Yoruba history, folklore, and institutions, defense of Yoruba culture against the "cultural imperialism" of the European Christian mission churches (even as the Christian message and Western education were being avidly accepted), introduction of Yoruba historical and social studies into the curriculum of schools (including the Christian mission schools), introduction of Yoruba music and songs into Christian church services, promotion of pride in Yoruba clothes and fashions, etc. When, through the efforts of the Christian missions and the growing literate elite, an orthography was developed for writing the Yoruba language, Yoruba cultural nationalism received a very powerful stimulus. One of the leading Yoruba clergymen of the time, Rev. Henry Johnson, exuberated that the creation of Yoruba orthography had laid the foundation for "progress to any extent" for the Yoruba nation.

There was a strong and growing possibility that all of these developments among the Yoruba, if left to evolve on their own, might together produce a modern Yoruba nation-state in West Africa (similar to what happened about the same time with Japan in Asia). As of the 1870s, the Yoruba and Japanese appear to have been about equal in population size, and Japan and Yorubaland were politically similar in that each was a land broken up into many small domains ruled by local rulers. The Yoruba had much more of Western education than the Japanese – as well as a stronger Western-educated professional class. But in the decades that followed, while Japan evolved into a modern nation-state and quickly became one of the economically and technologically strongest countries in the world, Yorubaland did not – thanks to European invasions, conquests, fragmentation, and imperialism. The first British attack on any part of Yorubaland was against the coastal Lagos kingdom. A succession contest was on between two princes of this kingdom, and the British, in order to seize a dominant share of the trade of the kingdom, supported one against the other. Because the kingdom was very stoutly and masterfully defended, the British had to resort to bombarding it from naval ships from the open sea. Ultimately, the kingdom was proclaimed a British royal colony – thus making the first part of Yorubaland to be conquered by Europeans.

For the following few decades, Europeans did not seem to pose any further threat. In fact, Lagos became, for Yoruba people, a buoyant center of trade, Christian missions, and Western education. But from the 1890s, British, French and German colonial agents aggressively began to seize Yorubaland. Of the military actions in this process, the landmarks were the British invasions of the Ijebu-Ode kingdom in 1892, the Ode-Itshekiri kingdom in 1894, the Oyo kingdom in 1895, and Ilorin in 1897, and the French invasion of the Dahomey kingdom and its western Yoruba neighbors in 1892. In each case, the invaders were met with very determined and sophisticated resistance, and were only able to win because they were able to bring up the latest and most advanced firearms, especially the Maxim field guns.

By 1897, then, Yorubaland had been carved into five European possessions – three owned by various agencies of British power, one owned by France, and one owned by Germany. Even after all three British possessions were included in a large country named Nigeria in 1914, they continued to be managed as two separate administrations in the new country, and thus the splitting up of British-owned Yorubaland was preserved – in spite of protests by the Yoruba people. The Nigeria which came into existence in 1914 consisted of about 300 nationalities. To the west of British-owned Yorubaland in Nigeria, French-owned Yorubaland became part of the French Protectorate of Dahomey (today's Benin Republic), consisting of some forty small nations. Further to the west, German-owned Yorubaland became part of the German Protectorate of Togo, consisting of over thirty small nations. In 1918 (following the First World War), German Togo was assigned to France as a mandated territory by the League of Nations – and is today the French-speaking Republic of Togo. Thus the large and proudly civilized Yoruba nation was set up for the fragmentations and brutalization that would be its lot in the course of the 20th century.

The Sokoto Sultanate [6]

Next, we will look at the experience of the Hausa-Fulani of the country now known as Northern Nigeria. A large grassland territory here was homeland to the Hausa people, the largest single nationality of the West African grasslands north of the middle Niger valley. Somewhat similar to the Yoruba of the south of the same middle Niger valley, the Hausa had developed into a few kingdoms (each with a town) centuries before the 19th – kingdoms of the same national culture and language, with great grassland distances between them, but interconnected by powerful traditions, with culturally and commercially rich contacts with their non-Hausa neighbors. Located immediately south of the Sahara Desert, the Hausa country benefited greatly from the trans-Saharan trade, and some of its towns ranked among the leading trading centers in the grasslands south of the Sahara and north of the River Niger. With this trade also had come Islam, with the result that the Hausa kingdoms and rulers were mostly Muslims, with the important cultural asset of literacy in Arabic. Another ethnic group, the Fulani, a mostly nomadic people, who had for centuries migrated slowly from the grasslands far to the west of Hausaland, had become part of the Hausa towns and countryside by the 18th century. It is in those far western grasslands beyond Hausaland that the early empires of Ghana, Mali and Songhai had flourished in succession until the 16th century. As would be remembered, following the fall of the Songhai Empire in the early 16th century, the peoples of that vast grassland territory had gone back to living in many small states. But, in the late 18th century, larger states began again to evolve among them – each created with the force of arms by a leader who was a founder of a strong Islamic movement. Emulating such movements, one of the few Fulani settlers in the Hausa towns, a Muslim cleric, founded an Islamic movement, and launched a jihad against the Hausa kingdoms. His Fulani immigrant people were very few in comparison with the Hausa, but his call for radical reforms in Islam won the support of the masses of Hausa Muslim folks, and the jihad quickly subdued the rulers of the old Hausa kingdoms and replaced them with Fulani rulers with the title of Emirs – and much of Hausaland became one large and loosely connected Fulani Muslim empire or sultanate.

This homeland of the Hausa (more correctly Hausa-Fulani henceforth) then grew more rapidly in commerce and wealth, as well as in Islamic literacy and scholarship. There is no doubt whatsoever that this sultanate, as it stood by the late 19th century, commanded the capacity to evolve into a dynamic and prosperous modern country in the heart of West Africa in our times. But, like most of West Africa, it was invaded and overrun by European (British) forces in the last years of the 19th century and incorporated into the British empire in West Africa, becoming ultimately a major part of the Northern Region of Nigeria. This was one large state with clear attributes of a state – a common government, reasonably clear boundaries, common language (the Hausa language), etc. But because, as a British protectorate, it did not immediately produce enough revenue for sustaining its British administration, the British had to merge it with other territories that commanded enough revenues to provide for its administration. And so it was that, in order to ensure a self-financing protectorate, Hausaland was amalgamated with the territories to the south, all becoming Nigeria, in 1914. The territories of the expansive grasslands beyond the western borders of Hausaland, with some

Hausa populations, fell to the French (and are today the Republics of Niger and Burkina Faso).

Kanem-Bornu Empire

Next, we will move to the northeast of Hausaland, to the land of the Kanuri. In the territory of the Lake Chad, the Kanuri and related peoples early created a number of kingdoms, and these had, by as early as the 14th century, developed into a large empire, the Kanem-Bornu Empire, under emperors who bore the title of Mai. Very successful farming in the lands watered by the great lake and its rivers made this empire a land of prosperity and thick population. To this prosperity, long distance trade contributed enormously. Northwards, trade routes connected the empire of Kanem-Bornu with the Mediterranean lands of Libya directly to the north, and with the lands of the Nile and Arabia to the northeast. With such connections came the Religion of Islam, and with it came literacy in Arabic. Westwards and southwards, trade routes linked this rich empire with the lands of Hausa and of Mali and, later, Songhai, and, across the Niger, with the countries of the Yoruba and other forest peoples of West Africa. Before the 16th century, probably most of the trade of the peoples of the country now known as Nigeria with the outside world through the Mediterranean, passed through the lands of Kanem-Bornu as center of exchange. By the late 16th century, the government of Kanem-Bornu maintained regular diplomatic relationships and embassies with the Ottoman Empire in the Mediterranean world. The court officials of one Mai who ruled in the first years of the 17th century gave the world perhaps the earliest history book written in the interior of West Africa.[7] This empire suffered some decline in the course of the 18th century. In the early 19th century, the Fulani-led jihad movement in Hausaland made a bid to conquer Kanem-Bornu, but the attempt failed. While defending itself, the empire revived much of its old strength and glory. Without doubt, this was a coherent and strong state by the late 19th century, a state with a lot of proud history – until the British and French empire builders came in the last years of the 19th century, seized the area, set up boundaries of their own making, and created new countries. The heart of the old Kanem-Bornu kingdom was ultimately incorporated into British-owned Nigeria and the rest into French possessions to the east and north.

Benin Kingdom [8]

Next, we will go to the southeast of Yorubaland, the thick forest country of the Edo and related peoples. Here, the old Edo kingdom of Benin was, by the 19th century, a rich land of commerce, culture, power and pride. Its capital city boasted broad streets, great market centers, a splendid palace and collections of art, gorgeous royal ceremonies, and an impressive system of city walls. Its central province was the homeland of the Edo nation, and its subordinate provinces the territories of Edo-related nationalities (like the Ishan and the Afenmai). Altogether, territorially, it was larger than many of today's nation states of Europe – and definitely commanded a first-rate capacity to become a prosperous nation state or country in the evolving modern world. The Benin kingdom had been one of the foremost centers of trade with Europeans along the West African coast since as early as the late 15th century. Benefiting massively from the trade, the kingdom had evolved into a powerful commercial empire, with commercial tentacles reaching out for hundreds of miles in neighboring counties.

Alarmed by the news of the activities of European imperialist agents in other parts of West Africa in the course of the 1890's, the Benin kingdom adopted a defensive mode. While still fully welcoming trade with the Europeans, the Benin authorities tried to limit contacts with agents of European imperialism operating on the coast. But the British, already active in seizing territories in West Africa, were determined to seize the Benin kingdom. In 1897, the British asked for permission to send a delegation to the Benin palace, and the Benin government refused to grant the permission. In defiance of the explicit Benin refusal, the British sent envoys from the coast to the palace of Benin, accompanied by some troops. Benin's security forces ambushed and wiped out the intruders. Seizing on that as declaration of war, the British mounted a massive invasion, and overran the Benin kingdom. This proud kingdom was ultimately forced into the British Protectorate of Southern Nigeria, and then into Nigeria –

where it became one of the many small, virtually voiceless, entities in a large multi-nation country.

The Igbo Nation [9]

From Benin, we will go eastwards and across the Lower Niger to the country of the Igbo people, numbering today over 40 million. Here, the Igbo nation early evolved a rich and artistic culture and built a couple of kingdoms, the rest living in small village polities that were parts of larger entities such as clans – all united by one cultural heritage, language, religion and customs. By the 19th century, the Igbo were a great trading people, and the available evidence indicates that they had been a trading people long before then. They were a major contributor to the very substantial trade that evolved with the outside world along the Lower Niger in the course of the century.

Probably more than that of any other major Black African people, the image of the Igbo nation has, since the beginning of the 20th century, suffered much distortion and downgrading at the hands of European colonial agents, colonial scholars, and colonial propagandists, and even some Nigerians who believe that building Nigeria requires that the various nations in Nigeria be pushed down and suppressed. In general, the tendency among such writers has been to take the absence of large political structures (kingdoms, empires, etc.) among most of the Igbo as proof that the Igbo were a primitive people – or that they were not even a definite people or nation at all. Happily, in more recent times, though that tone has not been completely silenced, stronger and more scholarly voices have arisen to restore to the Igbo nation a more balanced picture for its image. It would be difficult to doubt today that the Igbo nation had the cultural attributes that might have transformed their nation, on its own, into a virile and dynamic nation state in the modern world. But then, in the last decades of the 19th century, the Igbo were forcibly incorporated into the evolving British empire in West Africa, ultimately becoming part of Nigeria. The Igbo have proved to be one of Africa's most dynamic and modernizing peoples in the course of the 20th century – an indisputable example of an African nation denied the chance, by

European imperialism, of growing into a prosperous country on its own in the modern world.

Once, in Obafemi Awolowo University in Nigeria, in one of the classes that I taught on Nigerian History, one of my young Igbo students asked me: "I strongly believe that if we Igbo people had been allowed to have our own country in the modern world, we would be easily competing with a country like Japan today in technology, industries and world trade. What do you think?" I answered that I agreed absolutely with him. Nobody who really knows the Igbo, Yoruba, Hausa-Fulani, Kanuri, Edo, (and some other peoples that are now parts of Nigeria) can deny that these are proudly achieving nations that have been denied their true destinies by British rule and by inclusion in Nigeria.

The Dahomey Kingdom[10]

West of the country of the Yoruba (and outside the borders of modern Nigeria) is the smaller county of the people known as the Adja. A number of small kingdoms crystallized here in the course of the 17th and 18th centuries, some along the coast, others in the interior. The one located farthest in the interior (where Adja and Yoruba peoples were intermixed), the Dahomey kingdom, soon began to expand its borders in various directions, but particularly towards the coast, in order to share in the coastal trade. This brought it into trouble with the much more powerful Yoruba Oyo kingdom to the east, because the Oyo had long controlled most of the trade through the area to the coast. From about 1730, conquered by Oyo, Dahomey lived in subjection to Oyo, in the Oyo Empire. But when the Oyo Empire ran into serious political troubles of its own early in the 19th century, Dahomey was at last free to fulfill its ambitions. It absorbed almost all the Adja country and became a sizeable and powerful kingdom. Aggressively ambitious, Dahomey became one of the most notable states in West Africa in the course of the late 19th century. In the growing rejection of the slave trade by Europeans, Dahomey's resolute determination to continue that trade earned it a very poor image in European accounts of late 19th century West Africa. But this kingdom was also notable for its very strong monarchical government, its huge and closely controlled commerce, its well

94

organized and formidable military establishment, and its love of art. Left to grow as it was, and on its own, into the 20th century, Dahomey would undoubtedly have evolved into one of Africa's best ordered, most dynamic, and most ambitious countries in the West African coastlands. When attacked by the French in 1892, Dahomey stoutly defended itself – but, ultimately, it had no answer to the latest firearms at the disposal of the invading French. Its territories, the rest of the Adja country, most of the farthest western Yoruba, and a number of small peoples to the north, were then constituted by the French into a protectorate given the name Dahomey (which, after independence, changed its name to Benin Republic).

The Akan [11]

Still in West Africa, we will go to the homeland of the extraordinary people called the Akan, in the modern Republic of Ghana. One of Black Africa's most dynamic nations, the Akan early developed many small kingdoms. In addition to being very good farmers, the Akan were also great manufacturers and artisans, and their country was rich from a virile culture of local and long-distance trade – northwards with the trans-Niger grasslands and the trans-Saharan trade channels, and later southwards with the Atlantic coast. In the course of the 18th century, one of their kingdoms, the Ashanti kingdom, became very rich and powerful, and expanded to absorb some of the other Akan kingdoms. The ruler of this expanded kingdom, with the title of Asantihene, owned one of the most splendid courts in Africa; and his famous golden stool was the symbol of unity of all the Akan groups in his kingdom.

From the first decade of the 19th century, the ambition of the Ashanti kingdom to expand towards the south and control the territories and trade routes of the southern Akan states increasingly clashed with the schemes of British traders to control the trade of the area. The result was a series of wars throughout the 19th century between the British and the Ashanti, in many of which wars the Ashanti proudly held their own against the British and even defeated the British. However, in 1874, a strong British force pushed north and reached the Ashanti capital, Kumasi, meticulously looted it of its treasures (including large stores of gold, large collections of sculpture and royal furniture, ivory and other assets), and then proceeded needlessly to burn down the city. The Ashanti rulers therefore reluctantly entered into a treaty with the British, though they were determined to sustain their kingdom's economic and political independence. Over and over throughout these conflicts, the Ashanti had given clear notice to their British adversaries that their desire was a peaceful relationship which would guarantee British commercial interests in the area and the independence of their own kingdom. And, even in those encounters in which the Ashanti defeated the British, they conducted themselves with consummate honor and gallantry, allowing the British to re-supply their beleaguered forts, or permitting defeated British armies to retreat in order and go away.

As the European scramble for African territories came into full swing in the 1890's, the British intensified pressure on the Ashanti kingdom. Accusing the Ashanti of failure to implement the terms of the 1874 treaty, they demanded that the kingdom should accept to become a British Protectorate. The Asantihene refused to accept some of the British terms and, in response, the British launched another invasion in 1896. The Ashanti kingdom, like the other Akan kingdoms, thus became forcibly a British Protectorate, and the reigning Asantihene was exiled from his kingdom. Even after that, however, the Ashanti rulers continued to hold up their heads in great pride. The British response, in 1900, was to demand that the Ashanti should surrender their sacred Golden Stool. The British Governor of the Gold Coast, Sir Frederick Hodges, demanded in a public assembly that the Ashanti should surrender the Golden Stool to him to sit on. The Ashanti said not a word and, when the assembly ended, they went home and prepared for war – even though they knew fully well that the British by then commanded all the military advantages. The Ashanti lost the war (just as they had known they would); but they claimed the victory, because they had achieved their objective – which was to prevent the violation of their Golden Stool. The Ashanti kingdom was then fully incorporated into the British Protectorate of the Gold Coast.

Thus the British destroyed an African kingdom which was not inferior to any European nation-state in anything but military

96

technology, and which was the equal, perhaps even the superior, of Britain in its concepts of nobility, honor, courage and duty. There is no doubt whatsoever that the Ashanti kingdom, if its sovereignty had not been hijacked, commanded the capacity to enter into the 20th century with all the attributes of a modern nation-state (with clear boundaries, a government commanding the allegiance and respect of all citizens, state institutions amenable to the demands of the 20th century, a national language, etc.), and to respond in order and dignity to the world of the 20th century. The chances were good too that, in the environment of the 20th century, the other smaller Akan states not part of Ashanti by 1900 might have gone on to be happily included into an Akan nation-state. But none of these was to be.

States of the Western Sudan [12]

From the Akan country, we go north to the Western Sudan – that vast expanse of grassland territory of West Africa, now consisting of the countries of Niger, Burkina Faso, Mali, Mauritania, Gambia, and Senegal. This is a land of rich political and cultural history. The home of crop farming peoples and pastoralist peoples, it had the great Niger River flowing through it, and it also had intensive exposure to the trans-Saharan trade. Trade with the Sahara and the Mediterranean in the north, and with the forest lands of tropical West Africa in the south, made the Western Sudan a land of great trade and cultural inter-fertilization. But rivalries over the trans-Saharan routes generated, from time to time, conflicts with some of the peoples of the Sahara and of the Mediterranean coasts of North Africa. Among the many national groups of this broad country, there early developed a plethora of small kingdoms. The first large state or empire in the history of West Africa – the Ghana Empire – emerged here in about the 5th century AD, unifying many small kingdoms. The Ghana Empire was supplanted by a larger empire (the Mali Empire) in the 11th century, and Mali was supplanted by a still larger empire (the Songhai Empire) in the 15th century. For some time after the capital of Songhai was destroyed by invading Moroccans in 1591, the wide grassland country reverted to many small kingdoms. However, in the 18th century, larger polities began to emerge again

97

– the Macina Empire, which was absorbed by the larger Segu Tokulor Empire (founded by Alhaj Umar Tall in 1848). After the death of Ahaj Umar Tall in 1864, his empire split into three large states, the most successful of which came to be the Wassoulou Empire led by Samori Ture. Samori Ture was undoubtedly one of the most resourceful men in the West Africa of his time.

As they emerged, these 19th century empires had the common experience of conflict with the French who were trying to establish territorial possessions from bases along the coast. In particular, wars between the French and Samori Ture became legendary from 1880 on. Samori Ture defeated the French forces again and again, his most memorable victory coming on April 2, 1882, over large French forces armed with heavy artillery. In the years that followed, however, as the French subdued other adversaries in the sub-region, the strategic advantage gradually shifted in their favor, and Samori Ture had to make territorial concessions to them. When he was captured by the French on September 29, 1898, his Wassoulou Empire came to an end, and its territory became part of French West African possessions. Here again, in this broad grasslands of the West African interior, there were countries with systems and leaderships that had the capabilities to develop into strong and prosperous states in the modern world. Today, after wrested opportunities, after decades of mangling by French colonialists and by indigenous governments of the post-independence years, and after recent decades of devastating droughts , the French-made countries of these historic grasslands rank among the most troublingly poor countries in the world.

Peoples and States of West-Central Africa [13]

The southern half of the African continent (comprising Central, East and Southern Africa) is home to a large Black African subfamily consisting of many ethnic groups speaking languages called Bantu languages. There is a consensus among historians that this subfamily of Black people originated in the eastern extremity of West Africa (the area that is now the Cameroons and parts of eastern Nigeria), and gradually spread southwards and eastwards, their oldest states crystallizing in the

Congo valley and in East Africa, and their youngest states in the territories of Southern Africa. In later centuries, small groups of immigrants, mostly pastoralists from the Nile territory in the northeast, added to the ethnic diversity of the interior of the Congo region, the lake region to the east of it, and parts of East Africa. Over the whole region, trade early developed – trade with various Asian peoples on the East African coast, and trade along a cobweb of trade routes, some of which penetrated all the way to the Atlantic coasts of Central Africa.

By the time that the earliest European explorers reached the coasts of west-central Africa (today's Congo and Angola) in the late 15th century, the many kingdoms there had attained various high levels of civilization. The best documented of these kingdoms, the Kongo kingdom ruled by kings who bore the title of Manikongo, controlled a large forest country consisting of the Bakongo people and some of their smaller neighbors. Another kingdom named Loango was also strong but was not as well-known as the Kongo kingdom. The Manikongo welcomed the earliest Portuguese traders and Catholic missionaries, and some of his subjects accepted conversion to Christianity. Their capital town, Mbaza Kongo, where churches arose, was given the name San Salvador by the Portuguese missionaries. Between the Manikongo and the king of Portugal there followed a time of friendship, marked by exchanges of correspondence and envoys. The Manikongo sent some of his chiefs as ambassadors to the courts of Portugal and the Pope. When a Christianized prince ascended the throne, taking the name Affonso I, relations with the Portuguese and papal courts flourished greatly, and so did Christian missionary enterprise, and trade – trade in the products of the country and of Europe.

But then a time came when the Portuguese traders introduced a demand for slaves. The rulers of the Kongo kingdom resisted, sending strongly worded letters to the king of Portugal; but the Portuguese traders, operating essentially out of control of the Portuguese government, encouraged and armed near-coastal peoples of the Kongo kingdom and vassal kingdoms for slave raids. As the Kongo kingdom faced these troubles from the coastal districts in its west, rebellious vassals of the kingdom from its eastern provinces also started trouble. The devastation became so intense that, by the end of the 17th century, the kingdom had disintegrated and disappeared, Mbaza Kongo had fallen into ruins, and its territories had become the scene of the most ruthlessly intensive practice of the Slave Trade and slave raids in Africa. Loango and the smaller kingdoms of the area were swept along in these devastations. The Slave Trade waned slowly in the 19th century, and finally ended in the 1860's.

About twenty years after that, the European scramble for Africa began, and various European nations began to carve up Africa into empires. The region of the Congo was carved up among Portugal, Belgium, and France. Slices of the Bakongo nation belong today to Congo (Kinshasa), Congo (Brazzaville), northern Angola, and Cabinda, and Central African Republic. Recent population estimates have the Bakongo as 15% of the population of Angola, 16% of Congo (Kinshasa), and 46% of Congo (Brazzaville).

It is difficult to say how this intensely battered region of Africa might have, on its own, without the imposition of European rule, adjusted to the conditions and demands of the modern world and restructured itself in the early 20th century. It is, however, very improbable that its peoples would have, out of their own free will, chosen the countries and boundaries that European empire-builders have imposed on the area. For instance, as will be seen later, Bakongo nationalism (manifesting as, among other things, the desire of the large Bakongo nation to separate from the countries to which they now belong and form one country of their own), constitutes a considerable part of the political undercurrents and complexity of this region of Africa.

Peoples of the Interior of Central Africa [14]

The country east of the Congo basin is picturesque plateau country, with Africa's Great Lakes region (the home of Lakes Tanganyika, Victoria, etc.) to its further east. In the lands of this region, Bantu-speaking peoples intermixed with peoples from lands of the Upper Nile had started to create various state systems by the 15th century. Only the states of the countries that are now Rwanda and Burundi will be touched upon here; the rest (especially Buganda and the other kingdoms of present-day Uganda) will be treated as states of Eastern Africa.

Farming populations of Bahutu (better known today as Hutu) had established a spread of small kingdoms here as early as the 14th century. In the course of the next century, Batutsi (Tutsi) pastoralists, migrating from the northeast, increased the ethnic diversity of the region. The ethnic theories and ethnic-based historiography of the Belgian colonial era have so distorted the facts of the existence of the people of Burundi and Rwanda that Tutsi and Hutu now accept of themselves that they are two sharply different peoples – and historically two mutually hostile entities. However, what a closer look at their traditions reveals seems considerably different from that picture.

The farming folks and the pastoralist folks lived together in the same territory, and over time, became intermixed spatially – with the former (the farming people) constituting the overwhelming majority everywhere. Also, intermarriage was common among them. The ethnic lines slowly became blurred, though the original ethnic names, Hutu and Tutsi, continued to be used. Ultimately, one language (the language of the vast majority, the farming folks, the Hutu) came to be spoken by all. In essence, therefore, one ethnic group or nationality was in the process of evolving here, speaking one language, and possessing one common homeland and one culture, and even one religion. Within that common culture, "Tutsi" and "Hutu" gradually ceased being strictly racial or ethnic categories and gradually became like class categories. A third class known as Ganwa enjoyed the highest status, being the class associated with political leadership and ruling. Richer persons (owning cattle and land) came to be categorized as Tutsi, and the economically lesser persons as Hutu. But these class lines were by no means rigid; they were considerably fluid. Since cattle was regarded as the repository of high wealth, being a Tutsi came to mean owning many heads of cattle, and being a Hutu came to mean owning few or no cattle and being a cultivator. A Hutu person who became rich (in cattle) thereby became a Tutsi, while a Tutsi person who became poor became a Hutu. Moreover, intermarriage was common across the evolving class line and affected people's classifications – so that a Hutu man who married a Tutsi woman tended to become Tutsi. A

Tutsi or Hutu person who attained some high achievements or merits in the community could be elevated to the status of a Ganwa. There were even traditional ceremonies by which status changes upwards were celebrated.

Economically and socially, a unique pattern of patron-client relationships evolved in the culture. Unfortunately, the process of the evolution and the details of this system are heavily obscured today by the literature, practices and traditions of the Belgian colonial era. The pre-colonial practice seems to have been that a particular Hutu person or family gave (in addition to their own farming) some services to a particular Tutsi person by taking care of his cattle – and were paid in cattle for such services. In that way, many of the Hutu had access to cattle, and could grow in the ownership of cattle – and, if prudent and fortunate, could become rich enough to join the ranks of the Tutsi.

It seems fairly certain that this whole social and economic system was developed by the people of this beautiful territory as their answer to the question of how to control the sort of conflicts that can be characteristic of the contacts between sedentary farming people and cattle herding people. And to that end, it appears to have been considerably successful. That is not to say that the system did not have its weaknesses and bumps. Its practices of societal control could be harsh, allowing society to humiliate and demote the offender – through depriving him of his belongings, or publicly hanging him, or selling him to traders of the coastal slave trade. Moreover, just as among the rich in every culture, there were rich citizens who used the power of their wealth to impoverish the poorer – especially by lending him cattle or land that he was manifestly incapable of paying back. But all of these were weaknesses in the system and did not define the system. Moreover, they were not necessarily a Tutsi-versus-Hutu phenomenon. The notion that the Hutu and Tutsi are historically inveterate enemies of each other is not borne out by any careful sifting of the traditions of Burundi and Rwanda; it is a creation of modern times – a creation of Belgian colonial times, built upon by the politics and the economic pressures of independent Burundi and Rwanda. Furthermore, categorizing their conflicts as "inter-ethnic" conflicts does not seem to have much merit to it – beyond the sad fact that the Tutsi and Hutu have been conditioned under Belgian rule to regard themselves as different ethnic groups.

Politically, kingdoms evolved in most places in the region in the course of the centuries. The rulers of these belonged to the Ganwa class. In the area which was to become the protectorate (and later the Republic) of Burundi, a more centralized political structure evolved. Here, resistance to the pressures of wars and slave raids linked to the slave trade on the East African coast seems to have contributed, from the late 18th century, to the emergence of a more strongly centralized state. The ruler of this state, bearing the title of Mwami, came to rule over most of Burundi, with many provincial chiefs owing allegiance to him, and with his influence underpinned by the myth that he was of divine origin. In the course of the 19th century, the authority and territory of the Mwami expanded.

This was the situation when the Germans in the last years of the 19th century, and later the Belgians, came onto the scene. As will be seen further on, the Belgian colonial administrators, too arrogant and unfocused to seek a clear understanding of the nuances of Tutsi-Hutu society, proceeded to act on the pseudo-scientific race theories then prevalent in European scholarship, and thereby turned the Hutu and the Tutsi into two rigid ethnic groups that were irreconcilable enemies of each other. Belgian racial theories cast the Tutsi as a race of tall and elegant people – much like the Caucasoid it was said – who were naturally suited to ruling and had always ruled, and the Hutu as a lower race who were naturally suited to serving and had always been servants. The Ganwa were conceived as part of the Tutsi. Belgian colonial practice then gave most of the educational opportunities to the Tutsi, as well as virtually all of the opportunities for appointments into positions in the colonial civil service and military. The tradition of intense, even murderous, enmity between Hutu and Tutsi was thus planted.

Peoples of Eastern Africa [15]

East of these lands, in the broad eastern African territory that is now the home of Uganda, Kenya and Tanzania, bounded on the east by the Indian Ocean and on the west by the lands of the

Great Lakes, Bantu-speaking farmers and pastoralists, and Upper Nile immigrant pastoralists, early created various kinds of states. These lands became particularly rich in agricultural production, as well as in trade. From trading centers along the coast, trade routes fanned out into the interior, to the Great Lakes and beyond. In the Rift Valley, and in the country around Mont Kenya, many different nationalities (now known as Kikuyu, Luhya, Luo, Kalenjin, Kisii, etc.) established homelands. As earlier pointed out, the peoples of the various regions of this wide territory (in the uplands, the Rift Valley, the Lake country) had strong traditions of mutually beneficial relationships dating to early times – in intermarriages, trade, all intertwined with long-distance trade with the coast. While some of the peoples were considerably well defined, others were much less so. For instance, the people now known as the Kalenjin in Kenya were, even until the 1940s, still referred to as "Nandi speaking people" and were recognized as different small fragments such as Kipsigis, Nandi, Keiyo, Turgen, Marakwet, Teriki, etc. Similarly, today's Luhya people (also of Kenya), before colonialism, consisted of separate entities like the Wanga, Bukusu, Banyore, Maragoli, etc.

In the further interior, in the country that is now Uganda, a few peoples evolved into kingdoms (Bunyoro, Buganda, Kitara, Busoga, Toro, Ankole, etc.) as early as the 15th century. Typically, these kingdoms were ruled by kings wielding much power and surrounded by great ceremonies and grandeur. Some other peoples of the area were somewhat more loosely organized. Of these, one of the largest were the Acholi of today's northern Uganda, who lived in groups of clans presided over by headmen known as Rwot. Of the nationality kingdoms, the oldest was Bunyoro. Over time, however, Buganda became the largest and strongest, and the most successfully expansionist, and that expansion was still actively progressing in the 19th century when Europeans came to the area. Earliest European explorers in the East African interior in the 19th century wrote of the Buganda kingdom that it was a rich, highly civilized, and well-ordered kingdom. According to their accounts, the capital city of the Kabaka (king) had a population of about 40,000. The king's palace, situated on a commanding hill, was surrounded by a high wall more than four kilometers in circumference. Henry Stanley, the English journalist and explorer, wrote in 1875 that he witnessed 125,000 Bagandan troops marching out to war, and that on Lake Victoria the Kabaka had a naval force of some 230 outrigger canoes – which gave him strength to strike at will at distant parts of the shores of the lake.

In the course of the late 19th century, the Buganda kingdom's open-door policy resulted in the coming and rapid growth of various Christian missionary denominations as well as of Islam. As elsewhere in Africa, the coming of the Christian missionaries fostered the growth of education and literacy in the Buganda kingdom. The intense rivalry that then developed among all of the foreign influences (Christian denominations and the Muslims) was to result, ultimately, in Buganda becoming a British protectorate through treaties. Buganda thereafter became a strong partner in expanding British influence (through military and other means) to the other kingdoms of the area. Meanwhile, very much like among the Yoruba of West Africa, a literate elite and modern professional and entrepreneurial classes was emerging among the Baganda. Moreover, the Buganda kingdom's help to the British resulted in a further expansion of the Buganda kingdom's territory, and much expansion of the greatness and prestige of the Buganda king. Ultimately, the British carved out their protectorate of Uganda bringing many of these different peoples together. In short, then, this area of Africa had evolved its own dynamics before the establishment of British imperial rule, dynamics that had great possibilities of developing rich and strong modern states here through an interplay of the established historical trends with the various influences that the advancing modern world was bringing.

States of Southern Africa [16]

The history of the southernmost sub-region of Africa was made more complex by the fact that it received the earliest European settlement in Black Africa. European explorations of the late 16th century had resulted, among other things, in the development of European trade with the lands of the Indian Ocean, through a sea passage that rounded the Cape of Good Hope. First exclusively owned by the Portuguese, the trade soon attracted other European nations, notably the Dutch, English and French. In the 1650's, the Dutch East Indian Company established a small settlement at the Cape to supply water, vegetables and fresh meat to its ships on the long voyage. Over the next century and a half, the settlement attracted more settlers of Dutch, German, and French origin, and the white population gradually evolved into a unique cultural group which ultimately called itself Afrikaner and its language Afrikaans. From its inception, the settlement encountered an African people, the Khoikhoi, who lived on and near the Cape. From them the settlers initially bought cows for meat supplies to passing ships. However, the relationship, as it developed, was not friendly; the Khoikhoi resisted their loss of land, and a series of wars resulted. The Khoikhoi were rapidly decimated – not so much by the wars, but by the diseases imported by the settlers, especially small pox. Meanwhile, the settlers also began to encounter the Bantu-speaking peoples who constituted the vast majority of the inhabitants of the southern African region.

As the numbers of the white settlers increased, they mostly became farmers, raising crops as well as livestock. For labor supply, they had many slaves imported for them from south-eastern Asia – from Indonesia, Malaysia, India, etc. There developed a strange practice among the Afrikaner whereby a family would move far into the interior and set up its farm in considerable distance from other families, and this gradually produced a tradition of land disputes and conflicts between them and the Bantu-speaking peoples. The Bantu-speaking peoples had arrived in South Africa as early as 500 AD, gradually spreading south from the north and northeast, setting up various types of states ruled by sacred kings, and establishing strong traditions of trade which linked the Indian Ocean coast of present-day Mozambique with important centers of their civilization in the interior. These folk movements had come in two main waves – and produced the situation whereby the Nguni were settled in the eastern coastal areas and the Sotho and Tswana in the interior plateau, with the Tswana furthest to the west, close to the Kalahari Desert. Among these peoples, some fairly large iron-age states had started to evolve from about the 11th century. Of the earliest of these, the most famous was the kingdom of Mapungubwe. Not long after Mapungubwe, the civilization of the region reached a very high peak in the time of the kingdom now known as Great Zimbabwe, in about the 12th and 13th centuries. By the time of the coming of the Portuguese explorers to the eastern coast of Southern Africa in the last years of the 15th century, the greatest kingdom in Southern Africa was the Monomotapa kingdom, about which we have considerably more information than the earlier kingdoms. This, however, is no place for a detailed account of the history of this powerful and rich kingdom whose authority covered most of the land between the Zambezi and Limpopo rivers, encompassing most of what is now the modern states of Zimbabwe and Mozambique. Suffice it to say that by the late 16th century, this kingdom was in decline and was being supplanted by other kingdoms, especially Butua and Changamire, each of which was destined to decline in short order also – much of this due to the confusions brought by Portuguese aggressive ambitions and the slave trade. By the end of the 18th century, major states had given place all over Southern Africa to a series of small chiefdoms.

But then, as the 19th century opened, Southern Africa, like the rest of Africa, began to experience dramatic political transformations. A major movement towards the creation of a larger and stronger state emerged, initiated by one of the small Nguni-speaking chiefdoms – the Zulu chiefdom. Under a spectacularly talented young ruler named Shaka, the Zulus transformed the traditional Bantu weapons and methods of war, as well as state institutions, and launched into wide-ranging conquests of other Bantu chiefdoms. Far and wide, other chiefdoms in the way of the Zulu juggernaut fled and, in turn, became aggressors against others – thus creating widespread confusion, and causing large expanses of territory to look uninhabited. The originally small Zulu chiefdom quickly spread out to include a large expanse of country incorporating many subdued groups integrated into the new Zulu state system. Though erratic and unpredictable, Shaka deserves to be seen as one of the greatest African revolutionaries of the early 19th century. Shaka's death in 1828 stalled the Zulu expansion, but the Zulu state inherited by his successors was a fairly large, well organized, and militarily very powerful state. Moreover, the Zulu-led revolution generated, in many parts of the sub-continent, the disappearance of virtually all the old chiefdoms, and the emergence of new states which, like the Zulu state, were much larger and better organized than the old chiefdoms, and culturally incorporated elements from various groups that had been different culturally as well as politically. Of these new states, the most notable were the Sotho, Swazi and Ndebele kingdoms, this last kingdom crystallizing in the further northeast (in today's Republic of Zimbabwe)..

In short, southern Africa was restructuring itself, and producing new states that commanded the capacity to grow and enter into the evolving modern world as strong and dynamic states. Only brief notes will be here made about some of these states. In general, the measure of their virility as states came to be the quality of their responses to the challenges which emerged for them from the 1840's in the form of pressures by the Afrikaners and then by the British.

The Zulu kingdom was, militarily, the most powerful of these new states. While Shaka lived, his kingdom was more or less secure from attack. But almost as soon as he was removed from the scene, the kingdom began to be confronted by a strong push of some of the Afrikaner people into the further interior – the Afrikaner movements which came to be known as the Great Trek. Finding the territorial spaces which had been temporarily depopulated by the Zulu wars, the Afrikaners rushed to take possession, believing that those spaces were in fact unpopulated. The Trek Boers, as they were then called, evolved into three separate independent Afrikaner states or republics: Transvaal, Orange Free State and Natal. This large-scale penetration of the Afrikaners into the interior soon sparked a series of conflicts between them and the Zulu state. In these conflicts, some victories went to the Zulu and some to the Afrikaners, but the Zulu people more or less easily sustained the boundaries of their kingdom

But then, British imperialism appeared on the scene, intent on seizing control of the whole of southern Africa. After the British overcame the resistance of the Afrikaners and annexed the Afrikaner republics, the conflicts over territory became mostly a series of wars by the British against the Zulu state, as well as against the other Bantu states. Knowledge about the enormous mineral wealth of southern Africa was growing, and agents of British business were itching to rush in to seize control. Rather than seeing the Bantu states as countries that could develop into self-sustaining states, the British saw them as places from which much mineral wealth was waiting to be possessed, as rich sources of labor for British mining enterprises, and therefore as territories that the British must seize and control. From Natal (close to the southern border of Zululand), the British embarked on very determined maneuvers to seize the Zulu state. Further to the north, agents of British business led by Cecil Rhodes began, from 1890, to enter and seize Matabeleland and Mashonaland – the country that later was to be named Rhodesia. How strong and capable the young Bantu states were is attested to by their very impressive performances in their wars of resistance against British attempts to hijack their sovereignties. The Zulu state routed a large British force at Isandlwana in January 1879. The Matabele kingdom defeated a strong British force at Shangani in 1893; again in 1896, they held a clear military advantage over the British, but chose to yield to British appeals for peace. Both of these kingdoms, however, were ultimately taken over by the British. Botswana (called Bechuanaland by the British) voluntarily sought British protection.

The Basuto kingdom proved the most successful of the southern African states in the resistance against the British. In fact, in all of the resistance of African states and peoples against British imperialist adventures in the late 19th century, the Basuto kingdom proved to be one of the most successful in combat and one of the most astute in diplomacy. The architect of all of that was King Moshoeshoe, founder of the new Basuto kingdom and its ruler until 1870. His most memorable victory came in December 1852 against a large, well-armed and well trained army led by one of the best generals who ever served the British in Africa, George Cataract, Governor of Cape Colony. After the Basuto king had allowed the enemy to come deep into his kingdom and seize some cattle, he unleashed his army on them and very decisively routed them. Then, as the vanquished Cathcart stumbled away from the field, Moshoeshoe invoked his diplomatic skills, and sent after Cathcart a letter that must rank among the greatest pieces of diplomacy in history. His letter reads partly as follows:

Your Excellency: This day you have fought against my people and taken much cattle. I beg you will be satisfied with what you have taken. I entreat peace from you. You have chastised. Let it be enough I pray you, and let me no longer be considered as an enemy of the Queen.

Your humble servant. Moshesh.[17]

Not surprisingly, this amazing letter achieved the purposes intended by its writer. It helped Cathcart to feel his honor restored; it warmed the hearts of the British public back in Europe; and it therefore insured the Basuto kingdom against further British aggression. In the years that followed, the Basuto kingdom's wars against the Afrikaner republics became fierce and exhausting, but Moshoeshoe, ever the great general, always proved superior to the very best that the Afrikaners could send against him in arms or men.

Fig. 7: *King Moshoeshoe I with his ministers*

But that was not all. Moshoeshoe perceived that accepting Christianity into his kingdom would bring some benefits, and he took steps to invite missionaries to come and propagate the gospel among his people, and he made them his personal friends (even though he never really converted to Christianity) and adopted some aspects of their culture. He was right. In the turbulent relationships of the peoples of southern Africa with the European imperialist agents in the late 19th century, the missionaries served to promote a good image for the Basuto kingdom. As personal friends, missionaries served as scribes for the king, so that he dictated letters to them to write for him. Finally, in his great old age, two years before he died, seeing the trend of things all around southern Africa, Moshoeshoe invited the British to establish a protectorate over his kingdom, in order to secure peace for it and protect its integrity after he would have gone.

Moshoeshoe's successes and greatness did not end with his high qualities as general and diplomat; he was, first and foremost, an excellent nation builder and leader of men. Starting as chief of a tiny chiefdom, he had gathered fragments from chiefdoms shattered by the Zulu wars, and proceeded with consummate fairness and statesmanship to include all in his new state. Prominent persons who came fleeing to him with some followers he set up as leaders in his growing kingdom, and gave them and their men land to settle, as well as cattle for a new beginning. In the process, he built a kingdom that steadily grew in size and strength, to which all the new comers could be strongly loyal, and to whose culture all were proud to belong. The armies that he led to victories after victories came out of this wonderfully inclusive society. No human polity is without some internal weakness, and Moshoeshoe had his own share of troubles among his subjects; but the kingdom that he built compared with any other in the world in the quality of its cohesion and order. After the Basuto kingdom became a British protectorate, the British merged it with their South Africa possession. When the Basuto had occasion to revolt in 1879 against some laws of British South Africa, they proved far too strong to be suppressed – and, after three years of the stand-off, their country had to be excised from South Africa and constituted into a separate possession with a special relationship with the British.

In short, then, the African states which were confronted by European imperialist aggression in the last years of the 19th century in southern Africa were considerable and respectable states – each with a strong government commanding the allegiance and loyalty of its citizens, and with clear boundaries, a national language, and highly developed defense system. Most, moreover, commanded enormous natural resources in their territories (especially gold and diamonds) – resources upon which a prosperous entry into the evolving world economy of the 20th century could have been built by their African owners.

Overview

All over Africa, the coming of European imperialism thus effectively cut off any chance that any Black African peoples or states might enter and develop on their own, and in their own way, into the modern world. It is tempting to assume that the victories of the European invaders necessarily prove that the European states of the 19th century were, as states, intrinsically superior to all the African states of the time. However, as would already be fairly obvious in the paragraphs above, such an assumption is not, in many cases, borne out by the facts. In the probing that has gone on since the 20th century among historians about the reasons for the European victories in their wars of conquest against African states and peoples in the late 19th century, a case for the essential superiority of the European states over the African states can be made in some cases, but it cannot be made in many other cases – most of which have been discussed above in this chapter. In such cases, all the emphasis has had to be on the differentials in fire power between the invaders and the defenders, the frequent lack of collaboration by African states against the invaders, the not so rare willingness of African states to assist the foreign aggressor against African neighbors (sometimes as a result of old animosities generated by the Slave Trade), the fact that, in many cases, this or that particular African state found itself assailed at the same time by two or more European states from different directions, and finally, the fact that some African peoples were too preoccupied with their own affairs to pay adequate attention to what was brewing around them, etc.

By the last years of the 19th century, many African armies were armed with advanced fire-arms, but because fire-arms technology was changing very rapidly then in Europe, the European invader usually had the latest types of guns. In many cases, it was artillery and the machine gun (especially the Maxim gun) that gave the invaders the thin, but unanswerable, margin of advantage. Moreover, in every case, the fighting men (though not the highest officers) in the invading armies were African men recruited from a distance or even locally – a classic tactic of divide and conquer, that made the human expenditure of the African wars affordable to the European states. In many cases, sharp differences in culturally acceptable standards of political morality worked in favor of the European colonizers. Many an African ruler, requested to sign a so-called treaty of friendship and commerce written in a European language and presented to him by a missionary or the agent of a European country, trusted the translation of it given to him – only to discover later that the translation had hidden the true intent of the document. By then, the African ruler could only fight from a position of weakness, since the colonizers would have meanwhile established strategically strong footings in neighboring states. African states also universally suffered the important strategic disadvantage of not being able to perceive that the invaders were out to conquer all of Africa. Everywhere, Africans continued to see the Europeans as no more than the peoples that had for centuries rivaled one another for commercial advantages along the coast. It was for these many reasons, and in these many ways, that all African states, with the singular exception of the Empire of Ethiopia, fell to European imperialism. In 1896, Ethiopia, using breech-loading guns, annihilated an invading Italian army at Adowa, and thus became the only old African state that decisively preserved its sovereignty.

Many of the African states involved in this great confrontation between Europeans and Africans were, as states, about as old as the oldest of the European states (like Spain, Portugal, Britain and France), and much older than other European states such as Belgium, Italy and Germany. This was particularly true of many of the states of West Africa, west-central and eastern Africa. The peoples of southern Africa were ancient cultures, but their states were young, being founded in the midst of the Zulu-led revolution of the early years of the 19th century.

The Industrial Revolution in Europe generally put the very latest weaponry in the hands of European armies, but the considerable and accelerating influence of worldwide commerce often nearly evened the odds. In important considerations such as national cohesion, well ordered government, quality of leadership, loyalty, patriotism, national pride, and soldierly qualities, the European states of the late 19th century certainly did not excel many of their African contemporaries. Quite often, in such noble qualities as sense of honor and respect for human life, some of the African states far excelled their European assailants. And the very important fact must not be forgotten that it was not military power, or even any sort of national power or strength, but the collective favor and collusion of all of Europe, that enabled a small and internally disunited European state like Belgium to come to possess an African territory hundreds of times its own size – an empire that it was later to prove significantly incapable of ruling properly.

The African states that resisted European conquest in all parts of Africa, then, were not inferior as states to the invading European states, they were only different – different in culture, different in their state constitutions, different in their patterns of allegiance and of the relationship of the ruler to the citizen, different in their perception of emerging trends in contacts among the peoples of the world. The picture of generally barbarous and oppressive governments often painted by European imperialists about Africa (in order to justify European colonization and colonial disruption of Africa) does not hold up in the light of serious and objective research. Some African states, in fact, were more democratic than some of the states of Europe by the late 19th century.

CHAPTER FOUR

Kneading Troubles Into Countries

Having thus become owners and rulers of African territorial possessions by roughly the first decade of the 20th century, the European countries proceeded with structuring and managing their possessions – the new countries of Black Africa. In general, the steps thenceforth taken by the colonial authorities and administrators would lay the foundations and fashion the patterns of all aspects of the future of these new countries – their internal boundaries and administration, the nature of the relationship among the nationalities contained in them, the direction of their economic growth and social development, and their link with the evolving economy of the wider world . On the new map of Africa, generally straight lines marked the borders of most of the new countries. Only two countries appearing on the map lived under their own sovereignty – Liberia in West Africa, and Ethiopia in northeastern Africa. Everywhere else, from roughly 1900 to about the sixth decade of the 20th century, the self-assured agent of European imperialism bestrode the African earth "like a colossus", and the agent of European business enterprise kept busy extracting and evacuating valuable resources and wealth to his homeland in Europe. To assist this pillage, colonial governments took various steps to suppress indigenous African entrepreneurial initiatives. One of the most important chapters in the modern history of the world was being enacted.

For the impact of a historic movement of the magnitude of European imperialism in Africa, divergent assessments are inevitable. European imperialism in Africa was multi-faceted in operation and consequences. Its apologists would naturally harp on what can be argued as its beneficial effects. Some would emphasize that it was responsible for opening up vast areas of Africa to the influence of the Industrial Revolution. Others would point to its role in the expansion of Christian missionary activities in Africa. Christian missions (and European traders), they would point out, opened up and provided knowledge of the African interior, and the agents of European imperialism followed. Then the establishment of European colonial authority greatly facilitated the work of the Christian missionaries who, apart from bringing the Christian gospel, spread education and literacy, and thus contributed in a major way to the making of modern Africa.

On the surface, much of that cannot be denied. However, at greater depths, much of it bears re-assessing. As earlier pointed out, before the onslaught by European imperialist agents, much of Black Africa was already finding its own ways to absorb the Christian gospel as well as literacy and international trade, and thus charting its own course, in its own way, to the world of the Industrial Revolution and the evolving world economy. European colonialism's most important impact on Black Africa was in the political realm. It crafted virtually all of Black Africa's modern countries – the political framework within which Black Africa has had to navigate its path in the modern world. And its ways and means for getting that done, and the structures and directions that it bequeathed to each country of its creation, were such as were destined to lay the foundations for deep and intractable problems and pains for African peoples. In its ultimate and most impactful ramification, what imperialism did was to twist and distort Africa's emerging future.

Factors in European Colonialism in Africa

The fundamental presuppositions, and the consequent arrogance and disruptiveness of most of European rule in Africa, stemmed from a number of underlying factors. One underlying factor was the all-pervading influence of the heritage of the Atlantic Slave Trade, and of African slavery in Europe and the New World, in the molding of Euro-African relations up to the 19th century. In the course of over three centuries of the Atlantic Slave Trade and African slavery, European peoples had come to create and deeply hold the image of Africans as servile barbarians who had achieved no cultural progress in their history, and who had made, and were capable of making, no contributions to human civilization. All foreign conquerors tend to regard the peoples whom they conquer and rule as culturally inferior to themselves; in the case of European conquest of, and rule over, Africa in modern times, the degree of the contempt of the conquerors and rulers for their African subjects was exceptional. And most of the reason for that was the Slave Trade antecedent to European colonialism. Modern European conquests and imperialism were not limited to Africa, they also happened to Asia. But, in general, the European conquerors and imperialists, though they encountered cultures that were strange to them in both Africa and Asia, operated from the basic attitude that Asian peoples and heritages were more worthy of respect than African peoples and heritages.

Anybody familiar with Western scholarship and views concerning Africa in the era of the Slave Trade would easily recognize the genesis of the statements by Margery Perham (quoted above)[1] and similar utterances by many others like her. For instance, the following is a statement by Frederick Lugard, the founder of Nigeria, and about the most distinguished servant of British imperialism in tropical Africa:

"In character and temperament, the typical African of this race-type is a happy, thriftless, excitable person, lacking in self-control, discipline, and foresight, naturally courageous, and naturally courteous and polite, full of personal vanity, with little sense of veracity, fond of music and loving weapons as an oriental loves jewelry. His thoughts are concentrated on the events and feelings of the moment, and he suffers little from the apprehension for the future, or grief for the past. His mind is far nearer to the animal world than that of the European or Asiatic, and exhibits something of the animals' placidity and want of desire to rise beyond the state he has reached. Through the ages the African appears to have evolved no organized religious creed, and though some tribes appear to believe in a deity, the religious sense seldom rises above pantheistic animalism and seems more often to take the form of a vague dread of the supernatural.

He lacks the power of organization, and is conspicuously deficient in the management and control alike of men or business. He loves the display of power, but fails to realize its responsibility... he will work hard with a less incentive than most races.

He has the courage of the fighting animal, an instinct rather than a moral virtue...

In brief, the virtues and defects of this race-type are those of attractive children, whose confidence when it is won is given ungrudgingly as to an older and wiser superior and without envy...Perhaps the two traits which have impressed me as those most characteristic of the African native are his lack of apprehension and his lack of ability to visualize the future"[2]

After three centuries in which Black Africans had been the slaves to Westerners, and in which Westerners had had to devise various ways of repressing their African slaves in order to protect themselves against the danger of revolts and reprisals by the slaves, it was inevitable that rationalizations of the downtrodden status and condition of the slaves would result. Happily for the peoples of the West, Darwin's theory of evolution, when it appeared in the middle of the 19th century, seemed to nail such rationalizations beyond doubt. The Black man of Africa belonged, indeed, to some lower rung of the ladder in the evolution of the human race! And that was why he was so manifestly inferior, culturally and morally! By the last years of the 19th century, such thoughts and beliefs came to serve as significant strains in the battle cry for the conquest of Africa and its subjugation to the service of the interests of various European states. For Europeans, it was the "white man's burden" to bring the benefits of civilization to Africans. And in the decades that followed, in the era of European imperialism in Africa, the same thoughts and beliefs provided the rationale and justification for blatant, rough-shod, European trampling on African peoples, cultures and institutions. For the agents of European conquest and imperialism in Africa, what existed on the ground in terms of cultures and institutions, and even peoples, became irrelevant or even non-existent; only those things which existed in their own preconceptions and objectives were real and respectable.

Added to the heritage of the Atlantic Slave Trade was the heritage of the Industrial Revolution and some of economic culture and attitudes that it nurtured. From the 1870's, a higher order of industrialization (known as the Second Industrial Revolution among historians) had begun in Europe. While the "First Industrial Revolution" had reached its peak with the invention and development of steam energy, the Second Industrial Revolution was, in the last three decades of the 19th century, spinning out such mighty discoveries as electricity, petroleum, steel, the internal combustion engine, and a myriad of chemical products (like pharmaceuticals, polymers, chemical fertilizers, chemical resins, etc.). From these bases, staggeringly new products were making their appearance in the market. Up to the 1870's, about the most valuable product sought by most Europeans from Africa's thickest forests were ivory. But when, from the 1870's, an African forest tree yielded the latex that was processed into rubber, and the rubber was made into tyres for automobiles, the quest for natural resources from Africa rose to fever pitch. This generated the thrust that Europeans came seeking principally to control African resources that could advance the industrialization of their countries in Europe – in the words of Richard Dowden, to seize territories "for pillage".[3]

Where a particularly valuable natural resource was known or believed to exist in Africa, the objective was to go after it, and seize and control its territory – gold and diamonds in Southern Africa, rubber and copper in Central Africa, various minerals and plant resources all over. The human groups in the place did not really matter – beyond the fact that they might constitute some impediment, or be expendable as conscript labor for carrying out the pillage. Their cultures, institutions and boundaries and even their probable aspirations as humans and groups of humans - were of no consequence. All conquerors and imperialists in history have exploited the resources of conquered lands; the human race never before experienced anything like the magnitude of the knowledge of, and the hunger for, natural materials that propelled European imperialism in Africa.

Another factor that contributed enormously to the character of European imperialism in Africa was its plurality of thrusts. Europe did not come to Africa as one country or as one power, but as many competing countries. This was not like Greece under the command of Alexander the Great conquering the many peoples of western Asia, or the power of one Rome conquering and ruling the various peoples of Europe. It was Europe's Britain, France, Portugal, Spain, Germany, Belgium, Italy – each in its own way and for its own purposes, in competition with the others, scrambling to carve some territorial possession for itself in an Africa that was largely unknown to all of them, and then imposing its own kind of solutions to the political, economic and cultural challenges on the ground. Some, lacking the kinds of resources needed to make meaning of their possessions, resorted to blatant and crude pillage. Others proceeded to attempt to construct new societies based upon ideas of their own, with little or no contact with the realities on the ground.

Yet another important factor in the making of the impact of European imperialism in Black Africa was its brevity and its lack of stability. Not only was European rule in Africa ultimately so brief as to be incapable of producing thoughtful and beneficial political transformations, its makers also came to be too preoccupied with big problems of their own to conceive and engineer any such transformations. Effectively, European rule lasted no more than forty or fifty years in most African countries. In some countries in fact, it lasted fewer years. In many countries, boys who were already strong enough to help on the farms when the European colonialists first came to their homelands, went to Christian mission schools, and later became members of the modern ruling elite of their European-made countries at independence – and then survived colonialism by many years.[4]

And almost throughout those few decades of colonial rule over Africa, the countries of Europe stumbled from one huge problem of their own to another. First came the First World War, or the Great War, in which all the countries of Europe were engaged from 1914 (the year Nigeria, the most populous European protectorate in Africa, was created) until 1918. The reverberations from this Great War continued on until about the middle of the 1920's, with Europe continuing to be distressed by the economic disruptions occasioned by the war, as well as by the reparations disputes between France and Germany. Then in 1929 came the Great Depression, blasting the economies of all Europe for most of the 1930's and causing enormous losses of assets, massive unemployment, and massive pauperizations of European governments and people. From this great disaster, Europe plunged straight into another, and even greater, general war than the First World War – the Second World War, 1939-45. Largely ruined and exhausted from this war, Europe was in no shape to hold on to its African colonies, whose citizens, meanwhile, were rising and demanding freedom. And, beholding unto the United States of America, the new economic super-power in the world, for help to rebuild its economies, Europe could not afford to ignore America's subtle disapproval of colonial empires. In totality, therefore, European rule in Africa was a sudden, spasmodic, and rapidly ending storm. It lasted long enough, and commanded enough erratic energy, to destroy the political structures that Africans had spent hundreds or thousands of years building. But it did not last long enough, nor did it command enough of steady and stable energy, to build rational political structures.

Finally, it can be easily forgotten that the Western liberal democratic message, such as reached colonial Africa through the colonial experience, was not without powerful non-democratic rivals also from Europe. Indeed, for most of the colonial era, there were very powerful non-democratic political lessons emanating from Europe. From the 1920's, just as European rule was beginning to be spelt out in most parts of Africa, liberal political traditions collapsed in many countries of Europe, and produced totalitarianisms of the right in Italy, Germany, Spain, etc., and totalitarianisms of the left in Russia (and the Soviet Union) and ultimately all countries of Eastern Europe. For one thing, these regimes were, in essence, considerably akin to the nature of the various European colonial administrations in Africa. For another, the charisma and the aura of raw power emanating from the European totalitarian and authoritarian regimes did not pass over the literate African elite that were evolving into Africa's modern political elite. It was no accident that, later, the rigidly clenched fist and the explosive shout of "Power" were popular trademarks of many African political parties and politicians. Some in the emerging African leadership even wrote admiringly of fascist political methods, especially of fascist revolutionary methods of acquiring power and of eliminating all opposition. And for many a self-proclaimed socialist in the Africa of the independence era, the attraction to socialism was not so much the equalitarian doctrines of popular socialist dogma but, first, the communist revolutionary methods of seizing power and, second, the sort of absolute powers (including the elimination of all opposition) exercised by Stalin and the many communist bosses of Eastern Europe, as well as by Mao in China. Even as late as 2009, the national chairman of the party that had been rigging its members into ruling positions at all levels of government in Nigeria since 1999, had the bravado to say (in unabashed Nazi style) that his party would control all governments at all levels in the Nigerian federation for the next sixty years.

These Conditions and Ideas in Action

All of these conditions, experiences and ideas combined to impart a certain kind of character to state formation, and to all governance and behavior of administrations, in tropical Africa throughout the colonial era. The first major step was the determination and demarcation of boundaries for the countries that were created all over Black Africa. A Briton, Lord Salisbury, said of the Berlin Conference of 1884-5 at which European countries agreed on how to share Africa among them:

> "We have been engaged in drawing lines on maps where no white man's foot ever trod; we have been giving away mountains and rivers and lakes to each other, only hindered by the small impediment that we have never known where the rivers and lakes and mountains were."[5]

Another Briton, a British colonial agent who took part in the making of the southern stretch of the border between British-owned Nigeria and then German-owned Cameroons, said years later:

> "In those days, we just took a blue pencil and ruler, and we put it down at Old Calabar, and drew that blue line to Yola. I recollect thinking when I was sitting having an audience with the Emir (of Yola) surrounded by his tribe, that it was a very good thing that he did not know that I, with a blue pencil, had drawn a line through his territory."[5]

Those "blue lines", products of minds that were almost totally ignorant of the territories with which they were dealing, established the boundaries that African peoples are now required to worship as the borders of their countries. They also established, within each country, the boundaries of administrative districts and provinces. The problems thus created all over Black Africa are easy to see. Virtually all Black African countries were handed international and internal borders that, from the first day to now, have been beset by extremely destabilizing problems.

Moreover, in every country, the goal of imperial administration was not to "build" a country, but to wring from it the maximum economic advantage for the "mother country." Agents who came to a strange land and carved out some territory containing many different ancient peoples and states, and gave the territory a common administration and name, should have owed that territory the duty of helping it to evolve into a coherent entity. Nowhere was that duty avowed or acknowledged in practice or consciously pursued by European agents in Africa. Imperial investments, such as there were, targeted the exploitation of resources capable of the highest and quickest yields—mineral deposits, forest resources, export produce. In some countries, European companies were given concessions to exploit certain resources or even whole regions. The development of roads, railways and ports was designed to serve the goals of economic exploitation, to facilitate the evacuation of resources from the interior to the coast, and had no interest in facilitating the growth of a country. Areas without instantly manifest resources for exploitation remained essentially ignored and remote. In those countries where the climate permitted the introduction of farmers from Europe, developments were focused on helping the European farmers by opening up the areas where their farms concentrated. In order to give the European companies free rein, imperial policy discouraged indigenous entrepreneurship—or even destroyed it where it already existed. For instance, on the River Niger where indigenous traders were already a strong factor in the import-export trade with various European companies before the British imperial agents took over, the British administrators took steps to discourage the indigenous traders in order to ensure free and full control by European companies and merchants. The Yoruba merchant class and business class, already growing quite strongly in Lagos and some other parts of Yorubaland by the 1880s, were repressed by British colonial policy in the early 20th century, and replaced by European businesses and business people. The British Royal Niger Company was made to own, rule and control the commerce, and the administration, of whole territories. Cecil Rhodes' private businesses owned whole countries in southern Africa. Many parts of tropical Africa saw that same pattern – of private companies controlling whole territories or particular resources such as minerals.

Worse still, and very portentous for Black Africa's political future, even the administrative unity was nominal for most of the countries of tropical Africa for most of the colonial period. For instance, even after two protectorates were amalgamated to form Nigeria in 1914, the administrations of the two regions continued with more or less separate and different policies. Tentative constitutional advances introduced in the 1920s in Lagos and Calabar in the south did not touch the expansive northern region. It was not until 1949 that representative institutions, bringing the two protectorates together, were created—and that was only eleven years to independence. Belgian Congo (Congo Kinshasa), territorially the largest country in Africa, was a country only in name even until independence—its widely dispersed provinces virtually out of touch with one another. Sierra Leone started as two administrative entities, the "colony" and the "protectorate," and the two did not become administratively unified until 1924. In 1919, the French formed the territories of Upper Volta into one colony. In 1932, they split it up and shared it between neighboring French colonies. Then in 1947 they brought its parts together again as one country called Upper Volta (now Burkina Faso)—only a few years before independence. In Ghana (then known as the Gold Coast), the coastal areas (called the "colony") were not unified with the large territory of the Ashanti in the interior until 1946; and the more distant northern territories were not given representation in the Gold Coast Legislative Council until 1950-51—i.e., only six years before independence.

Furthermore, policies of the imperialists commonly promoted disunity and distrust among their African subjects. For instance, some inexplicable caprice of the British formulators of Nigeria produced a policy which, while presenting Nigeria to the British government and people as a glorious British possession,

124

nevertheless kept the northern and southern parts of Nigeria resolutely separate. Such a policy produced the outcome that the northern and southern parts of Nigeria essentially went in different directions for almost all the years of British rule, perhaps the strongest links between them being the use of revenue from the south to meet the expenses of administration in the north. British colonial administrators even discouraged Christian missionary enterprise from continuing to spread in the Nigerian Northern provinces – in the strange official assessment that Christian evangelism was good for the "pagans" of the south but not for the Muslims of the north.

In most countries, the few scattered nodal centers of colonial administration, and the areas where resources were being exploited, tended to receive all of the colonial government's inputs into infrastructural and social development. In the outcome, government schools, for instance, were very few in every colony or protectorate, and were always located in the centers of colonial administration or in the new communities emerging in locations of such ventures as mining. Any wider provision of educational opportunities in any colony or protectorate was the gift of the Christian missions. Thus, in every country, the roots were planted of socio-economic development that is orientated to a few urban centers, to the neglect of rural areas and of the concentrations of population that were regarded as less important. The negative consequences of such a mode of socio-economic development have been many and, in some places, have been serious. In particular, in a country with many different ethnic national territories, it holds the potential of labeling some peoples as superior and others as inferior, thereby establishing the seeds of unhealthy inter-people rivalries and even hostilities.

Most colonial powers employed, in their tropical African possessions, policies and practices based on the prevalent race theories of the colonial era, race theories, as earlier pointed out, originating during the centuries of the Slave Trade and particularly accentuated in Western scholarship in the 19th century and the early 20th. In Nigeria, for instance, it suited the British to play the race theory from time to time to support their chosen policy of discrimination in favor of one of the three largest Nigerian nationalities. In general, the French used the race theories much

125

more widely than the British, while the Belgians employed them very intensively in their colonies of the Congo, Burundi and Rwanda. In Burundi and Rwanda, as earlier pointed out, the Tutsi and Hutu had for centuries lived intermixed in the same country, and had gradually evolved as a people of one culture with one language and one religion. Nevertheless, on the basis of supposed race "facts", the Belgian administration promoted beliefs and myths of racial differences between Tutsi and Hutu, singled out the Tutsi for preference, and pursued policies that prepared the ground for horrible conflicts between the two. In no other tropical African country did racial and ethnic theories become as profoundly influential as in Rwanda and Burundi, and the Belgian Congo, but they were made a factor of life in almost every country under colonialism. The heritage of these theories and policies has been the growth of inter-ethnic animosities and hostilities even where none had existed before European colonialism, and their intensification where some had existed.

Still more, as independence seemed more and more inevitable in Africa generally in the years after the Second World War, each imperial power sought out a preferred people to hand power to in each colony at independence, as a means of protecting their own interests after the independence of their colonies. Working towards this objective usually called for various kinds of maneuvers and manipulations. In many cases, these involved crafting constitutions with features aimed at benefiting a particular nationality and giving it secure political advantages over other peoples in its country. In other cases, they involved the falsification of politically important national statistics, such as censuses. And in yet other cases, they involved unfair manipulations of the electoral process – with a view to giving political advantage to a favored people. And usually too, once the colonial rulers of a country had thus engineered their chosen pattern for its political life, they gave it support, even for long after independence – meddling with and guiding its affairs from the shadows. In such situations, the objective always has been to promote and protect the interests of the former colonial overlord and not of the African country concerned, and the consequence has commonly been the promotion or intensification of strife and conflict among the country's various sections.

In every country, the colonial administration was confronted inevitably by the problem of what to do with a multiplicity of indigenous governments and political traditions. In its response, every colonial power was motivated by the determination to simplify the administrative situation and minimize the expenses of administration. Some embarked on suppressing the indigenous governments and institutions and pursuing policies of "assimilation" – which meant that they created incentives for the rising class of educated citizens (products mostly of Christian mission schools) to strive to become Europeans and help to perpetuate European rule. Others pursued policies of "Indirect Rule" – using the indigenous rulers to do the dirtier tasks of administration (like tax collection, and the recruitment of people for forced labor on the public works, especially roads and railways, that were needed for the exploitation of the natural resources – but also, in some cases, on the forced production and gathering of natural resources for export). In some cases (such as in Nigeria), Indirect Rule worked out as taking a system that was designed to address the peculiar conditions of a particular people and forcibly applying it to the vastly different conditions of other peoples, thereby generating revolts and conflicts. In the exceptionally ugly case of the Belgian Congo under Belgium's King Leopold, the indigenous rulers were made to round up people (men and women) to produce quotas of rubber, and to provide some persons who would be held as hostages by King Leopold's officials in order to ensure performance of the quotas.

In virtually every case, though in different ways, the outcome was the elimination of the indigenous governments and institutions as effective factors in the lives of their people. In many cases, they were swept aside and more or less ultimately made to disappear, even though some vestiges might remain as inconsequential antiques. In some other cases they still seemed to possess some visible virility, but they had so negated their traditional roles and values, and become so unpopular, as to be inconsequential. In a very few cases, they continued to enjoy some significance among their people, but in a country in which they and their people were essentially a voiceless minority. However, in every case, as each colonial power was forced to prepare to give up its African colony in the years after the Second World War, it was not the indigenous rulers and institutions, but a new elite – the commonly small class of literate citizens – that was groomed to take over the governance. Thus, all over Black Africa, African peoples came to be component parts of countries not chosen by them, countries into whose founding and making they had made no inputs whatsoever, and entered into independent statehood under rulers with, at best, seriously doubtful legitimacy – and with no sort of legitimacy that was sanctified by the history and culture of the ruled.

Consequent Problems

The fruits of all these manner and styles of colonial governance came to manifest as soon as independence was achieved in every country. As a result of the largely irrational borders created by imperialist agents, practically all Sub-Saharan African countries were faced immediately at independence by serious border problems. Just any African country amply illustrates this picture of border confusions, but we will start with Nigeria, Africa's largest country in population and third largest in territorial size at independence. Hardly any one mile of Nigeria's thousands of miles of borders stands free of serious, and potentially explosive, border conflicts. In its southwestern length it cuts through the homeland of the Yoruba; further north from there, it cuts through the homeland of the Bariba; in the northwest, through the country of the Hausa; in the northeast through the country of the Kanuri and related peoples; in the southeast through the homelands of peoples who straddle the Nigerian-Cameroons border in the Adamawa Mountains and the Cross River swamps. Naturally, since independence, Nigeria has more or less regularly had one border problem or other. The most publicized of such problems has been the dispute with the Cameroons over the Bakassi Peninsula. This dispute started soon after independence, was occasionally marked by armed conflicts, and sometimes threatened outright war between the two countries. It was resolved in 2006 as a result of intensive mediation by the United Nations. Even after that, significant residues of the bad blood have continued to linger. Even as recently as the first months of 2010, there were reports that Nigeria might send, or was sending, troops to the area because of seriously deteriorating security conditions for Nigerians living there.

Though the Bakassi situation has attracted the most attention in the world, it has by no means been the only cause of dispute between Nigeria and the Cameroons. All along their 1,600 miles of border from Lake Chad in the north to the Gulf of Guinea in the south, Nigeria and the Cameroons have been locked in disputes since the 1960's. Indeed, but for Nigeria's intimidating size and influence in African affairs, the comparative weakness of the countries that are her neighbors, and her own cautious restraint in her attitudes to border uncertainties, Nigeria should be perpetually engulfed in destabilizing border storms.

Most other African countries have not been that fortunate. In fact, border conflicts became such a great potential threat to peace in the new Africa in the first years of independence that the OAU had to pass a resolution in 1964 binding all African countries to agree to maintain the borders bequeathed to them by the colonial powers. Even though most members of the OAU subscribed to that resolution, many neighbors have never been able specifically to settle their border disputes.

In eastern Africa, Somalia and Kenya have suffered from serious border difficulties since independence. In fact, the great crisis that destroyed all order and government in Somalia started with multiple border problems – especially with Kenya and with Ethiopia. With a substantial ethnic Somali population inside the Kenyan border provinces, independent Somalia has never recognized the border with Kenya. As soon as Somalia became independent, she began actively to encourage ethnic Somali insurgency inside Kenya and Ethiopia. Her quest for military help for these border situations pushed her into an alliance with the Soviet Union. Receiving substantial military help from the Soviet Union, Somalia became deeply involved in the Cold War, and that meant very influential enemies from among the Western powers. When a revolution came in Ethiopia and the Ethiopian revolutionary government became Soviet allies, Somalia more or less found herself abandoned by the Soviets – and the fragile political system of Somalia (of clans and clan leaders) fractured under the pressure, and then in 1991 totally collapsed. With the collapse of orderly government in Somalia, her border conflicts became more tense and more confused, producing serious complications with Kenya and then with Ethiopia, and forcing Ethiopia to send troops into Somalia in order to keep peace there.

While battling border troubles with Somalia, Kenya has also had to face border problems with Uganda and, to some extent, with Ethiopia and Sudan. The British took some trouble to demarcate the Kenyan-Ugandan border in 1926, and the two countries subscribed to the 1964 OAU resolution on the preservation of colonial borders. Even so, their border remains unsettled. On their land borders, conflicts are caused by irregular crossings from either side, especially by livestock herders. In the area known as Migingo, the dispute has been particularly intense. The border through Lake Victoria, where no agreed demarcations exist, is even more problematic. And so also is the uncertainty of the border in the Bukwa and Morumeri area where the three countries, Kenya, Uganda and Sudan, have conflicting claims. The Kenyan-Ethiopian border has been comparatively peaceful, but it too is occasionally disturbed by conflicting claims of pastoralist communities from both sides. A stretch of territory known as the Elemi Triangle, administered by Kenya, is claimed by Sudan and partly also by Ethiopia. This region of Africa is also the scene of one of the worst inter-state wars on the continent – the war over a disputed borders between Ethiopia and Eritrea. For two years, 1998-2000, this border war reached a peak. In 2000, negotiations produced a settlement, but in spite of that, tension has continued between the two countries. An estimated 70,000 people have lost their lives in these hostilities.

An even more destabilizing effect of the chaotic seizures of territory by European imperialist agents is that every country created by them in Sub-Saharan Africa is a 'ramshackle state". Each is a country comprising many peoples who, if they had been free to choose, are very unlikely to have chosen to belong together in the same country. Since African peoples in many parts of Africa are small in population and territory, it seems inevitable (as earlier pointed out) that, if Africa had had the chance to enter into the 20th century in its own way, many countries that would have evolved in Africa would have been made up of various peoples. However, the circumstances would have been different, and so would the resulting countries. The important fact of history here is that people from another continent came and, without caring about the peoples before them, or about the future of each country they were forcibly creating, or about the future of the peoples they were forcing together into that country, drew up an unthinking map for Africa. The scenario was more or less the same in most cases. Agents of a European nation came to an African ruler and solicited for preferential trade relations for their nationals to the exclusion of other European nationals; a treaty was entered into; when, later, representatives of the said European nation began to assume some authority over the African ruler's country, the ruler rejected their claims; the European nation declared war and launched an invasion. Various territories acquired in this way in a contiguous swathe were then given one colonial administration and, ultimately, a name – all in order to minimize the human and financial expenses of colonial administration. And so, a country was born. Each eclectic agglomeration of peoples and territories which was thus created and given a common administration and a name could only be, and has been, a panacea for instability and troubles.

As should be obvious from these modes of structuring and managing of the various European possessions in the colonial years, it is not merely the combination of many nationalities in each country that has generated the conflicts experienced since independence in the countries of tropical Africa. While the mere act of grouping various nationalities together in a country has some potential for conflicts, conflicts are not necessarily inevitable in multi-nation countries. It is also naturally tempting to make the assumption that most of the conflicts have their roots in pre-colonial patterns of hostility among neighboring peoples. Certainly, there would be conflict situations that can be so traced, but in most cases, it is the discriminations and manipulations perpetrated by the colonial administrations that have set most of the stage for troubles and conflicts. In fact, the inter-ethnic conflicts are a very significant part of the heritage of colonialism in tropical Africa.

Another heritage of colonialism is the lack of stable value systems in the politics and governance of tropical African countries. For members of the new literate elite who had to rule each African country at independence, there was, in all essence, nothing of a solid value system to work with. They were not being called upon to rule according to the norms and values that any of their peoples had evolved and lived by in their history. In their own indigenous systems, Africans and their indigenous rulers had known what rulers might or might not do. That is the essence of legitimacy. Under European colonial rule, there had been essentially nothing that the European colonial ruler might not do. Now that the new leaders of independent Africa were taking over, who knew what value system would, or should, guide their conduct as rulers? As the citizens of every country were being told by their new rulers to feast and dance to welcome independence in, they faced a very uncertain, a very precarious future indeed. Uprooted from their indigenous political and value systems, these new rulers had only the values of the colonizers to hold on to – and that was, to put it mildly, a very shaky pillar indeed. Since the heart of the legitimacy of each European state's sovereignty over its African possessions had been its power to hold and coerce, the African indigenous successors of the European rulers came to consider the power to hold and coerce as sufficient legitimacy for their own positions as rulers of those possessions. It was blissfully assumed by the new rulers of Africa that each ruler, in order to hold his new country together, only needed to maintain the strength and rigor of the institutions and coercive powers of the new state.

Beyond that, the new rulers had been allowed by the colonial authorities to participate in some veneer of Western democratic political practice in the final years of European colonial rule, but their grafting onto that system was fickle and shoddy in extreme – not only because their apprenticeship had been flighty and chaotic, but also because the system as shown to them was crooked and heavily corrupted. Under the African colonial versions of Western democracy, rigid limits to association and expression were enforced, and those Africans who dared to test those boundaries by criticizing certain aspects of colonial rule invariably ended up in prison. For instance, the Irish, Welsh or Scottish citizen of Britain enjoyed, throughout the 20th century, the protection of British law to voice Irish, Welsh or Scottish nationalist demands for separation from Britain; but it was a crime for the Yoruba traditional ruler in French Dahomey to make contacts with his traditional subjects beyond the border in British

Nigeria – a crime, as would be remembered, punishable by imprisonment and banishment. And the more outspoken African nationalists (like Kwame Nkrumah, Jomo Kenyatta, Kamuzu Banda, etc.) served prison terms. In Nigeria, it was acceptable to the British that Yoruba people who were consigned to northern Nigeria, separate from the large body of their people who were in southern Nigeria, if they demanded to be regrouped with southern Nigeria, could be treated as criminal insurrectionists. For the men who became the new rulers of African countries after independence, listening to, or discussing with, their subjects was out of the question, and the more outspoken or more irreconcilable critics deserved imprisonment or even detention without trial. Before European colonial rule, indigenous African governments had generally been based on consensus and conciliation, and had been free of all the hash pressures on the citizen that came to be characteristic of colonial and post-colonial rule in Africa. Yet another kind of corruption of the so-called democratic system of the last years of colonial rule was the falsification of national data and the rigging of elections – all of which the imperial rulers, as will be explained a little more hereunder, commonly engaged in – and passed on to their successors.

Moreover, as a direct consequence of the colonizer's policies of divide and rule, as well as of repression of all dissent, the men who found themselves standing under the new national flag of every newly independent country and haranguing the citizens were, essentially, strangers to one another. Among them, the task of mutual discovery would soon prove daunting. They had spun about the same rhetoric while demanding liberation from foreign rule. But when that noise was over, did they know or understand one another? Could they trust one another? The answer was swift to come in many countries. Almost as soon as the independence celebrations ended in Ghana, Kwameh Nkrumah, the hero who had led Ghana into independence, was heard to rant against those whom he called "tribalists," "balkanizers," "imperialist stooges" — meaning the political elite of the proud kingdom of Ashanti and others. The principal crime of these tribalists and balkanizers was that they happened to believe that a federal constitution, or some sort of arrangement that ensured some local autonomy to the component peoples of their new country, would better serve the interests of all in their new country than the strongly centralized arrangement favored by Dr. Nkrumah. It needs to be added, in fairness to Dr. Nkrumah and some other leaders of his generation, that Dr. Nkrumah's efforts to acquire maximum power for the government of his new country was almost unanimously welcomed by the younger generation of educated Africans of the time (the youth generation to which this author belonged) as the very best course for Ghana and the rest of Africa. The great pity is that, even today, after decades of experiencing the pitfalls and pains of that manner of leadership and nation-building, our leading politicians all over Africa still cling to it.

In Congo (Kinshasa), an enormous country with some of the world's thickest forests and biggest rivers, and with concentrations of human population far removed by vast forests from one another, the hurried alliance which led the country to independence disintegrated within days after independence. Widespread chaos ensued, including secessionist demands by the elite (the handful of men who constituted the literate elite) of some of the provinces. The first Prime Minister, Patrice Lumumba, unrepentantly passionate about his new country and its unity, and about a strongly unifying government for it, quickly fell out with virtually all prominent politicians from other regions of his country. His acceptance of help from the Soviet Union greatly compounded the confusion into which he thus plunged, because it pushed him into the eye of an international storm that he did not know much about. Those who had access to him knew that he was no communist, and that he did not have much clear knowledge or understanding about communism – and that his thinking was apparently to use Soviet help to survive and then, later, to ask the Soviets to go away. But he did not survive the intensified confusion.

In Nigeria, Africa's most populous country, and the most promising African country at independence, trouble started almost immediately after independence. In less than fifteen months after independence, the country began to unravel. Thus, developments were essentially the same in every country after independence, though troubles were less dramatic in some and slower to come in others.

Each African country confronted at independence then, and has continued to confront, a potpourri of destabilizing problems. On the morning of the day after the independence celebrations in each country, in fact, the attributes of a state were more assumed than real – even though they were assumed exuberantly. The borders were uncertain, shaky, and potentially explosive. Many of the men who were supposed to be in control, the literate elite of various patches of each country, were nervous, uncertain what would be their peoples' shares in the new dispensation and how it was all going to affect them and their peoples. The traditional political elite, even in the few countries where the masses of the people were still attached to their traditional institutions, had been suppressed and repressed, and could see that they were not going to be consulted or even respected in the new dispensation. Consequently, huge question marks hung over every country and its so-called Independence Constitution.

In the historiography of European colonial rule in Africa, one often encounters the suggestion that each country's colonial army, comprising persons drawn from various ethnic backgrounds and trained together to defend their common country, represented a nucleus of national unity at independence. In reality, however, ethnic cleavages were very real in the so-called national army of every country; and the pressures exerted on all by the rivalries common in politics tended in every country to affect the cohesion of the military – thus posing strong potential threats to national security. Quite commonly, hostile actions against the government of an African country from the army of the country are not by the army as an establishment, but by some faction within the army. And such actions are often not just against the civilian rulers, but also against some other faction within the army itself. Moreover, the sorts of men commonly recruited into colonial armies were usually the semi-literate (men with, at best, a couple of years of elementary schooling), sometimes even illiterate – men whose capacity to understand country, or duty to country, in the new context, was minimal. Even worse, many a national army, having been created by the colonial administration as a tool for controlling the colony, had in fact been trained and orientated to despise the rising political elite. European colonial officials all over Africa despised the rising African literate elite, and those colonial officials who trained and commanded the colonial armies usually passed such attitudes to their soldiers. Not infrequently, after independence, the indigenous soldiers who became the new commanders were only waiting for the slightest signs of political pitfalls to boot out the ones whom they were used to calling "bloody civilians". Finally, in any case in which the army boss happened to belong to a nationality different from, and rival to, that of the political bosses, trouble lurked only a little below the surface. In every country, the new leader of government was unknown or unacceptable in large parts of his country.

In most countries, rulers cast around for some slogan, some claptrap, some battle cry, that could ignite "national unity" – Nkrumah's "African Socialism" or "Pan-Africanism" in Ghana, Leopold Sedar Senghor's "Negritude" in Senegal, Nigerian leaders' "Unity in Diversity", Jomo Kenyatta's "Harambee" in Kenya, etc. All proved unavailing – and were soon forgotten.

Decades after independence, and in spite of military coups, civil wars, ethnic cleansing and genocide in nearly all countries, the variegated ethnic and cultural composition of each country still loads its political system with extremely heavy burdens. The refusal of the leadership of every country to seek appropriately to find political and constitutional arrangements based on consensus among its various peoples results in endless, willful, constitutional experimentations by the leadership – usually without seeking any inputs from the broad mass of citizens or from the various peoples that make up the country. In virtually every country, therefore, no sooner is a new constitution written than the need for another, a "better" one, becomes pressing.

While growing literacy may appear to foster, to some extent and for some occasions, an acceptance of the new country by some members of its various peoples, the stronger tendency has been that, in the context of bruising inter-ethnic rivalries and hostilities inherited from colonial times, literacy strengthens each people's awareness of itself as a distinct cultural entity in the world, with the result that it tends to become more conscious of its cultural heritage, more emphatic about the differences between itself and other groups, more defensive of its interests, and more desirous to control its own affairs and determine its own future. Consequently, relationships between nationalities in each country, rather than mellowing out, tend to grow sharper. The common experience is that, under the pressure of rivalry with other nations in the same country, nations are highlighting and rediscovering their history and, in the context of the rivalries, are employing the new knowledge to argue some superiority or better claim over their rivals. Dominant nationalities in each country seek to sustain their dominance or even to hold on to a monopoly control of their country's government; and the other nationalities mount various types of resistance. Nationalities that had had little or no contacts with each other in pre-colonial times, and therefore no historical reason to be hostile to each other, nevertheless become bitter political rivals, or even enemies, in the modern country. For instance, the highly literate Yoruba and Igbo of Nigeria (two of Africa's most literate peoples and, incidentally, two of Africa's largest peoples in population and territory), though they have no record of contacts or mutual hostility in their pre-colonial history, today harbor deep, virtually irresoluble suspicions of each other, even while both solidly oppose, and would do anything to resist, Hausa-Fulani pretensions of domination over Nigeria. As Sudan and Rwanda, and later South Sudan, have shown, in the hands of two peoples with some history of conflicts or of subordination of one to the other under European colonial rule, competition for political positioning in the new country can be unimaginably bitter and produce the darkest of horrors.

Furthermore, in the midst of the sometimes nebulous promotion of "national unity" by rulers or dominant groups, component nationalities that evince some distinctive strengths or capabilities often risk becoming suspect or even odious. In Nigeria since independence, the large Yoruba of Southwestern Nigeria, who had evolved Black Africa's most advanced urban civilization centuries before the advent of British colonialism, who adopted Western education more quickly in the mid-19th century, and more seriously, than all the other peoples of the later country of Nigeria, and whose homeland has remained consistently in the forefront of development and modernization in Nigeria, have usually lived under hostility from every federal administration of the Nigerian federation. Any nationality that is split between neighboring countries and manifests strong feelings of attachment with the other part of itself in the other country also risks being odious in the country to which it belongs. In the worst of cases, such suspect or odious groups risk actual danger of attack from other groups or from even their country's government. Among the worst cases, Idi Amin as ruler of Uganda seemed dead set on exterminating the Acholi people of his country. The world hears little or nothing of the nationalism of the Bakongo of west-central Africa, the large people of the once considerable kingdom of the Kongo who are today estimated to constitute about 14% of the population of Angola, about 16% of Congo (Kinshasa), and about 48% of Congo (Brazzaville) – a total population variously estimated at as low as five million and as high as about eleven million. Bakongo nationalism is a persistent feature of the politics of these countries. Its shape tends to differ from country to country, sometimes with a tendency towards secessionism. Increasingly since the 1960s, one of its strong manifestation has been a Bakongo fundamentalist movement for the unification of all Bakongo into one country with the name Kongo Dia Ntotela (Kongo United States) – in order to revive the historic glory of their Bakongo nation of the time of 15th century Kongo Kingdom. Not surprisingly, while the Bakongo are influential in some of the countries to which they belong, they are suspect in others. ABAKO, the party founded by the Bakongo literate elite of the Belgian Congo in the last years of Belgian rule, was a major member of the alliance of parties that led the Congo to independence. Its leader, Joseph Kasavubu, served as the country's first president – with Patrice Lumumba from another part of the country and another party serving as Prime Minister. In Angola, in contrast, the Portuguese came down particularly heavily on the Bakongo following the Angolan anti-Portuguese revolt of 1961, displacing hundreds of thousands of them, who then took refuge in Congo (Kinshasa). In the Angolan civil war, Bakongo nationalism played a considerable role in the groups fighting against the MPLA, whose leaders were mostly men of mestizo origin (people of mixed African and Portuguese blood living mostly in and around the capital city and on the coast). Bakongo solidarity also played some part in the Mobutu support for such Angolan groups as the FLNA of Holden Roberto, a member of the Bakongo nationality. With Angolan rulers, therefore, the Bakongo have been sometimes suspect, and that has earned them repression and mass killings. In a 1993 Angolan incident now known as "Bloody

Friday", some 4,000 to 6,000 Bakongo were killed in one day. In many African countries, some national groups dare not freely express their true desires, out of fear of having latent hostilities whipped up against them by the powerful agencies of government.

A strong, pervasive, culture of democracy, if introduced early by the European founders of these African countries and operated honestly, might probably have enabled each country to chart a more stable political path. In response to this, the former imperial overlords often claim, with much of the world believing them, that before they gave up Africa, they taught democracy to their African subjects. Their claims are not true. European rule in Africa was, as earlier pointed out, always ultimately a dictatorship by a few white officials, upheld by police and military force, with absolute powers to limit or prevent freedom of expression and association. Its most outspoken critics invariably ended up in prison, so that many of the first rulers of independent African countries were alumni of colonial prisons. As independence became inevitable after the Second World War, most imperial overlords began to introduce some aspects of representative government, resulting in political parties and elections, as preparation for post-independence governments. Almost in every country, however, these developments came too late. In Congo (Kinshasa) the only election before independence came on the eve of independence.

But even worse, the imperial authorities did not let the nascent political development operate freely and fairly. The imperial policy of promoting a favored group to power usually resulted in official tampering with the political process. The pre-independence elections in many countries were rigged by the colonial governments. The lessons from the widespread official fraud sank, and were to become the vogue among African rulers after independence. The well-known technique is to speak the mellifluous language of popular politics; acknowledge the people as source of political power; do the electioneering campaign rounds; then, at election, use the power of position as ruler to manufacture the election results. And if voices of protest arise, the African ruler knows what the colonial administration used to do in such situations – namely, manipulate the courts to uphold the fraud, face the world with a fait accompli, and go on. At any point in this whole process, the ultimate answer exists in reserve - to unleash the coercive agencies of government to intimidate and repress opponents and silence the press and other organizations like labor unions, students' bodies, etc. That, for Africa by and large, is democracy as it was taught by former imperialist rulers.

For these reasons, loyalty to the true purposes and intentions of democracy, and faith in democracy and in elections, rather than growing, have both steadily declined in independent African countries. According to the Guinea Bissau economist, Carlos Lopes, who was for some time the resident United Nations representative in independent Zimbabwe, Africans would perhaps fare better if they gave more priority to the concept of "tolerance" over that of "democracy", because elections have commonly been used on the continent to "legitimize authoritarian governments", often to annihilate the opposition, often to exclude those who are "different" ethnically or linguistically – as a result of which election has tended to become "a recipe for using democracy perversely, for obtaining a result opposite to democracy's real aims."[6]

CHAPTER FIVE

Further Factors In Our Conflicts

Almost all of the conflicts in African countries since independence have tended to play out in some sort of inter-ethnic confrontation or violence (pogroms, ethnic cleansing, genocide, etc.). However, as has been pointed out above, that is not to say that the ethnic diversity *per se* has been the sole and inevitable cause of the conflicts. It is worth repeating that though ethnic diversity in a country has an inherent potential for conflict, whether and how conflict will actually be produced depends on a lot of other factors. As should already be obvious from the above, the roots of the problem in each Sub-Saharan African country crystallized, not merely from the grouping of different ethnic nations together, but from a complex interplay of historical circumstances – namely, the basic fact of ethnic heterogeneity of the countries, the manner in which the peoples of each country were thrown together without any knowledge or input of theirs and without any deference to their peculiarities, differences or desires, the cavalier manner in which their political institutions were trampled under and disrupted or destroyed, the patterns (in particular) of inter-relationships and politics fashioned and fostered by the foreign rulers in each country, the nature of the new leadership generated by the situation, the almost inevitable mismanagement and poor governance of Africa's countries after independence and the corruption resulting from the mix, the warped structuring of the economy of each country by its imperial rulers, the consequent economic ignorance and poverty of each country at independence, the meddling of former imperialist overlords in the post-independence affairs of each country, etc.

In the final analysis, however, after all factors have been accounted for, the most decisive factor has to be the drastic failure of leadership in virtually every independent country of tropical Africa. This central weakness, while it did not create the roots of the political problems and difficulties that our countries and peoples have had to live and struggle with, has been responsible for transforming the problems and difficulties into outright disasters. This is the central factor in the political disasters that have befallen the countries of Black Africa since independence. Particular focus on it will come in the very next chapter, but attention to it belongs to nearly all the rest of this short book.

Meanwhile, we will consider here the other main factors in the making of the troubles and conflicts. Of course, the primary foundations for instability and disorder were laid in the European colonial experience, and that has been the burden of the chapters preceding this one. Of the many other factors, we shall examine the following most crucial ones.

One is the role of the poor performance on the economic front.[1] Many countries at independence started off from a weak economic base. The basic structure of the economy of most countries, as designed by the former colonial rulers, was an economy exporting raw materials (minerals or cash crops) and importing manufactured goods. In most cases, the export base featured just one primary product – like a particular mineral or cash crop. In general, the pricing mechanisms were controlled by external, non-African, interests, and each country suffered from varying disadvantages in its struggle against powerful trends and entrenched patterns and interests in the world market. Periodic fluctuations in world commodity prices would later create challenges that the new African countries would need to struggle to understand or master, a situation that, for many countries, would result in economic distress. Widening this economic base was made very difficult in many countries by the fact that the directions of the colonial economy had prevented the emergence of an entrepreneurial class or middle class, and the formation of indigenous private capital. The literacy and educational base was also very fragile in many countries – for instance, the large country of Congo (Kinshasa) had less than a dozen college graduates at independence.

It is tempting for Africans to conclude from all these that the economic situation was generally impossible, that the economic problems were simply intractable, following independence. But that, on the whole, was not true at independence and in the immediate years after independence. On the contrary, many African countries showed some success in the years immediately following independence. In the three Regions of

142

Nigeria (Northern, Eastern and Western), serious attention to the export farming economy that was inherited from the colonial regime created, in the late 1950s and early 1960s, considerable bases of success upon which wider successes could be nurtured. Between the Eastern and Western Regions, a lively development rivalry ensued, and many programs of socio-economic development, funded mostly by the export crop earnings, reinforced rising hopes of wider successes. An ambitious educational program in the Western Region (the first Free Primary Education Program on the continent), created promises of fast socio-economic growth on a wide front in that Region. In the Eastern Region, a growing culture of small modern businesses gradually arose. Besides Nigeria in West Africa, the Ivory Coast, by also strengthening the export farming economy inherited from the colonial times, became immediately tropical Africa's greatest success story. Cameroon also followed more or less in the footpaths of the Ivory Coast, with considerable success. Ghana too started on a very hopeful footing, based on the strong performance of its cocoa export crop. With bases also in agriculture, some other countries - Kenya, Malawi, and Swaziland – also showed promising beginnings.

In the field of social services, school enrolment increased rapidly in Africa during the independence decade, though not on a scale comparable to Latin America's or Asia's. So too did health delivery services. The development of infrastructures, especially of durable roads and city water installations, also witnessed a strong showing. Some of the best ports in modern Africa, and many large water dams, were constructed in these years

In many countries, manufacturing also saw sudden increases. In fact, the most rapid growth in many countries immediately after independence was in the building of manufacturing industries. It was widely believed among African leaders that Africa's central development push should be in industrialization, and that the greatest need of the times was the establishment of import-substituting industries. Ambitious industrial estates sprang up in many countries. In the field of international commerce, Africa's share in world trade showed considerable increases.

The general African economic performance was lower than those of other Third World regions, but it was nevertheless sufficient to inspire hope. For most of the 1960s, in fact, most of the world's opinion about Africa's economic prospects was one of optimism.

But then, from the late 1960s on, various economic and natural problems began to arise to weaken economic performance. Declines, from time to time, in the world prices of commodities like cocoa or coffee brought distress upon the countries that were mostly dependent on those commodity exports. Even a country like the Ivory Coast, doing considerably better than most other countries, suffered sharply as a result of the 1978 collapse in world cocoa and coffee prices. The worldwide recession in the 1970s led to slumps in the prices of minerals, especially copper – resulting, for instance, for major copper producers like Zambia and Congo (Kinshasa) the harsh condition whereby they even sometimes produced copper at a loss. Droughts beginning from about 1968 in the West African Sahel region south of the Sahara Desert destroyed much of the agricultural production in many countries of that region, especially in Mauritania, Mali, Senegal, Niger, Burkina Faso, Nigeria and Chad. For instance, the production of groundnuts in Northern Nigeria fell from 765,000 tons in 1968-9 to only 25,000 tons in 1972-3. By 1972, Mali had lost some 40% of both its food production and its cattle. Similar devastations were wrought by droughts in the grassland areas of East Africa and then in countries of the Horn region – Ethiopia, Somalia, Eritrea. Then came the sharp rises in oil prices as a result of events in the Middle East – first the Arab-Israeli war and then the war between Iraq and Iran. From $3 per barrel in 1973, the price of oil rose in the next seven years until it reached $55 and then dropped sharply to $38 per barrel by 1981. Only few tropical African countries (like Nigeria, Gabon and Congo-Brazzaville) were oil producers; the rest were oil importers and they all plunged into serious balance of payments difficulties.

To make all these worse, the population of Africa rose rapidly, beginning from the early 1960s, mostly as a result of successes in the improvements of health delivery services, and improvements in hygiene consequent on growing literacy. Population increase was generally faster in Africa than in other parts of the world. Total African population jumped from about 200 million in 1960 to about 450 million by 1990. In many countries, the impact of the rapid population growth on land use – on the availability of arable land – was very serious. In many countries, food production failed to keep pace with the population growth, resulting in cataclysmic shortages of food. Massive programs of food aid by the rest of the world became the only means of warding off unthinkable losses of human life in the countries of the West African Sahel, parts of the Horn of Africa, and Ethiopia.

To top it all, as these difficulties developed, nearly every country in Black Africa began to experience very serious political instability. Authoritarian regimes sprang up across the sub-continent, and then followed a rash of military seizures of government, and then vicious military dictatorships – all compounded by a growing political culture of ethnic conflicts. In the midst of all these, orderly attention to the demands of economic development virtually perished in most countries. A vicious cycle of authoritarian rule, political turmoil and intensified economic decline settled into the life of Black Africa. Poverty escalated. By the 1980s, most of the earlier hope about tropical Africa's prospects in the world had disappeared.

In the face of all these multiple challenges, the countries of Africa needed, in the economic sphere, informed changes and redirections in economic policy. Unfortunately, the African governments (civilian and military – but particularly the military governments) proved disastrously incapable of conceiving and pursuing the needed economic policy changes. The failure of leadership to grapple with economic problems at this critical juncture converted the problems into long-lasting disasters. For most countries, balance of payment difficulties forced restrictions on imports, including imports needed to keep the new industries running. Therefore, many new factories were forced to operate at low capacity or even to close. In spite of that, most governments continued to hold on to state-led industrialization as the only route to economic growth. By the end of the 1970s, many of these industries had failed in many countries. By the 1980s, many countries were even experiencing a process of 'de-industrialization'. As a result of commonly poor attitudes towards

145

business people, poorly conceived business laws and regulations, and the escalating influence of corruption and fraud, most of the countries failed to attract private capital (even indigenous private capital) – in a world in which the flow of private capital was generally multiplying.

In particular, a vigorous development of agriculture and strong growth in agricultural production was badly needed all over Africa. But most Black African governments and leaderships viewed only industrialization as the soul of modern economic development – refusing to take cognizance of the fact that success in agriculture was a pillar of the economy of the most industrialized countries of the world. Focusing virtually all attention on industrialization as the road to modern economic development, African governments and leaders let farming acquire the image of an archaic occupation fit only for the old, illiterate and poor members of the population. All over tropical Africa, therefore, farming failed to attract the younger generation of people and literate folks, and agricultural production per head declined steadily. In many countries, it would be remembered, natural disasters like droughts heavily compounded the decline of agriculture.

For many countries, the neglect and decline of agriculture proved particularly damaging to the whole economy. For instance, at independence in 1960, Nigeria was the world's largest exporter of groundnuts and palm produce and the second largest exporter of cocoa; by the end of the 1970s, Nigeria had almost totally ceased exporting any of these. Cocoa was the strong pillar of Ghana's economy at independence; between the mid-1960s and 1980, its cocoa production fell by half. Nearly every country of tropical Africa began to spend heavily on food imports, while the poorer countries began to rely on international food aid. Huge balance of payment deficits began to build up heavy foreign debts for many countries. In addition, to meet the socio-economic needs of their people, most countries began to borrow large amounts of money abroad – rather than pursue needed austerity measures. Each country thus created for itself an enormous debt problem.

In the years after the Second World War, just before the independence of African countries, the imperial powers had set up some public corporations and businesses in their African colonies, as support to their own war recovery programs. After independence, many African countries continued to expand on this tradition of state-owned enterprises, the rulers often arguing that the lack of both an indigenous entrepreneurial class and indigenous private capital made it incumbent on government to step up as entrepreneur and investor, especially in the establishment of industries. Almost everywhere after independence, the resulting state-owned businesses became objects of sordid public corruption. Influential politicians treated loans from state-owned banks as their reward for helping the ruling party to win elections, and state-owned industries as places where jobs, distributorships, soft contracts and other kinds of favor were provided for the benefit of their relatives and political supporters. Under such battering, state-owned businesses tended generally to decline in efficiency and performance, and a lot ultimately failed – thus becoming a heavy burden on the economy in many countries.

Ghana, Black Africa's first independent country, pursued the most radical and systematic state-enterprise strategy for development. The government of Dr. Nkrumah had started off initially after independence in 1957 in the way that was to become common with newly independent countries in all parts of tropical Africa – promoting private enterprise, investing heavily in state-owned enterprises, and ambitiously investing in social services and infrastructures. However, after the first four years (1957-61), he became dissatisfied with the pace of private-sector industrial growth. In particular, the influx of foreign private capital did not prove as strong as he had hoped for. In response, he chose to embark on a wholesale change of policy. After a visit to the Soviet Union in 1961, he announced that Ghana would thenceforth pursue a socialist strategy of economic development. In 1962, his party (the CPP) adopted the new socialist policy, and in March 1963, the Ghanaian parliament passed the first socialist development plan, the Seven-Year Development Plan 1963-70.

Under the plan, the Ghanaian state went ambitiously into agriculture, industries and commerce. A State Farms Corporation owned, by 1965, 135 state farms employing 21,000 farm workers. The Workers Brigade also owned some 34 farms. Private farmers were still allowed under the system, but these must now sell most of their crops to government corporations. A United Ghana

147

Farmers Council was established to promote farmers' cooperatives among the private farmers. State-owned industries sprang up. By 1965, there were 64 state-owned factories. A State Enterprises Secretariat was established to coordinate the management of the state factories. The state acquired a large private commercial company and turned it into a National Trading Corporation engaging in imports and exports. Regulations were introduced to enable the government to control prices, imports and foreign exchange.

Much of these investments, especially in agriculture and industries, quickly turned into disasters. Widespread lack of faith in the whole system, poor employment policies and practices, unsuitable personnel, crushing mismanagement, outright thefts of assets – all these soon led to the accumulation of heavy losses and debts. Since a lot of the money invested in the enterprises was from foreign loans, Ghana's foreign debt surged from $16.3 million in 1961 to $395 million by 1965-6. Meanwhile, the government regulations gradually ruined Ghana's small traders and owners of small businesses. Much of the country seethed with disaffection. The market women, faithful allies of Dr. Nkrumah since the independence struggle days, turned against him. Farmers became discouraged and despondent, and agricultural production fell sharply, resulting in serious food shortages and high food prices. And while the life of the masses of Ghana's people was thus progressively gripped by poverty and hardship, prominent functionaries in the government and ruling party became rich through various kinds of corrupt practices. Partly influenced by the euphoric propaganda by the rulers of Ghana, socialism began to acquire some popularity in some other countries of Black Africa, and a few countries, notably Uganda under Obote, took steps to adopt a socialist strategy of development also – with outcomes similar to Ghana's.

In summary, poor knowledge and poor understanding of economic factors by independent African governments and leaders, and poor choices of economic policy, exerted devastating impact on most tropical African countries. Most of these countries showed no understanding, or even awareness, of international economic realities and processes. In the circumstance, sloppy management of international trade processes and obligations created a situation whereby the products of these countries were gradually edged out in the world market by products of other regions of the Third World. In a world in which tourism was becoming a major factor in the economies of countries, hardly any tropical African country showed any awareness of the importance of tourism – other than the four countries (Kenya, Senegal, Botswana and Tanzania) that had developed some tourist industries since colonial times. By 1990, Africa had lost about half of its 1970 world trade volume, or an estimated $70 billion per year. By then, dependence on foreign aid had become almost universal in Black Africa.

Even a country like Nigeria, whose enormous petroleum wealth began to yield huge revenues from about 1970, plunged into serious distress from the 1980s as a result of a combination of natural disasters, fluctuations in the world market prices of commodities, all massively exacerbated by poor management and corruption. Until 1979 Nigeria still had a favorable balance of trade, and healthy foreign reserves. But growing weaknesses in the management of this country's affairs were already building towards serious down-turns in its economy. Under the centralizing and controlling zeal of successive military regimes, and the almost total shift of attention to petroleum as the pillar of the economy, the Regional and local initiatives and energies that had been fundamental to economic development in Nigeria up to the 1960s were progressively destroyed. Most of the Regional attention to the main Nigerian cash crops – cocoa in the Western Region, palm produce in the Eastern Region, and groundnuts in the Northern Region – disappeared, and Nigeria's produce exports declined dramatically. The Northern Region suffered the most – because the general mismanagement of the Nigerian economy was given very devastating effect here by the droughts in the far northern provinces. By 1982, Nigeria's foreign reserves had fallen by about 60%; Nigeria had built up a balance of payments deficit of $7.3 billion and foreign debts of over $6 billion. In 1983, the petroleum earnings expectations, on which Nigerian rulers had built grandiose national budgets and a mammoth culture of corruption, collapsed when the world price of oil fell by 25% and Nigeria's share of oil exports under the OPEC agreements was reduced by 60%. Nigeria's foreign debt shot up to over $18 billion and capital began to flee from the country. Serious distress gripped the country and its people, much like other countries in the subcontinent. The economic distress has grown relentlessly even until the time of this writing. In 2011, as earlier stated, the Nigerian National Bureau of Statistics announced that 61.9% of Nigerians lived in 'absolute poverty'. And in many parts of the country, the crushing poverty was intensifying various kinds of conflicts.

Similarly in country after country in the subcontinent, the escalation of economic distress has accentuated political tensions and inter-group conflicts. And most governments and political leaders have abandoned even the weak attention that had earlier been paid to economic matters, and given all their attention to issues of political control.

We will illustrate this picture with one or two examples. Though bad blood between the Tutsi and Hutu had risen and grown under Belgian colonial rule and had generated a growing culture of mutual attacks, the making of the horrendous Hutu-Tutsi genocide of 1994 had significant inputs in the economic distress that grew in Rwanda beginning from the late 1980's.[2] As it had been structured under Belgian colonialism, Rwanda's economy depended heavily on coffee exports at independence. In 1987, the system of coffee quotas set up under the International Coffee Agreement (ICA) began to collapse, and the world prices of coffee fell precipitously, plunging Rwanda into serious economic distress. Next year, the World Bank and the International Monetary Fund (IMF) stepped in and, among other things, recommended a Structural Adjustment Program for Rwanda's economy, involving special soft loans to Rwanda on the "conditionalities" usually attached to such loans for poor countries. As in all poor countries thus needing assistance by the IMF and offered these conditionalities (including especially the devaluation of the national currency, and the withdrawal of subsidies to certain weak parts of the economy), the initial effect was some increased economic distress for the broad masses of the people. In Rwanda, this hit the peasant farmers particularly hard, as general inflation escalated and the prices of food rose sharply. Unfortunately, Rwanda did not command the inner coherence and strength to wade through this phase. Under the pressure, the Hutu political elite began to fracture, the Tutsi rebel army in exile (the RPF) invaded the country, and the government weakened markedly. When the special loans began to come in 1990, the embattled government funneled them into the purchase of arms for the fight against the invading rebel army rather than into the economy. By 1992, the government was near bankrupt, public services were collapsing, and the country was gripped in famine. Incidents of inter-ethnic violence and killings spread, especially in the poor rural areas. When the president's aircraft fatally crashed (widely believed to have been shot down) in 1994, the explosion that had been building finally materialized.

In some countries, the economic distress was underlined by sharp declines of certain vital resources. Perhaps the best example here is in the Darfur province of Sudan. In general, the almost perpetual political conflicts and civil wars in Sudan have been explained as stemming from confrontations between racially or ethnically different peoples (Arabs and Black Africans), or between predominantly Muslim and predominantly non-Muslim peoples, or between oppressors and the oppressed, etc. While all these are factors in the conflicts, certain economic factors have also been very influential in the making and character of the troubles in Darfur. Dwindling land, water and grazing resources due mostly to droughts had, since the 1970s, progressively threatened the wellbeing of the inhabitants of this part of Africa. This increasingly generated hostilities, and intensified the established patterns of conflict, between the predominantly pastoralist Arab groups and the predominantly farming Black African peoples. When the government responded to the situation with solutions that were manifestly discriminatory, typically in favor of the Arabs and against the Black Africans, the latter's sense of outrage at the inequity generated rebellion and insurgency. Powerful rebel militias arose to confront the Sudanese army. But besides that, under the aegis of a government that was determined only to impose order and strengthen the Arab population, the Arab communities were encouraged and assisted to spawn the Janjaweed death squads to effect ethnic cleansing and genocide in the villages.[3]

Resources – notably minerals and petroleum – that feature in international trade and produce the largest foreign exchange and national revenues, have also played roles in political conflicts in tropical African countries. In Nigeria, the peoples of the petroleum-rich Niger Delta have, for decades, been engaged in an insurgency against Nigeria's federal government. Cabinda's petroleum is important in Cabinda's secessionist temper against Angola. In the civil wars in the Congo Democratic Republic, Liberia, Sierra Leone, etc., control over rich mineral resources frequently constituted tactical objectives in the conflicts between opposing forces. In Sudan, disagreements over the sharing of petroleum wealth were a major factor in the stalemate between the national government and the petroleum-rich southern provinces for many years.

Not surprisingly, there are different opinions as to the particular significance of these resources in African political conflicts. The situation in most cases is usually very complex. For instance, the peoples of Nigeria's Niger Delta are not fighting for, or over, petroleum *per se*, but against the gross inequity of their position in the Nigerian scheme of things. Like all other of the smallest peoples in Nigeria, the Niger Delta peoples are essentially voiceless and marginalized in Nigerian affairs, and the unique needs of their part of Nigeria have very little chance of receiving appropriate and adequate national attention. The Niger Delta therefore remains one of the poorest corners of Nigeria (in transportation, social services, schools, etc.), even though it supplies a preponderance of Nigeria's national wealth. Moreover, even their traditional natural resources (the little land they have in the swamps and creeks, and their fishing waters) have been steadily degraded by the activities of petroleum explorations and mining – and they have been thus progressively pauperized. At the same time, they can, in the context of Nigeria's enormous culture of public corruption, see politicians from other parts of Nigeria (especially from among the larger and therefore more influential peoples) live in great opulence from unearned wealth – all of which comes from the petroleum revenues. Furthermore, when some citizens of the Niger Delta raised voices against these inequities and the degradation of their homeland, the federal government's response was to throw Nigeria's law enforcement machinery against them, and to indict, convict and execute them. It is on these circumstances that the insurgency in the Niger Delta has grown. Inevitably, conflicts of this nature develop into demands for equitable sharing of resources – such as revenues from oil in the Nigerian Niger Delta or in Southern Sudan. Ultimately, therefore, resource sharing has commonly become a major bone of contention in many African conflicts. As for the civil wars in which competing rebel groups try to seize rich mines (such as diamond mines in Sierra Leone), such actions are often merely parts of the means of executing the conflict – either to acquire the resources for the purchase of weapons, or to use the control of important resource-bearing territory to bargain for recognition and assistance. All in all, the intrinsic picture can be very complex indeed.

In the course of the last two decades of the twentieth century, religion (Islam) has increasingly showed up as a factor in the politics of some African countries, especially in East, Southern, and West Africa. In Nigeria, for instance, religion first showed up strongly in the political leaders' discussions leading to the creation of the 1979 constitution. The northern Islamic voices led a move to have the Sharia law enshrined in the Nigerian constitution, in spite of the manifest religious plurality of the country. Then in the 1980s, considerable rumblings arose over the suspicion that some elements wanted to use federal power secretly to enroll Nigeria as a member of the Organization of Islamic Countries. At the same time, for the first time, some Northern Muslim clerics raised the call to Muslims to refuse to be ruled by non-Muslims - and certain voices began to urge "total Islamization of Nigeria." In the Sudan before the partition, the influence of Islam in politics was much more established and stronger, featuring relentless efforts by the Islamic Arab peoples of Northern Sudan to enforce Islamic conversion of the peoples of the Southern Sudan who are the partly Christian, and partly devotees of traditional religions. Ripples of religion's intrusion into politics have also appeared in countries like Uganda and Tanzania.

In these countries, the escalation of religious division tends to go hand-in-hand with the well-established patterns of inter-ethnic and political relationships. The reality usually is that while some nationalities are predominantly Muslim, others are predominantly Christian or non-Muslim. For instance, in Nigeria, the peoples of the far Northern Nigeria are predominantly Muslim, while most of the peoples of Southern Nigeria are predominantly

Christian. Similarly, in the Sudan (until the partition into Sudan and South Sudan), the Northern Arab populations are Muslim, while many of the peoples of the South are predominantly non-Muslim or Christian. These realities tend to forge an alliance between religion and politics or ethnic groups' political goals. In Nigeria, the introduction of Islam into politics has been generally perceived by most peoples as a devise aimed at reinforcing the political dominance of the Muslim Hausa-Fulani of Northern Nigeria in Nigerian affairs. In the Sudan, forcible Islamization of the Southern provinces by the Northern Arab-led governments was simply a devise for reinforcing the entrenched pattern of Northern Arab domination. Because of this convergence of religion and politics, religion has come to exercise a very divisive influence in some African countries.

In this matter of linkage between politics and religion, two special notes need to be made about the Nigerian situation. First, the two peoples, Hausa and Fulani, who live intermingled in Nigeria's far northwestern provinces, have been Muslims for many centuries. As would be remembered, the Hausa are a very large people and are the indigenes of the country. The Fulani, who began to migrate from the grasslands of the west into Hausaland in about the 18th century, are much smaller in numbers, compared to the Hausa who are one of the largest nations in Africa. In the early 19th century, as would be remembered, the radical Islamic movement which emerged among the immigrant Fulani, with a call for a jihad for a purer Islam, succeeded in winning the support of the Hausa masses into a war against the Hausa rulers. The war ended with destruction of the indigenous Hausa leadership and system of government , and the substitution of Fulani men as rulers over the Hausa states. Since then, the Fulani have ruled virtually everywhere in Hausaland. Having achieved their phenomenal success over such a large and civilized people as the Hausa, the Fulani have, in the context of multi-nation Nigeria since about the time of independence, confidently developed the ambition to extend that success, their objective being to control all the peoples of Nigeria, employing the numerical weight of the Hausa and the call to a purer Islam and a jihad. More will be said about this circumstance in other contexts subsequently; suffice it to say here that it is this that has steadily advanced the religion of Islam as a very major factor in the politics of Nigeria.

The second note is about the large Yoruba nationality of southwestern Nigeria – Nigeria's second largest nationality. In the linkage of religion with politics, the Yoruba represent an exception. Though Islam and Christianity and traditional Yoruba religion are all strong among the Yoruba, the Yoruba have sustained their traditional culture of religious toleration and accommodation. Among them therefore, religion has never noticeably intruded into political life. The Muslim Hausa-Fulani sometimes seem baffled by this, and sometimes seem to despise it – and have made efforts to infuse their own kind of jihadist Islam into the religious life of Yoruba Muslims. But that has not worked, and Yoruba people have proudly continued to sustain their culture of religious accommodation. Their greatest writer, the Nobel laureate Wole Soyinka, has written that the Yoruba response to religious diversity is *"an eternal bequest to a world riven by religious intolerance and xenophobia"*.

Finally, another factor that has played significant roles in the stimulation of conflicts in African countries is the factor of interference and meddling by external, extra-African, influences. Since the independence of African countries, such interferences and meddling have usually taken two forms, though the two may often be interrelated. One is the direct meddling by a country's former colonial overlord, for the purpose of protecting and preserving its own interests in its former colony; and the other the entanglements that commonly arose for African countries in the Cold War as they came into the world comity of nations. Most commonly, the thrust has been to manipulate the inherent weaknesses and divisions in an African country for purposes that are not related to its interests – for purposes that may even seriously hurt its interests while serving the economic and strategic interests of a former colonial overlord or the strategic interests of a power or a power bloc in the world. Such manipulations from abroad have been commonly effective and damaging since virtually every Sub-Saharan African country has been vulnerable on account of its poverty and its lack of cohesion. Consequently, many of the conflicts in tropical African countries have been either engineered or complicated by influences and manipulations from abroad. And the continued weakness and disunity of nearly every one of these countries continue to invite these external manipulations, and continue to give them clout.

Many factors, then, interwoven in countless series of complexes in each case, have been contributory to the making of the political conflicts that have wracked the countries of Black Africa since independence. For the many reasons earlier explained, however, the ethnic factor tends always to stand out most visibly in virtually every case, and to serve as the vehicle of political relationships and mobilizations, political successes or failures, political fears and passions, political action, protest, rebellion, and conflict. As widespread experiences in all parts of the world in our time show, a country in which many nations are co-citizens, each living in its own ancestral homeland, and all sharing the same sovereignty and from the same body of opportunities, tends to be prone to such rivalries, hostilities, and conflicts among its component nations – although other factors will contribute to the nature, the timing, the provocation, and severity of the conflicts. Of these other factors, the most damaging in the case of Sub-Saharan African countries, it needs to be repeated, has been the character of leadership in each country – the refusal to view the national make-up of each country realistically and rationally, to be receptive to the voices of the people, and to involve the people in the making of policies of "nation building".

The African Scene by 2010-11

What then are the observable states of things in Sub-Saharan Africa by the end of the first decade of the 21st century – or the end of the first half-century of independence? In many countries, active conflicts and wars have recently subsided. Some welcome situations have evolved in a few countries. In the small country of Botswana in Southern Africa, fortunate to be the home of only one culturally homogenous people, the Tswana people (though with traces of San folks), political stability and peace have been continuously a fact of life, and economic and social progress is impressive. When this country of about 1.6 million people became independent in 1966, it had, in the words of Richard

156

Dowden's recently published book on contemporary Africa, *"nothing - - - except a few cows and a lot of bush"*. The development of diamond mining commenced in the country in 1967, pouring billions of dollars into its economy. But the really important thing is that the country has remained democratic and peaceful – unlike most other resource-rich African countries whose resources have tended to become a curse. Between 1970 and 2006, Botswana's income per capita rose from $122 to $4,755. And its democratically elected governments have used this surge of wealth to improve the quality of life of their people, through education, improved health programs, roads, water supply, etc. Botswana came under the scourge of HIV/AIDS infection, with one of the highest rates of the infection in Africa; but it developed one of the world's most progressive programs for dealing with the epidemic. The total effect of all these is that Botswana's economy is one of the most dynamic economies on the African continent. Mining continues to be the pillar of its economy, but tourism is growing fast, owing to the country's extensive nature resources and conservation policies. Botswana is thus an example of what a culturally homogenous African country can develop to become in the world.[4]

Naturally, that conclusion about Botswana raises questions about Somalia and Lesotho, both of which are ethnically homogenous too. Like Botswana, Somalia is a country of one people – the Somali people - speaking the same language, living the same culture. In addition, Somalia is also unified by one religion, Islam. In spite of all this, Somalia has been, and continues to be, one of Africa's worst nightmares. Its system of governance and order disintegrated in 1991, and its full revival is not yet in sight even as this is being written in 2012. Like Botswana too, Lesotho is an ethnically and culturally homogenous country – even though its people, the Basuto, crystallized into one ethnic nation from various ethnic fragments only in the course of the 19th century. "Lesotho" means "land of the Basuto people". Yet, the Lesotho modern elite battered and brutalized their country politically almost consistently for decades after independence.

Why has Botswana been so successful, Lesotho so pitiful, and Somalia such a shocking disaster? In the case of Somalia, the answer is mostly in its border profile. Somalia was saddled by crippling border problems at independence (because the Somali people were fragmented among the countries of Somalia, Kenya, Eritrea, Ethiopia), while Botswana has had no known border problems. Unable to live with their people's fragmentation across so many borders, the Somali government at independence launched into efforts to round off Somalia's borders and bring in all Somali. That way, they pushed their young and fragile country into early wars and entrapped it in risky international relationships and commitments. The country's political and economic strength soon proved incapable of sustaining such heavy pressures, and it ultimately stumbled and collapsed. In addition, this broken country has been further battered by devastating droughts and famine. And further still, Somalia has experienced destabilizing influences from its particular geographical location. The Horn of Africa, only a short distance across the sea from Yemen in the southern tip of the Arabian Peninsula, has long been an area of the strongest impact of Islamic influences from Arabia into Eastern Africa. In the course of the late 20th century, radical fundamentalist Islam has tended to filter quite easily through Yemen to Somalia – thereby compounding Somalia's political instability. A group named Al-Shabaab became the most powerful terrorist organization in the country. For a long time, Al-Shabaab held parts of the Somali capital, Mogadishu, until they were dislodged by forces of the African Union in late 2011. Mogadishu then began to experience some reconstruction, but, as this is being written, the huge camps of displaced persons remain, and the prospects for an orderly and stable Somalia still look far away.

Lesotho's problems have been different. This small country inset in the Union of South Africa has had no significant border problems. Moreover, of the countless peoples of Africa, hardly any has demonstrated as much loyalty and adherence to its traditional political institutions as the Basuto have demonstrated towards theirs – a fact that ought to have helped political stability. But Lesotho, as earlier pointed out, suffers seriously from its natural poverty as a country. Not only is its mountainous and largely barren country sparsely populated and scarcely urbanized (having no more than three towns), it is also very difficult to develop and connect with modern infrastructures. For much of the 20th century, the most reliable source of income for most Somali workers was in mining jobs in South African mines. But even this has weakened markedly since the later years of the 20th century as a result retrenchments in those mines. Lesotho's prospects for the development of a tourist industry look fairly good, but even in this Lesotho faces tough competition from many attractive places in southern Africa. Altogether, therefore, Lesotho is trapped in a prospect of economic poverty. All it has held onto since independence is a tenuous status of *de jure* sovereignty. It is against this unfortunate backdrop that the politics of Lesotho sometimes hovered close to a circus show for many decades after independence..

Another country with happy developments to show has been the Union of South Africa. In this county, apartheid is dead. Incredibly, the Black peoples of the country (unified to some extent by a near century of struggle against an oppressive white minority dictatorship) are working with the white population to find together the road to a new and dynamic nationhood. But it is yet impossible to tell how the picture of unity and stability now prevalent in this country will grow. There are observers who warn that certain disturbing signs that have already begun to appear (such as residual inter-ethnic tensions and emerging signs of public corruption) need to be watched.

Tanzania is another country in which some reasonably solid gains have been made for stable order. An unusually perceptive leader, Julius Nyerere, led the citizens of this not particularly endowed country to march together in a proud struggle for their new country. Nyerere's bold economic engineering did not yield much of the fruits that he envisaged, but, of the tens of top leaders who ruled African countries until about 1999 (Ali Mazrui puts their number at 170), Nyerere was one of only three who ever willingly gave up power. When Nyerere voluntarily retired from the presidency of Tanzania in 1985, admonished his countrymen to rally round their new president (former Vice-President Ali Hassan Mwinyi), and returned to a humble life as a common citizen, he bequeathed an inestimable political legacy to his country and to its politicians. Given its difficult economic prospects, Tanzania is an unbelievably hopeful country.

Ghana too is increasingly being celebrated as a country that has recently turned the corner for the better – in a West Africa where nearly every other country is rattled by turmoil and corruption. Jerry Rawlings, first seen on the political stage of this country as a young military coup leader, matured surprisingly into a statesman and nation builder, and showed the citizens of his country the path to accountability in public life and to stability of democratic processes. Almost unbelievably, Ghanaians today hold free and fair elections, and have one of the most respectable governments in Africa.

Unhappily, however, for most of the rest of Black Africa, the fundamental realities and weaknesses are not going away or even abating. And the turmoil, conflicts, blood-letting, wars, massive human displacements internally and across national borders, desperately barbarous refugee camps, and more, are still with us. In some countries where some quiet has been achieved, it seems that what has happened in each case is a truce, or temporary exhaustion, or temporary victory of some party, rather than a final and abiding peace acceptable to most. In some countries, the decades of conflicts, coups, counter coups, civil wars and horrendous blood-letting have changed little or nothing. No informed observer believes that the peace that exists in Angola, or Rwanda, or Central African Republic, or Uganda, or Zimbabwe, or Nigeria, or some other countries of West Africa, is so meaningfully structured and so stable as to prove final and abiding. Disruption, insecurity and blood-letting have remained facts of life in much of the eastern provinces of the Congo (Kinshasa). In Rwanda, the regime that seized control in 1994 has continued to hold the country in its grip for over seventeen years. As a result, serious groups of opposition and resistance have crystallized. Even from among the group that took power in this country in 1994, some prominent members have fled abroad to protect their lives. In fact, there are already observers who fear that the authoritarianism of the Rwandan regime could be contributing significantly to the preparation of the ground for another round of hideous bloodletting in this country. In Uganda, the man who seized power in 1886 is still holding it, and increasingly shows no sign of ever wanting to bow out. For most of the countries of Black Africa, the political prospects still did not look good as 2010 wound to a close.

As if to startle and wake up any observer who might be slipping into over-optimism, the year 2010 even closed with some very troubling developments in some countries. In Nigeria, some of the most bizarre series of inter-ethnic and religious mass killings ever to be recorded in the frequently troubled Nigerian Middle Belt occurred. Further to the North, the Islamic fundamentalist terror gangs struck in a series of their most devastating explosions yet, resulting in massive killings of people and destruction of property in some Northern cities. At least one of these terror gangs with the name Boko Haram, frighteningly upgraded the sophistication of its terror tools and methods and, in the process, initiated Nigeria's era of bombs in crowded places, sudden termination of the lives of many innocent men, women and children, and sudden destruction of a lot of property. To Nigeria, a particularly strange feature of this growing sophistication of terror by Boko Haram was the use of suicide bombers. As of this writing (2013), Boko Haram has operated virtually unrestrained, and repeatedly issued threats to bring its devastations south to the cities of Southern Nigeria. A hideous peak for Boko Haram's bombing campaigns was reached on August 26, 2011, when a bomb set by them blew up the headquarters of the United Nations Organization in Abuja, killing many UN employees and many other persons. There have been indications too that Boko Haram is seeking some sort of relationship with the Somali terrorist organization, Al-Shabaab, towards a *jihad* in Nigeria.

Apart from the mass killings and destructions by Boko Haram and lesser known terror gangs in parts of Nigeria, there have been other signs of deep undercurrents of coming violence and trouble. In August 2010, large quantities of arms (including grenades, grenade launchers, assault rifles, etc.) were discovered at the Lagos port, illegally imported by unknown persons – raising the probability that some influential Nigerians might be engaged in illegal importation of arms for political purposes. On October 1, Nigeria's Independence Day, car bombs exploded, killing tens of people in the Nigerian capital city of Abuja, and responsibility for them was later claimed by elements of the Niger Delta liberation movement known as MEND – Movement for the Emancipation of the Niger Delta. Meanwhile, arguments over the Nigerian national elections, finally scheduled for April 2011, developed into very bitter and hostile confrontations between various sectional groups, with some prominent leaders of some sections threatening to make

Nigeria "ungovernable" if certain things did not go their way in the elections.

As the year was ending, therefore, all of this jangled mass of discordance, hostility, and killings, created widespread fears that the election year 2011 might prove to be a very violent year for Nigeria. Under the cloud of the uncertainty and fears, some foreign oil companies announced their withdrawal from participation in Nigeria's oil exploration and production – citing loss of profits as a result of violence in the country, and fears of much bigger violence in coming years. And, as can be seen from the paragraphs above, 2011 indeed proved a year of great violence and uncertainties for Nigeria. In some of the last months of the year, almost every day saw bomb blasts in some place or other in Nigeria, causing the loss of countless lives. Inter-ethnic conflicts in various parts of Nigeria forced countless thousands of Nigerians to flee from the places where they have long lived and done business, back to their native homelands. Even in some parts where such conflicts have usually been absent, retaliatory killings and destruction of property became quite common. Altogether the picture of Nigeria has been of a country beginning to disintegrate and rip apart. Thereafter, stories of Nigerians secretly and illegally buying arms abroad, and detection and seizure of illegal caches of arms in various parts of Nigeria, have steadily increased – thereby painting the picture of a country in which the various elite groups are preparing for some sort of ultimate show-down.

Meanwhile, as Nigeria thus seemed to slide towards heightened trouble or even generalized conflagration or even disintegration by 2011, a political storm began to rage in the Ivory Coast. Presidential elections held in November-December 2010 in this country resulted in the defeat of the incumbent president, Laurent Gbagbo, and victory for his opponent, Alassane Ouantara. Gbagbo refused to surrender power, had himself re-sworn as president, and continued to hold the machineries of power. But the winner, Ouantara, was accorded recognition as new president of Ivory Coast by the United Nations, the United States and many other countries, as well as by the countries of the West African sub-region (members of ECOWAS). Ouantara, protected by United Nations peace-keeping forces, was holed up in a hotel in the capital city in the last days of 2010, as Gbagbo's supporters

162

escalated threats that they would storm the hotel, and as the United Nations issued dire warnings against such a criminal act. Repeated calls by ECOWAS on Gbagbo to step down went unheeded. Obviously, Gbagbo and his supporters were aware of what the whole world was aware of – namely, that, as things stood, ECOWAS did not command the ability to enforce its will. Nigeria, the backbone of the military strength of ECOMOG (the military arm of ECOWAS), was hopelessly mired in its own complex problems and unsure how it would manage to make its own forthcoming elections peaceful. Apparently because of Nigeria's handicap also, the African Union could not act.

At various points in the Ivorian crisis, fears mounted of the probability of resumed civil war between the southern and northern halves of the Ivory Coast. In the end, it was forces of the United Nations, not of ECOWAS or the African Union, that brought this situation to some resolution in 2011. Gbagbo was overpowered and apprehended, and Ouantara was sworn in as president.

But just as that was being accomplished, signs of serious turmoil began to appear in the Republic of Mali, the large country in the West African Sahel, and heartland of the early Islamic civilizations of Mali and Songhai. Historically, conflicts have periodically flared up between the mostly nomadic Tuareg peoples of the desert in the north, and the peoples of the south. In recent decades, economic distress, exacerbated by long droughts in this sub-region of West Africa, has seriously buffeted Mali, and added to the spirit of insurrection among the Tuaregs, some of whom began to demand secession of the northern provinces from the country. In early 2012, the military toppled the government of Mali, and created a vacuum which enabled Tuareg insurrectionists to overrun some of the towns of the south and destroy the ancient monuments of the old city of Timbuktu. Thereafter, the insurrectionists established their hold on Mali's northern provinces, representing nearly two-thirds of the country. The world's most feared Islamic terrorist organization, Al-Qaida, through its Northern African affiliate, Alqaida in the Islamic Maghreb (AQIM), immediately took advantage of the situation, moved into northern Mali, and took possession of the insurrection. Thus, yet another scene of war emerged in the interior of West

Africa. Even more troubling to the rest of West Africa, Africa and the wider world, the interior grassland and Sahel territories of West Africa, consisting of countries like Mauritania, Mali, Burkina Faso, northern Senegal, Niger, northern Nigeria and Chad, moved close to becoming a major base of terrorism in the world.

Moreover, as these storms raged in West Africa, old storms continued or resumed, and new ones arose, in other regions of the sub-continent. In Somalia, Al-Shabaab, having been driven from the capital city of Mogadishu and other main cities, continued to hold patches of the country. In Congo (Kinshasa), rebel forces continued to hold parts of the eastern provinces. The Central African Republic, continually rattled by conflicts since independence, had finally produced a somewhat stable government in 2003 under the leadership of the military dictator, Francois Bozize. However, many fragmented opposition groups remained alive, continually attacking the Bozize government. Finally, in 2013 these coalesced into a major force claiming to be united by Islam, launched a major assault, forced Bozize to flee, and imposed their own leader, Michel Djotodia, as president. Their continued rampage after that, and the development of divisions in the Djotodia government, soon resulted in the coalescing of their opponents into a strong force which then tried to use an appeal to Christian unity to recruit fighters. In the circumstance, this very complex conflict came to be known in the wide world as a religious war. Djotodia was forced out in January 2014, and was replaced by a woman president, in the hope that that would produce peace – but the fighting and the carnage continued. With both sides killing civilians indiscriminately, international observers were soon reporting the killing of tens of thousands of people and the displacement of very many more. Most of the killed and displaced have been from among the country's Muslim minority.

These situations have thus demonstrated most profoundly the inherent weaknesses of the Pan-African and regional security arrangements on the African continent. The Pan-African and regional constructs are not unimportant (and have shown some effect in most of the conflict situations). However, the decisive factor in the making of Black Africa's better political prospects has to be the character and quality of the management of each country, as well as meaningful responses to the fundamental issues in the making of these countries – altogether resulting in the generation of greatly increased chances for stability, prosperity and peace in each country and on the sub-continent.

Prospects for Afro-Arab Relations in Africa[5]

By 2010, also, some of what have long seemed likely to prove the most tenacious areas of conflict in Africa lay in the northernmost belt of Black Africa, the belt where Arab and Black African civilizations and peoples meet. An informative Black African statement of, and concerns about, the affairs of the countries of this belt is contained in a 2004 paper by Kwesi Prah, Director of the Center for Advanced Studies of African Society (CASAS, based in Cape Town, Union of South Africa). Dr. Prah voices the growing concern among Black African intellectuals about the obfuscations and outright silence surrounding the unrelenting Arab pressures on Black African peoples throughout this belt – from Mauritania in the west, through Mali, Niger, Chad, to the Republic of Sudan in the east. According to him, while Arab leaders have been doing a good job of sidestepping and covering the truth about developments in this belt, most Black African leaders and thinkers have also been squeamish about them – afraid to hurt the image of Afro-Arab solidarity that has been promoted since the anti-colonial struggles, especially of the times of Nkrumah and Abdel Nasser. In fact, whenever African and Arab leaders get together in meetings, the focus of discussion, almost invariably, has been the mobilization of African influence to serve non-African Arab interests. While all this artful avoidance of facts and truth has been going on, the Arab entry into Africa and pressure on Africans that had begun in the seventh century have continued relentlessly in this belt till now. The attitudes manifested by the Arabs have steadfastly been that these Black African frontier lands are a civilizational vacuum that must be filled by Arab civilization, a legitimate *lebensraum* for Arab occupation. One of the oldest and most nefarious aspects of the pressure – the enslavement of Black Africans (Soninkes, Wolofs, Fulanis, Tukulors in the west, and Furs and Massalit in the east) by Arabs – has continued, in many cases with backing by the laws of the countries concerned.

Arabs have been enslaving Black Africans in this broad belt for nearly a thousand years. In some countries there (such as Mauritania) the slavery was still actively alive until the 1960s. Slavery did not become a crime in Mauritania until 2007, and even today, some estimates have it that over 10% of the people of Mauritania and up to 8% of the people of Niger are slaves. The bitterness generated by these circumstances has repeatedly generated civil wars or rebellions in most of the countries of this belt – in Mali, Niger, Chad and Sudan. In Mali where the Black African peoples of the south constitute a majority and control the reins of government, rebellions by the Tuaregs, Berbers and Arabs of the desert north have been frequent. In a major rebellion in 2012, the Tuaregs proclaimed secession and declared some northern provinces a separate new country of Azawad for some months.

The civil war in the province of Darfur formed, from 2003, the most internationally publicized front of the war between Africans and Arabs in this belt of Africa. The Arabs, who constitute a minority of Darfur's population, enjoyed the advantage of support by the Arab-led government of Sudan. Soon after the Darfur situation started in 2003, it developed into two different kinds of crisis – a war between the government's armed forces and some local Black African militias, and a totally different campaign by Arab Janjaweed death squads, armed by the government, against unarmed and defenseless villages throughout the province. Most members of the international community declared the government-supported Janjaweed activities as acts of genocide, and the government greatly increased its own criminal image by using its sovereign powers to resist the coming of international humanitarian help, as well as international observers, to the large refugee camps housing the displaced villagers.

In 2010, the International Criminal Court (ICC) issued warrants for the arrest of the president of Sudan, Omar al-Bashir, for war crimes and crimes against humanity in Darfur. That step opened up a very significant new angle to the situation. The world watched the evolving response of Black Africa and the Arab world to this new turn in the crisis. Surprisingly, however, the AU immediately refused to grant recognition to, and even denounced, the warrant of arrest.

But Kwesi Prah is much nearer to the position of most Black Africans when he writes:

"Afro-Arab relations will remain conflictual for as long as Arab slavery of Africans persists, and ethnic cleansing and claims of lebensraum - - - continue. - - Many Africans take great exception to the sentiments and views expressed by Col. Khadafi at the March 2001 Amman, Jordan, meeting of the Arab League where he said that, "the third of the Arab community living outside Africa should move in with the two-thirds on the continent and join the African Union 'which is the only space we have'".

Kwesi Prah then offers suggestions which, quite obviously, express the feelings and opinions of the overwhelming majority of informed Black Africans over the future relationship between Black Africans and Arabs in these critical borderlands:

"Africans and Arabs need to create platforms and bases for a civilizational dialogue, which will help to advance mutual understanding and foster coexistence in peace and prosperity. For as long as one party regards the other as a "civilization vacuum" which needs to be occupied civilizationally, there is little hope for long term peace on this continent. Afro-Arab cooperation will not be achievable in any serious sense if efforts are accompanied, willy nilly, by obfuscation, half-truths and the philandering of time. What we need is openness and critical discussion. No issues should be embargoed; the search should be for amicable, neighborly and brotherly or sisterly solutions, which bring democracy in all areas of social life. If this cannot be achieved, then we should be able to go our separate ways in peace in the Afro-Arab borderlands. Africans will be custodians of their own destiny and will fight to achieve this."

By late 2010, the prospect of a very significant change in the Republic of Sudan, the easternmost sector of the Afro-Arab borderlands, appeared in the horizon. The 2005 General Peace Agreement (GPA) between Southern Sudan and the Khartoum government had provided for a referendum in the South, to ascertain the wishes of the Southerners about a separate country of their own. Disagreements and disputes over various details held up the arrangements for the referendum after that. At last, however, by November 2010, voters' registration for the referendum was commenced – and the referendum was scheduled to be conducted in early January 2011. It was very obvious to all observers worldwide that a whole lot would depend on whether or not the Khartoum government would allow the conduct of this referendum to be free and fair. A manipulated or inconclusive referendum was almost certain to provoke a resumption of a bitter civil war between the government of Sudan and the peoples of Southern Sudan. Sudan's President Al-Bashir made repeated public statements promising to let the referendum run without interference, and to accept its outcome, but that did not reduce the massive and deep distrust of him in the South.

Adding significantly to the possibility of renewed conflict was the unresolved dispute between the North and the South over the status of the small province of Abyei. This province had historically been a sort of bridge-land between what later became the northern and southern provinces of Sudan. With the development of civil war between the North and South in the 1950s, the people who had long been settled residents of most of Abyei, the Ngok Dinka, associated themselves with the South, while another people, the Messiria (a nomadic Arab people) who had traditionally come in and out of Abyei seasonally, associated themselves with the North. With the discovery of oil in Abyei in the 1970s, the government of Sudan embarked on maneuvers to make the province decisively a part of the North. That turned the little province into a major factor in the North-South hostilities. The GPA of 2005 provided for a separate referendum for Abyei, but this was never held, and it was not clear whether it was being considered as part of the Southern referendum being planned for January 2011. In the circumstance, the little province of Abyei loomed like a big threat over the whole Southern referendum and the chances for peace or war in Sudan. On its part, the United Nations Organization announced arrangements to increase its peace-keeping force in the country prior to the date of the referendum – as, in the last days of 2010, Africa and the whole world waited for the outcome of this very historic resolution to the Sudan nightmare.

Republic of South Sudan!

Happily, the referendum went mostly peacefully. After that, however, anxieties over Abyei and other areas of the borders escalated, resulting in fighting between the armed forces of Northern and Southern Sudan. But, in spite of this, the new Republic of Southern Sudan came into being on July 9, 2011, appearing to end at last one of the longest and most devastating conflicts in modern African history.

However, conflicts continued off and on in Abyei and some other border areas for months between the two countries, among other things holding up the movement of South Sudan's crude oil exports through North Sudan. Most of the points of disagreement were resolved in late 2012 at a peace conference brokered by the African Union, and further talks were planned to resolve other difficulties that were still unresolved. The South's crude oil exports were therefore able to reach the outside world again through Northern Sudan. How this solution of the Sudan problem will impact the remaining areas of conflict in the Arab-African borderlands in northern Africa remained to be seen.

How too the new Republic of South Sudan, with its population of about 11 million, consisting of roughly 80 different small ethnic nationalities, would fare as one country, remained to be seen. Of the about 80 groups, the largest two are the Dinka (representing about 35% of the country's population) and the Nuer (about 15%). The country entered into independence with Salva Kiir (a Dinka) as president and Riek Machar (a Nuer) as vice-president. Many of the ethnic leaders proposed that their country be organized in such a way as to ensure voices for the nationalities – with a "House of Nationalities" (a sort of federal legislature) representing all the nationalities. However, Salva Kiir's government rejected the idea, even though he had said at the independence ceremony that his desire was that the new country, in which inter-ethnic conflicts had been common historically, would have "a new beginning of tolerance where cultural and ethnic diversity will be a source of pride".

In July 2013, Kiir dismissed his Vice-President, Machar, and all his minsters, saying that all he wanted to do was to reduce the size of the government. Machar charged that it was a step towards a dictatorship. The Dinka and Nuer in the military split apart. In

169

December 2013, civil war erupted and, when Dinka soldiers embarked on killing Nuer civilians, the civil war quickly degenerated into a horrific inter-ethnic blood-letting. Thus arose a brand new addition to the storms devastating country after country in Sub-Saharan Africa.

In less than three months, as many as 10,000 people (according to some human rights organizations) lost their lives. Desertions from both sides spawned more and more hostile militias. All reports have it that all sides have been grossly guilty of killing civilians indiscriminately. Agreement to end the war has been reached again and again – including even an agreement to organize the country as a federation; but each agreement has collapsed within hours. By December 2014, the number of people killed was being variously estimated at between 50,000 and 100,000, and the fighting and carnage were still continuing.

CHAPTER SIX

Quests For Solutions

The roots of the contemporary political problems of Black Africa, then, are multi-dimensional and complex. The experiences of the colonial era, the manner of creation of the countries, the nature and styles of colonial governance, the kinds of inter-relationships and indigenous leadership, and the complex economic, cultural and social difficulties consequently generated in every country – all these laid the foundations for strongly disoriented societies in every country.

Deep down, what the world should recognize is that the peoples of many countries of Sub-Saharan Africa feel trapped. They live in countries that are not of their own choosing, every small nation with other nations that they might not have chosen to belong with in a country if they had been free to choose, and, in most cases, under constitutional, political, economic and social arrangements inherited fundamentally from the colonial experience – arrangements which, in many cases, they fear to be working against their group interests. In many countries, there are some national groups that have been conditioned by experience to live in fear of attacks and mass killings – like the Igbo in Nigeria, the Bakongo in Angola, the Acholi in Uganda, many of the peoples of southern and western provinces of the Republic of Sudan (before the creation of the Republic of Southern Sudan), to mention only a few.

In some countries, national qualities, objectives or attainments that some nationalities cherish are frowned upon, and treated as cause of offence, by other nationalities in the same country. Notably in Nigeria, the Yoruba had been a strongly urbanized people for many centuries, and were already well advanced in Western education, before they were pulled together with other nationalities to form Nigeria in 1914. They also already had a strong and well-established tradition of religious tolerance and accommodation, whereby Yoruba Christians, Muslims and devotees of the traditional Yoruba religion live harmoniously and happily in Yoruba towns and households, and belong together in families, civic organizations, businesses, schools, etc, and share joyfully in one another's Christian, Muslim and traditional festivals – perhaps the best example of such religious sophistication in the world. Most other Nigerian peoples ultimately embarked on competition with the Yoruba in the development of Western education. Many also admire the Yoruba tradition of religious tolerance. A prominent Igbo citizen, Dr. Pius Ezeife, once said about the Yoruba: *"We use Yoruba today as an epitome of proper management of religion in the society. In a Yoruba family, you have Christians and Muslims. - - - In Yoruba land, whether it is Christmas time, Eid-malud or Eid-Kabir, it's all festivity"* He added that in the Nigerian world of violent religious conflicts generated by the extreme Muslims of Northern Nigeria, "it is possible to radicalize Yoruba Muslims" , but that people of good will "should do everything within our powers" to prevent it. In a 2013 major study of Nigeria's disunity and decline, two researchers for an important agency of the United States government wrote: *"The Yoruba serve as a modern example of coexistence, since many Muslim, Christian, and animist Yoruba dwell peacefully, not only in the same cities, but also in the same households"*. The famous Yoruba writer, Wole Soyinka (Africa's first Nobel Laureate for Literature) once wrote that the religious accommodation of the Yoruba people is an *"eternal bequest to a world that is riven by the spirit of intolerance, of xenophobia and suspicion"*.

But the Muslim Hausa-Fulani of Northern Nigeria, whom the British installed as the rulers and dominant group over Nigeria at independence in 1960, have been mostly opposed to, or at least lukewarm about, Western education, and strongly despised the Yoruba Muslims' toleration of people of other religions. Their attitudes to Western education, and maneuvers to impose their more radical form of Islam over all of Nigeria (especially to sell it to the large Muslim part of the Yoruba) have been significant factors in the Nigerian culture of conflicts and in the instability and decline of Nigeria. Another strong factor has been the fact that the large but historically mostly acephalous, stateless and pre-urban Igbo, since being brought together with the Yoruba and the other nationalities in Nigeria in 1914, have evinced an increasingly virulent hatred of the Yoruba. While migrating in increasing numbers from their own homeland since Nigeria's independence to come and benefit from the advantages of the heavily urbanized (and most modernized) Yoruba homeland, the Igbo (for the most part) operate and speak as if they view the Yoruba nation as an enemy that must be brought down. Even many of those Igbo who have come to live and prosper in the Yoruba homeland evince, not gratitude, but spite, for the Yoruba tradition of peaceful and open accommodation of foreigners, and often tend to behave as if they are compulsively hateful of the Yoruba nation. Usually proudly tenacious of their traditions of religious tolerance and hospitality to foreigners, the Yoruba are often painfully at a loss about how to deal with these separate Hausa-Fulani and Igbo phenomena – and have lost much of the development momentum and confidence that they brought into Nigeria. Also, in those vast territories of the Nigerian Middle Belt and Northeast, where tens of small Muslim and Christian peoples live closely side by side, inter-ethnic hostilities have grown relentlessly, and Islamic pressure has been very hard on the Christian peoples. Indeed, inter-ethnic conflicts have increasingly approached the realms of mutual attempts at genocide. And very importantly, the Nigerian federal establishment, mostly under the influence of Northern Muslims since independence, has caused serious declines in the quality of Western education in Nigeria, a matter which seriously hurts the interests of the large Yoruba and Igbo and the many smaller nationalities that desire Western education as an important asset. Periodically, therefore, Nigeria has tended to seem like a churning caldron.

Even when nationalities live manifestly at peace with their neighbors in the same country, they are aware that the cultures in their country, including theirs, are locked in a relentless subliminal conflict. They are uncomfortable at having to live under the impact of the ethical standards or religious attitudes of other people, about the decline and degeneration of their own group's ethical values, and about the widening influence of the culture of corruption in their countries' public affairs. Among the more informed, there is growing unease and fear that their cultures may be headed to extinction. Public officials live commonly under suspicions and accusations of nepotism in favor of members of their own nationality. For the smallest minority peoples in most African countries, inevitably regularly marginalized, the usual fate is, essentially, denial of a voice in the affairs of the country to which they belong. A member of such a small nationality has, in the ordinary order of things, essentially no chance of becoming ruler of his country, no matter the eminence of his personal qualifications and qualities. For such marginalized peoples, their experiences commonly translate to a feeling of being ruled by strangers who cannot be trusted. Peoples who happen to find themselves excluded from ruling groupings or alliances, even if they are large nationalities that cannot be easily outvoted and marginalized, know that their chances of sharing in power are still about nil – because the people who control the apparatus and power of state will manipulate and rig the elections any way. In many countries, military coups are the most effective way to protest against a ruler – or to change a government; and it is therefore common to hear frustrated sections of many countries wishing that the military would step in and put an end to a regime.

It is in this complex web of existential realities, therefore, that are generated the anger, suspicion and fear so easily observable among the peoples of most Black African countries. Responsive leaderships could go a long way in generating constructive solutions, traditions and arrangements of group justice, and a growing spirit of mutual accommodation, tolerance, peace and progress. But, in most countries, leadership has usually been of the "strong man" type characterized by "winner-take-all" and "power-is-everything" mentalities – almost invariably provoking divisions and factions (understandably, often along ethnic lines), and the probability of conflicts. Herein is generated the often horrifying news about Black Africa – news of unbelievable corruption and lawlessness in governments, of incurable urges to falsify elections, of military coups and assassinations, of civil wars, pogroms, ethnic cleansing, and genocide, of so-called "democratically elected" rulers posturing like absolute dictators, of insane warlords and rag-tag guerrilla bands out of control, of poor children abducted from their homes into the bush where they are trained and drugged to kill, of millions of displaced humans on the move to no destinations and dying in droves along the way, of sprawling and hideously primitive refugee camps where deprivation, disease and death reign over the uprooted lives of hundreds of thousands of men, women, and children.

Some Search for Solutions

Africans have, of course, since independence, sought solutions. In most countries, the political elite review, or create, constitutions frequently, trying to find some arrangement that could improve things according to their own light and desires. However, such efforts have almost universally had identical characteristics. The group in power would not take the risk of involving those who are out of power, or the risk of involving the general citizenry. For African leaders, "nation-building" means simply that which the rulers or ruling groups, in their infinite wisdom, do for their countries. The moment an African becomes president or prime minister of his country, he immediately begins to behave as if he sees himself as the only wise person in his country – and the only person who loves his country. And almost invariably, his and his cronies' agenda (his cronies being usually mostly members of his ethnic nationality), become the "national" agenda, or the "mainstream" agenda. More or less the same kinds of attributes characterize numerically or politically dominant nationalities. If the ruler happens to be a soldier who has seized power by force, his exhibition of arrogance and petulance can rise to insufferable heights. The so-called national or mainstream agenda, and the push for it, can often be very disrespectful of certain nationalities in the country – a disrespect that can sometimes be quite deliberate. In this regard, it is not uncommon for highly placed persons arguing for the so-called national or mainstream agenda to question, or even deny explicitly, the claim of certain nationalities in their country to any group pride, or even to any identity as a people.

The following is a very strong example of this latter kind of behavior – an example so blatant that one of Nigeria's foremost historians, Dr. Adiele Afigbo (former Chair of History at the University of Nigeria, Nsukka), felt compelled to write a long essay mostly on it. It was all started by a statement attributed to a citizen of the embattled Niger Delta, scene of decades of insurgency and civil war. The statement had, among other things, said as follows:

"The Federal Government is rampaging our land. - - - That land is Urhobo. And Urhobo people were there before Nigeria was founded. Nigeria is only 87 years old. We have been here for 6,000 years".

Thereupon, a very prominent Nigerian historian, Dr. Yusuf Bala Usman, working for the Center for Democratic Development Research and Training (CEDDERT, a federal government agency), responded under the name of the agency with two blazing papers denying the right of the Urhobo to claim to be a nation, and extending the same denial to some other Southern Nigerian peoples, especially the large Igbo nation of southeastern Nigeria. Quoting "facts and figures" and "authorities" Dr. Usman asserted that many of the Nigerian peoples now claiming to be nations are only "recent formations', that the Urhobo "are a congeries of ethnic fragments" from among the Igbo, the Ijaw and the Edo, and that it is wrong to treat such a congeries as a "monolithic nation", that many local fragments of the people now identified as one Igbo nation bore, until recent times, different names, and that "there is nothing like an Igbo nation". [1]

This is no place for the kind of erudite expose that Dr. Afigbo had to go into in order to deal with his historian colleague's power-packed statements. Suffice it to say that it is ordinary knowledge in the world today that some of the peoples (the ethno-linguistic groups) of Black Africa, and of many other parts of the world, though each undoubtedly culturally one people, became clearly identified as coherent groups or nations only in very recent history, and that such a fact does not negate their identity as nations, and their claims to be nations.

But for our purpose here, the more important point is that Dr. Usman's kind of response is not a helpful contribution to nation building in a country like Nigeria. Denying the identity or existence of some nations of Nigeria does not remove them as significant factors in the Nigerian enterprise, and it does not advance the debate over the appropriate pattern of relationships among the nations of the Nigerian federation, or the debate over the sharing of resources among the nations of Nigeria. Forcefully asserting that the Urhobo nation evolved from a congeries of ethnic fragments, or that some members of the Igbo nation did not identify themselves as Igbo until recent times, or that an Igbo or

Urhobo nation does not exist, or that the Yoruba are not one nation but many different nations, tends, in the context of Nigerian politics, to have the effect of grossly disrespecting and infuriating the peoples concerned, and further complicating inter-ethnic animosities in Nigeria – and that cannot be any positive step in quest for nation building. The kinds of statements made by Dr. Usman tend, particularly, to have strongly disruptive impact when the persons making such statements in the Nigerian debate happen to belong (as Dr. Usman did) to the nationality (the Fulani nation) that most other Nigerian nationalities see as wielding, undeservingly, too much influence over the affairs of Nigeria – as a result of their being so empowered by British manipulations.

But this is a style of nation building that is common in Black Africa. In not a few countries, in fact, this culture of nation building has been known to generate actual attacks on some nationalities by the rulers of their country, with the use of the security forces of their country. In the circumstance, it is not surprising that much of what goes as nation building in Sub-Saharan Africa tends to generate conflict.

Pan-African Solutions

Sub-Saharan African rulers and ruling groups have also made very loud efforts at a level beyond their immediate countries – namely, under the Pan-African umbrella, and in regional groupings, for peace and order on their continent. Thus, as soon as a good number of African countries had become independent in the first years of the 1960's, their governments began to interact in the spirit of the Pan-African Movement. The first major outcome was the coming together of thirty-two African heads of state to establish the Organization of African Unity (OAU) in 1963.

As the African governments worked together to create the structure of the OAU, the most pressing need of Africa was the completion of the liberation of the continent from European colonialism. Some African countries (especially the Portuguese colonies of Angola, Mozambique and Guinea-Bissau), expressly denied independence by their colonial rulers, had just embarked on armed struggles to free themselves. The white settlers of Southern Rhodesia (now Zimbabwe) were in the process of tightening their grip on that country. And apartheid was in the peak of its power in the Union of South Africa. Moreover, perceived by the African leaders as ancillary to the liberation struggle was the need for independent African countries to establish their freedom of action in the affairs of the wider world. The Cold War was raging between the Western Powers led by America and the Communist Block led by the Soviet Union, and each side was mounting action to bring the newly independent African countries under its influence. For the governments of the young countries of Africa, the paths out there in the wider world were being made very treacherous, and the threat was growing that Africa could become a major battle ground of the Cold War. What this could mean was already being made quite clear by the experiences of a country like Congo (Kinshasa) where the young Prime Minister, Patrice Lumumba, by appearing to be a friend of the Soviet Union, attracted the instant hostility of the West – and the exploitation of his country's weaknesses to wreck his government and eliminate him. Also, and finally, signs of internal troubles were already beginning to show up on the African continent itself. Border disputes between neighboring countries were spreading in parts of the continent, and inside some countries, the earliest political explosions and military coups were being reported.

The initial main aims of the OAU, therefore, were to pursue the anti-colonial struggle and, in particular, to fight apartheid, to defend the sovereignty and integrity of the newly independent African countries, promote cooperation in economic development among African countries, and promote cooperation among African countries in international matters, in accordance with the Charter of the United Nations. Conscious that each African country was in danger of suffering external meddling in its internal affairs, the OAU rejected, and bound itself to steer clear of, interferences in the internal affairs of its member states. To ensure that border disputes would not lead to wars among its member states, the OAU crafted a resolution in 1964 binding its members to preserve the national borders created on the African continent by the former colonial powers.

The 1964 resolution on borders curtailed the spread of border conflicts to some extent in the years that followed. Moreover, in the decades that followed, the OAU employed its influence to intervene in various troubles between African countries, and to promote the struggle for freedom from colonialism and from white minority dictatorships in Southern Africa. But the OAU was not prepared for, or attuned to, the negative political developments that increasingly came to materialize inside African countries – the rise of authoritarian and repressive governments, human rights abuses, corruption, and military coups, and civil wars. Its pledge of non-interference in the internal affairs of its members meant that it could not do much about these situations. The OAU lost much of its early allure; in fact some critics even denounced it as a club of autocrats and oppressors.

By the 1990's, the African political scene had changed radically. The last traces of formal European imperialism had been terminated. The liberation wars in the Portuguese colonies (Angola, Mozambique and Guinea-Bissau) and in Zimbabwe were won and over. Apartheid was dead in the Union of South Africa. The anti-colonial liberation struggle was over. But a vastly more urgent challenge had arisen in virtually all parts of Africa. Internally, nearly every Black African country was in the grip of political crises, civil wars, and turmoil. At the peak of the desperate situation stood the total collapse of order in Somalia, the horrific genocide in Rwanda, the wars in some countries of West Africa, Sudan, Uganda and Angola, the so-called "African World War" being waged in the Congo Democratic Republic, millions of displaced Africans in many countries, and the huge refugee camps that stood as monuments to Black Africa's folly and poverty.

The OAU kind of structure was no longer appropriate or adequate as the vehicle of Pan-African response to the needs of the African continent. And, as events were demonstrating quite pointedly, Africa could not depend on the international community to prevent African countries' political troubles or alleviate their consequences. As African trouble spots had multiplied, the United Nations Organization had had to respond to a rapidly increasing number of crises in Africa, and with more varied and complex missions (comprising military, police, and civilian observer components in peace-making and peace-keeping operations). But UN missions were commonly too late in arriving in African trouble spots, because of complications caused by negotiations and debates over mandates, and the delays caused by the UN's efforts to obtain commitments of men and resources from its member states. Moreover, in the course of the 1990's, the UN came increasingly to find it difficult to obtain commitments of peace-keeping troops from America and the Western European countries for African missions other than for observer or trainer purposes.

In these circumstances, some informed African observers could not avoid feeling that the international community attached less importance to African problems than to problems in other parts of the world (especially Europe) – as if African lives were less valuable than other lives. From various directions, African leaders began to speak of the need for a new African approach to African problems – a new initiative to provide African solutions to African problems. President Thabo Mbeki of South Africa spoke of the need for an "African Renaissance", and President Olusegun Obasanjo of Nigeria became a leading voice in the crusade for a new African arrangement capable of dealing with conflagrations on the African continent.

African Union

This new wave of Pan-African passion and commitment produced the African Union. A series of meetings of African rulers beginning from 1999 resulted in July 2000 in the agreement creating the African Union – the *Constitutive Act of the African Union*. By 2002, the African Union (AU) had completely replaced the OAU.[2]

The objectives of the African Union cover a very wide field of cooperation and collaboration among African states for the welfare of Africa and its peoples. They include the same old objectives that have always been important in the Pan-African agenda - like promotion of unity among African countries; economic cooperation among African countries for the purpose of advancing economic progress and alleviating poverty on the continent; the building of "an integrated Africa, a prosperous and peaceful Africa, driven by its own citizens and representing a dynamic force in the international arena"; promotion and defense of African common positions on issues of interest to Africa and its peoples. They also include such contemporary universal concerns as the protection of the African environment, and new objectives such as the provision of basic social services, and especially of basic education, for the population of every country, mitigation of the impact of diseases, and the alleviation of poverty. In the light of the experiences of Africa in the decades since independence (political conflicts, mass killings, displacement of millions, and the accumulation of millions in refugee camps, etc.), the stated objectives of the AU include a very major emphasis on the promotion and defense of security on the continent. For that purpose, very detailed and ambitious provisions were laid down for security and order in Africa.

The founders had, however, to give emphatic recognition to the obvious fact that the quality of governance in the countries of Africa was crucial to the prospects of security and order on the continent. Therefore, they laid down the principles of good governance that members of the AU must observe. Furthermore, the Constitutive Act affirmed the responsibility of Africa to protect life and human rights on the African continent (the so-called Responsibility to Protect, or R2P), and therefore established the right of the Union to intervene in a Member State pursuant to a decision of the Assembly in respect of grace circumstances – namely war crimes, genocide, and crimes against humanity.

They categorically rejected and renounced non-constitutional changes of government in African countries – that is, military coups against democratically elected governments, actions of mercenaries, rebels or dissidents for the purpose of replacing a democratically elected government, refusal of an incumbent ruler to relinquish power to the person democratically elected in a free and fair election, and any constitutional amendment that violates the principle of democratic change of government. In addition, the Constitutive Act lays down these other principles for good governance: rejection and renunciation of corruption, commitment to a transparent system of representative government, regular and transparently free and fair elections, separation of powers in government, effective participation of all citizens in democratic processes, promotion of gender balance, and transparency in the management of public affairs.

It was laid down that the decision to intervene in "grave circumstances" in a Member State required only the votes of two-thirds of members in the highest decision-making organ of the African Union, the AU Assembly. In effect, no Member State (not even the Member State concerned) can veto a decision of the Assembly to authorize AU organs to intervene in a Member State in which war crimes, genocide and crimes against humanity are assessed by the Assembly to be taking place. As this was articulated by one of the architects of the African Union, President Alpha Oumar Konare of Mali (1992-2002), this was a turning away from a Pan-African culture based on "non-intervention" to another based on "non-indifference". It established the important principle that the sovereignty and right of self-determination of an African country does not entail its freedom to inflict suffering on any of its citizens and abuse their human rights; and the principle of Africa's responsibility to protect the human rights of African persons anywhere on the continent. Not only does the Act authorize the AU to so intervene to protect the security of persons, it also authorizes it to penalize member states that flout the provisions of the Act, and lays down specific penalties for any country in which an unconstitutional change of government takes place.

A detailed superstructure of decision-making and administrative organs was set up for the purposes of this ambitious AU venture. Its highest decision-making organ is the Assembly, comprising the heads of state and governments of its member states. But a representative body is also provided for - namely, the African Parliament, comprising 265 members elected by the national parliaments of the member states. The Executive Council, a body comprising the Foreign Ministers of the member states, prepares matters for decision-making for the Assembly. The most important administrative organ is the secretariat. Known as the AU Commission, it is domiciled in Addis Ababa, Ethiopia. The main organs of the AU are deliberately located in different member states.

Of the organs provided for peace, order, security, and conflict management, the following are the most important: the Peace and Security Council (PSC), and the Peace and Security Directorate (PSD). The AU gives the PSC considerable influence and responsibility to implement the AU's common African security policy of defending life and property, with a view to ensuring permanent conditions for development on the continent. The PSC is thus mandated to set up machinery for predicting and preventing conflicts and, where conflicts happen to break out, to set up and dispatch peace-keeping missions. If the AU has to intervene in serious conditions such as war crimes, genocide, and crimes against humanity in any member country, the PSC has the mandate and duty to recommend to the Assembly of the AU appropriate measures for such intervention. The PSC is also empowered to impose sanctions on a country in which unconstitutional change of government occurs. The PSC is thus the AU's body for decision making in peace and security issues. As for the PSD, it is set up to execute and follow up the PSC's decisions, to be responsible for strategically and operationally leading the AU's peace and security operations, and to harmonize the AU's peace activities with those of other agencies (United Nations and regional organizations) on the African continent. For carrying out its functions, the PSD is equipped with a secretariat to assist the PSC, a Conflict Management Division (CMD), and a Peace Support Operations Division (PSOD). The CMD serves as its operational arm, and consists of an Early Warning Unit, and a Conflict Management and Post-Conflict Unit. The PSOD also consists of two units – an Operations and Support Unit, and an African Standby Force and Military Staff Committee. The PSOD is designed to operationally lead AU peace-keeping missions, deploy ambassadors, special liaison officers and observers, assist regional initiatives, and assist in national reconstruction efforts. The important point about all these details is that they show how far the rulers of Africa came in conceiving the kinds of response needed for meeting the demands of peace, order and security on their continent.

But in addition to charting all these ambitious agreements, conventions, and instruments of the African Union for the pursuit of peace and security on their continent, African governments have also generally shown increased readiness to make human and material contributions to peace operations. This willingness and readiness on the part of African governments has become particularly noticeable since about 1989 – in international peace operations in Africa and other continents, and in African operations on the African continent. Up to about 1989, no more than 12 African countries had made any contributions to international peace operations anywhere, most of them to just one operation in all. By 2002, as many as 41 African countries had made contributions, some of them to many different operations. With the founding of the new AU, African willingness to contribute to peace operations, especially on their own continent, but also on other continents, became even greater.

Yet another major development in this direction in Africa has been the emergence of many regional organizations dedicated principally to regional economic cooperation, but also to regional peace and security initiatives. Of these, the largest and most active to date has been the Economic Community of West African States (ECOWAS), established by the countries of West Africa, with its ECOWAS Cease-fire Monitoring Group (ECOMOG). ECOWAS distinguished itself in the peace missions in the Liberian civil war, as well as in the other troubled countries of the sub-region – Sierra Leone, Ivory Coast, Guinea (Conakry). In the same sub-region, a Treaty of Non-aggression, Assistance and Mutual Defense (ANAD) had been signed as early as 1977 by Ivory Coast, Mali, Burkina Faso, Mauritania, Niger, Senegal and Togo. In 1986, an ANAD military commission resolved a border dispute between Mali and Burkina Faso, but since the time of the Liberian civil war in the 1990's, ANAD has been completely overshadowed by ECOWAS and its ECOMOG in West Africa. The Southern African Development Community (SADC), established by the countries of southern Africa, sent peace-mission troops to the Democratic Republic of the Congo, and later to Lesotho, in the 1990's. Other regional organizations that have contributed to peace missions in their regions are the Economic and Monetary Community of Central African States (CEMAC), the Eastern African Community (EAC), the Community of Sahelo-Saharan States (CEN-SAD), and the Economic Market for East and Southern Africa (COMESA). All of these bodies started principally for economic cooperation purposes in their regions, but that objective has been commonly conceived to include peace and security commitments.

Though the United States and the European powers have, as would be remembered, been increasingly reluctant to contribute manpower to African peace-keeping missions, they however welcomed the AU as a very significant development on the African continent, and have generally stepped forth to find ways to give support to the African initiatives. The United States, Britain and France lead the way in all this. The objective of their actions is to help to improve the peace-keeping capabilities of the AU and the regional African organizations – mostly through special equipment donation programs, and through various programs of training for African peace-keeping personnel.

Without any doubt, these ambitious Pan-African and regional efforts and structures, and the African leaders, professionals and experts responsible for setting them up, deserve the gratitude of Africa and all Africans. However, for now at least, the whole structure represents no more than big and commendable ambitions. It suffers significant uncertainties. For one thing, resources lag behind the grand ambitions – with the result that the capacity and the implementing structures are feeble. And the weaknesses are deep-rooted, being due, not so much to limitations in the willingness, but in the ability, of the Member States of the AU to contribute the resources (in personnel and funds) that the whole ambitious structure requires for capacity. Many of the member states of the AU are among the poorest countries in the world. Only a few (like Nigeria and Libya, and then South Africa) have been really able to contribute reliably. The amount of Nigeria's offer of contribution has tended to determine the scale, effectiveness and duration of the African Union's peace programs. As for Libya's contribution, it has occasionally been problematic, because of the fact that Libya (under President Gaddafi) was known to encourage and support rebellions and terrorist movements in some African countries.

Given these circumstances, the African Union's peace programs must lean heavily on foreign assistance, but, in this too, there have been some constraints. The United Sates and other Western countries, as would be remembered, while willing to offer equipment, funding and training assistance, have been increasingly reluctant to offer personnel beyond the category of observers and trainers. Africa is very short in appropriately trained personnel for peace operations, and this can often mean that even the foreign offers of equipment are inadequately taken advantage of. But another face of this situation has been that, in the atmosphere of

"African solutions to African Problems", the African Union can sometimes be somewhat reluctant to accept certain types of foreign aid. To raise capacity and performance to match ambition, therefore, the new peace and security architecture of the AU has a long way to go.

In the course of the year 2011, as country after country in North Africa (Tunisia, Egypt, and Libya), all members of the African Union, plunged into massive popular revolts and violent changes of governments, these weaknesses of the African Union structure were very fully demonstrated. Particularly in Libya, where the government of President Muammar Gaddafi ordered the national armed forces to crush the revolt and thereby provoked a messy and drawn-out civil war, the AU looked very impotent indeed. High-powered AU delegations to Gaddafi achieved nothing. Nor was the AU able to do anything about what was developing, at some point in the confrontation, into an unrestrained use of force by the Libyan armed forces against excitable hordes of Libyan youths who very visibly lacked knowledge of arms or warfare. At that point, it fell to the United Nations to step forward in denunciation of the growing crime against humanity, and to NATO (with the support of the European Union and the United States) to offer some air cover to the masses of Libyans against the armed forces of their own country.

But capacity building has not been the only area of weakness. Another has been the difficulties with the harmonizing of functional relationships between the African Union's peace and security structure and the regional organizations. The African Union's continent-wide peace and security programs are structured to lean on the regional organizations for implementation – and a problem resides here in the fact that there are too many of the regional organizations. More than 40 regional organizations have arisen on the continent; and of the 54 member states of the AU, each of at least 26 has membership in two or more regional organizations. As an immediate measure, the African Union selected just seven regional organizations to work with – but that can only be a very temporary step, and solid action is needed to deal with this situation.

While showing no marked improvement in its capacity to deal with all these weaknesses, the AU diverted attention, from

2006 on, into a big project which, in the opinion of many observers, was extremely difficult and perhaps even unrealistic. To "complete the AU project", as it was said, the highest decision-making organs of the AU began to devote much attention to converting the AU into a political union of all of Africa. As ought to have been expected, different lines of approach immediately emerged in the counsels of the AU over this matter. Of the most prominent, one proposes a maximalist approach that would convert the AU into a United States of Africa with an African army; and another proposes a minimalist approach that would limit itself to strengthening the existing organs of the AU and making the AU, as it was structured, more effective. Since 2007, some final resolution on the matter has been put off from year to year.

Poor Perception & Poorer Leadership

But even when (or if) the day comes when the AU somehow becomes stronger and more effective, Africa will still be the home of deep political troubles. The ambitious AU architecture for peace and security, impressive though it is, and even if it works at full efficiency, cannot provide effective answers to the deep fundamentals in the Sub-Saharan African situation. The fundamentals will still remain – and remain very potent. As long as the Black African political elite fails, or refuses, to perceive, acknowledge, and respond realistically, to the fundamental reality of each country, not even the most successful Pan-African or regional African construct will ever solve the problems of Black Africa. The reality that is fundamental to the political difficulties of each of our countries in Black Africa is that each country is made up of many different nations, each of which nations is an ancient people in its own right, in its own homeland, product of its own history, possessed of its own culture, endowed with its own strength, tenacious of its own pride, and desirous to manage its own life and determine its own future. The manner in which these peoples were pushed together into countries, denied any voice in the making and structuring of those countries and, in many cases, broken up within the countries they belonged to and between neighboring countries - all of these are not going away and could not go away. As long as no country is seriously and realistically dealing with this fundamental, even the best that an African Union can give will fall short. The new African Union's ambitious structure proclaims hope to a battered Africa, but most of the structure's captains, ideologues and professionals are pitifully tainted and deflated in the eyes of Africa and the world because of the poor quality of governance that they uphold and practice in their various countries. To elucidate this, let us view some concrete examples.

West Africa's largest, richest, and most powerful country, Nigeria, invested a lot of its resources in the effort to bring the civil wars in Liberia, Ivory Coast and Sierra Leone to an end. In spite of the well-known criticisms of the Nigerian military in action, this was a great service to Africa and to the world. And Nigeria has also been usually forthcoming in contributing its resources in other African trouble spots. For all these, Nigeria deserves the gratitude of Africa and the world. And if any one man can be regarded as the architect and hero of most of these Nigerian contributions to peace in Africa in recent times, that one man would be Olusegun Obasanjo, President of Nigeria from 1999 to 2007. However, at home in Nigeria, and in the same years, Obasanjo was also, in the opinion of probably most informed Nigerians, the leader of that which qualifies as one of the most authoritarian elected governments in Nigeria's crooked and corrupt political history.

In fairness to Obasanjo, long before he was elected President in 1999, a certain coalition of "leaders" had long held a grip on Nigeria's political life. As would be remembered, the British founders and rulers of Nigeria had planted the seeds of the coalition in the late 1950's, the years before Nigeria became independent in 1960. A fuller detail of this Nigerian situation than has been given hitherto is necessary at this point. When, after the Second World War, the European colonial powers had realized that they would have to give up their African colonies, each had sought or created a group that it could trust in every African country to hand power to, a group that could be trusted to protect the former colonialist's interests after independence. In Nigeria, the British had chosen the leadership of the Northern Nigerian Hausa-Fulani to fill that role. The reasons for the British choice were obvious. The Hausa-Fulani, being ardent Muslims, had, under British rule, been very little exposed to Christian missionary influence, the providers of virtually all of Western education in colonial Africa. As a result, by the late 1950's they were far behind the peoples of Southern Nigeria in education, had almost none of the lawyers, doctors, professionals, journalists, etc., that the Southern peoples had plentifully, and were therefore not sure that they really would want British rule to end as soon as demanded by the southerners, out of fear of being dominated by the southern educated elite in an independent Nigeria. The British concluded from this that the Hausa-Fulani were much better disposed towards British rule and British interests, and could therefore be trusted to protect British interests after independence.

In the last years of the 1950's, the British administration took a series of steps to establish the dominance of the Hausa-Fulani group in the affairs of Nigeria. Constitutional changes effected between 1957 and 1960 firmly guaranteed that the Northern Region alone (out of the three Regions that comprised the Nigerian Federation – Northern, Eastern and Western Regions) had a clear majority in the Nigerian federal parliament. The powers of the federal government were then enhanced. A clause was even, as a last act of strengthening the Federal Government after independence, inserted into the Independence Constitution authorizing the Federal Government to, at its discretion, declare that law and order had broken down in any Region, and to then suspend the elected government of that Region and appoint an emergency administration for the Region. Political interferences in the 1959 pre-independence Nigerian elections by the British administrators guaranteed that the political party of the Hausa-Fulani was protected from competition by other political parties (led by Northern opposition elements and by Eastern and Western Regional politicians) in parts of the North. The Hausa-Fulani party, fielding electoral candidates in only the Northern Region, thus won the largest number of seats, of all parties, to the federal parliament. But because it did not win an over-all majority, there arose a chance that other parties could form a coalition to control the federal parliament and form the executive arm of the Federal Government. The British administration, it is now known, had had the foresight to prepare for this possibility also – by using a combination of arm-twisting and bribery to prepare a Southern party to be ready to enter into a coalition with the Hausa-Fulani party. The British Governor General of Nigeria quickly called the Hausa-Fulani party to form the government, and after some two days of play-acting, the bride that had been prepared ready signed on to the marriage contract. At Nigeria's independence on October 1, 1960, the Hausa-Fulani political elite were so strongly in control of the Federal Government that their leader, Sir Ahmadu Bello, could, according to a local newspaper, say on October 12:

"This new nation called Nigeria should be an estate of our great-grandfather Uthman Dan Fodio. We must ruthlessly prevent a change of power. We must use the minorities in the North as willing tools, and the South as conquered territory, and never allow them to rule over us, and never allow them to have control over their future.[3]

In the years that followed, the Northern political elite employed its control of the Federal Government to advance Northern military officers to a preponderance of place in the Nigerian army. Moreover, unhappy to share power with even a junior coalition partner, mostly from the Eastern Region, in the Federal Government, the Northern group attempted to create a subordinate following in the Western Region. By employing provisions of the constitution, they declared an emergency over the Western Region, suspended that Region's elected government, and installed over it a federally appointed administrator, and then exploited its new powers over the Region to rig the elections in the Region. Very illustrative of the political mood of the times were the following exuberant sentences in a letter by a Northern correspondent to a newspaper in the midst of the furor following the rigging of the federal election of 1964 in the Western Region:

The conquest to the sea is now in sight. When our God-send Ahmadu Bello said some years ago that our conquest will reach the sea shores of Nigeria, some idiots in the South were doubting its possibilities. Today, have we not reached the sea? Lagos is reached. It remains Port Harcourt. It must be conquered and taken.[4]

Lagos is the main southwestern city, and Port Harcourt the main southeastern city, on the coast. When the Western Region's regional election was even more blatantly rigged in the same ways in late 1965, the Yoruba people of the Western Region exploded in a widespread and prolonged rebellion, which shook the whole country to its foundations, and led to the first military coup in Nigeria. This was soon followed by a counter-coup by military officers of Northern Nigerian origin, by a series of pogroms against the southeastern Igbo people resident in the North, and, in reaction, by an attempt by the Eastern Region, led by the large Igbo nation, to secede from Nigeria. The federal attempt to suppress the secession led to a sanguinary thirty-month civil war which, according to certain accounts, took more than one million lives of Igbo people.

The decades after the civil war then featured a series of military coups, each of them led by Northern military officers and each producing a Northern military dictator. The large numbers of Northern military officers retiring from political public positions in the military regimes evolved into a political class, which then naturally allied with the Northern political elite to constitute a powerful political axis. Protecting and advancing the privileged position of the Northern leadership in the central government of Nigeria, and expanding the authority of the central government, have remained the nodal objectives of this Northern axis.

The big "enemy" of Nigeria (of "national unity"), in this context, is the strength inherent in each of Nigeria's nationalities – and naturally, the greatest "enemies" are the two largest southern nations, the Yoruba and the Igbo. Even the capabilities and achievements of these two are seen as threats to Nigeria, and everything must be done to circumvent, divide, confuse, and frustrate them. Of the two large nationalities, one is the immediate "enemy" one time, and the other at another time. And everything must be done to ensure that the two are perpetually enemies of each other. Meanwhile, to give itself a "national" image, the axis must recruit some leaders (especially retired military officers) of all Nigerian nationalities, using, as incentive, the offer of the chance to accumulate personal fortunes through a culture of corruption in the management of public money. Many top leaders and accomplices of the axis rank today among the richest persons in Africa (or even in the world). Thus, in Nigeria, public corruption has not been merely a matter of public officials stealing public resources; it is a deliberate tool employed by the people who control the powers and resources of the central government, for the purpose of subverting, weakening and controlling chosen members of the political elite of the various peoples of Nigeria. It is a tool for Nigeria's perverse brand of "nation building". Political parties have been founded from time to time to serve as front for the Northern axis and its political agenda.

In one of the few elections in these decades, the 1992 presidential election, a party based in the South fielded a candidate who proved capable of drawing electoral support from most parts of the country. Chief M.K.O. Abiola was a member of the Yoruba people of the Southwest. One of the richest businessmen in the country, he was widely known as a philanthropist who had given to many worthy causes across the country. He was also a Muslim with many personal friends and associations in the North. Consequently, his popularity overwhelmed the Northern candidate, and as the polls closed, there was no doubt that he had won quite easily. But the Northern military officer and Military Head of State who had organized the election announced without giving any clear reason that he was cancelling the election - and it quickly became obvious that it was the Northern axis that had pushed him into doing it. As popular reaction against this mounted in the South, especially in the Southwest, the head of the military regime could not hold on to power. He stepped down, but another Northern military officer then seized power and proceeded brutally to stamp out the reaction.

By 1998-9, as a result of all these relentless manipulations of the country's political life, and the crude violence and corruption of the most recent military regime (whose head died suddenly in 1998), Nigeria tottered on the brink of total dissolution. Some of the peoples of the country were openly talking of secession. As the very large Yoruba nation of Southwestern Nigeria evinced the most resentment and resolve, the Northern axis decided to concede the presidency of Nigeria to the Yoruba political elite in the 1999 federal elections in order to appease the Yoruba nation. The axis (operating with the political party front named Peoples Democratic Party, PDP)), then nominated retired General Olusegun Obasanjo, a Yoruba man, as its candidate for president. But then another strong party based in the South nominated another prominent Yoruba – Chief Olu Falae, a retired civil servant who had once held the position of Secretary to the Federal Government. Yoruba voters voted very overwhelmingly for Falae and against Obasanjo, but, countrywide, Obasanjo was elected anyway – leading, yet again, to allegations of rigging. This was the ideal situation desired by the axis in the circumstance – a non-Hausa-Fulani President who could be shown up as a Southern compromise president, who appeared to feel that he did not owe his own nationality anything, and who could therefore be trusted to pursue the goals of the axis.

In the next years under the Obasanjo presidency, more and more "leaders" were recruited from among the other nations of Nigeria – "leaders" grateful for easy unearned wealth, allowed to steal and share whatever public money came under their influence in public positions (Federal or State or Local Government positions), and assured of fraudulent victories at elections through election rigging with the assistance of federal agencies. Corruption boomed. For Obasanjo and for the axis, the 2003 federal elections became a specially desperate battle. The Yoruba resistance had to be crushed – happen as it might. In the name of "national unity", the political party of the axis(the PDP) and its local candidates must sweep, not only the elections to the federal government, but also the elections to the governments of all the 36 states to which the Nigerian Federation had been delimited.

So it was that, when the 2003 elections came, Nigeria witnessed the most desperate and most violent election rigging yet in its history. Massive fights, blood-letting and violent deaths were widespread, as local folks tried to resist the rigging, most especially in the Yoruba states. In Obasanjo's Ogun State (one of the six states of the Yoruba in southwestern Nigeria), where, like the other Yoruba states, Obasanjo had been very massively rejected at the polls in 1999, the votes reported for Obasanjo grossly outnumbered the registered voters – causing a court to muster the courage to throw out all the presidential votes in that state. In one Igbo state in the southeast, a man who had not even filed nomination papers with the National Electoral Commission was somehow declared elected as Senator, and was sworn in as member of the Nigerian Senate. Tens of election petitions clogged the courts – very many of them petitions over the reported results in the gubernatorial and other races in the six Yoruba states of the Southwest. After the election, one newly "elected" governor of an Igbo state came under intense harassment by some leaders of his party in his state – including their once kidnapping him and holding him hostage and, on another occasion, burning down his office. It ultimately came to public knowledge that these politicians were assailing their State Governor because he was refusing to honour the pledge on which they had rigged the election for him – namely, to use his position to steal large amounts of public money for them monthly.

Reports of assassinations filled the news media in these years. Hardly a month passed without some report of an assassination, or assassination attempt, or exposed or alleged assassination plot. After a crowded series of leaks of massive ongoing corruption in various branches of Nigeria's government in March and April 2005, President Obasanjo announced that he was starting a war against corruption, and vowed to employ all means at his disposal for the fight. For some time after that, an agency led by a surprisingly professional police officer pursued and published investigations of some leading men. But the whole exercise hit a rock when the agency published some very staggering allegations against President Obasanjo's Vice-President, and the Vice-President responded with his own very detailed allegations of financial corruption against the President himself.

And then came the biggest and worst under the Obasanjo presidency – namely, the 2007 national elections. Many international observers were in Nigeria for the 2007 elections, and their reports were, to say the least, shocking. The whole world watched in utter unbelief on television as Nigerian officials, attended by thugs, snatched ballot boxes at polling stations. But we will content ourselves here with an excerpt from a summary of the International Observers Report published by *Africa Report*: [5]

Africa Report No. 126
30 May, 2007

NIGERIA: FAILED ELECTIONS, FAILING STATE?
EXECUTIVE SUMMARY AND RECOMMENDATIONS

The elections, in the view of Nigerians and the many international observers alike, were the most poorly organized and massively rigged in the country's history. In a bitterly contentious

194

environment, outgoing President Obasanjo and his Peoples Democratic Party (PDP) acted with unbridled desperation to ensure sweeping, winner-take-all victories, not only in the presidency and federal legislature but also in state governorships and assemblies.

Characterized as a "do-or-die" battle by Obasanjo, the campaigns and elections also witnessed extensive violence, including over 200 people killed. Widespread electoral malpractice and the staggering scale of falsified results were possible because of serious shortcomings within the regulatory agencies, most notably the Independent National Electoral Commission (INEC). Vigorously manipulated by the presidency, INEC virtually abdicated its responsibility as impartial umpire. Inefficient and non-transparent in its operations, it became an accessory to active rigging. Similarly, the massively deployed police and other security services helped curb violence but largely turned blind eyes to, and in some cases helped in, the brazen falsification of results. INEC declared a landslide for Yar'Adua with 70 per cent of the votes, to 18 per cent for Muhammadu Buhari of the All Nigeria People's Party (ANPP). That victory is bitterly disputed by many Nigerians, however, including broad-based labor, religious and civil society groups. It has pushed the country further towards a one- party state and diminished citizen confidence in electoral institutions and processes.

Most ominously, it has undermined Nigeria's capacity to manage its internal conflicts, deepening already violent tensions in the Niger Delta and refueling Biafran separatism in the ethnically Ibo south east. It has also badly damaged the country's international image and Obasanjo's legacy as a statesman, thus diminishing their credibility to serve as leading forces for peace and democracy throughout West Africa.

I have gone to this length about President Obasanjo's domestic political record as president of Nigeria for a very important reason. In every Sub-Saharan African country, most of the politically influential citizens do not have a clear understanding of the political realities of their country, do not do anything about it, and even make it worse by their policies and actions. They believe that what the turmoil in every country calls for is a peace-making and peace-keeping response by a Pan-African or worldwide agency. They are ready to invest energy and resources in such efforts. And they have, to cap it all, given a lot of time and scope in recent times to discussing the possibility of converting the African Union to some sort of United States of Africa possessing an African army.

In fact what Africa needs, what Africa has needed since independence, is completely different. The reason the African countries are politically unstable and tumultuous is that, in the particular nature of their circumstances, they cannot be otherwise. The way each was put together as a country, its consequent composition and structure, and its ordering by its founders – all these have doomed these countries to be politically unstable from the beginning. But, much more importantly, leading Africans in every country have been wrong in assuming after independence that Africans in each country already had a complete and finished country – that the white man who came and gave them a country had done all that needed to be done for the composition and structure of that country. We Africans therefore have mostly ignored the manifest realities facing us – and either ignored or tried to suppress the uniqueness of our various peoples in each country in the quest for "nation building". And by doing so, we have brought unimaginable disasters upon ourselves as peoples.

To illustrate this point more strongly, let us continue a little more with President Obasanjo. Undeniably, this is a man gifted with capabilities that deserve respect. He also often claims to be committed to the survival of Nigeria as one country. Unfortunately, however, because he believes that Nigeria is a finished product, and that the uniqueness of Nigeria's various peoples needs to be suppressed and repressed in the interest of Nigeria's unity, he, as president, took actions that hurt Nigeria rather than build it, by massively suppressing and subduing the main peoples of Nigeria. As a Yoruba man from southwestern parts of Nigeria, he (like all non-Hausa-Fulani Nigerians) cannot openly endorse Hausa-Fulani pretensions of dominance over Nigeria. He has sometimes spoken out against it – especially since his leaving office as president. In particular, in the course of late 2010 when his interests in Nigerian politics diverged obviously from those of the Northern leadership group, he was again and again reported as saying that no one nationality has the right to claim dominance over Nigerian affairs, and that Nigeria belongs to all Nigerians. However, as president, because of the direction of his basic understanding of the Nigerian situation, he seemed to operate on the conviction that any means of binding Nigeria together was justified. During his eight-year presidency, he launched, with the power of his position and his considerable capabilities, into helping the axis to fuller strength and power, using the tools that the axis had always used - namely, corruption, bribery, election manipulation, and authoritarian exercise of power. For eight years, he was offered an eminent opportunity to diffuse any special Hausa-Fulani or any other ethnic prerogative over the Nigerian federal establishment, promote an open political system for Nigeria, and give the various peoples of Nigeria some room to grow in their own ways in the context of Nigeria. Since these are the things that most of his own Yoruba people, and many other peoples of Southern Nigeria, have always desired in Nigeria, a lot of people hoped, as he came into the presidency, that welcome changes would be wrought by him – in spite of his political affiliation. Outside of Nigeria too, in the wider world, there were great hopes that Obasanjo would turn Nigeria around onto an open democratic path. His star rose high in the international community, so high that many believed he would someday become Secretary General of the United Nations. But he did not only fail to diffuse the prerogative and the rigidity of federal hold and its authoritarianism and corruption, he actually reinforced it all. After he stepped down from the presidency, he claimed that his greatest achievement was that he had kept Nigeria together. In fact, apparently unknown to him, he probably took Nigeria much closer to disintegration and dissolution.

But, though many of the members of Nigeria's intelligentsia (especially the southern intelligentsia) are inclined to castigate Obasanjo in particular, they should realize that his perception of Nigeria is not peculiar to him, and that very many influential citizens like him do not see that Nigeria is a product yet to be properly made, a product that still needs to be properly formulated and structured. Many influential Nigerians might reject Obasanjo's particular line of actions, but they essentially agree with his perception that Nigeria, as it is, is complete and good, and

197

even that the inherent strengths of the various peoples or nations of Nigeria negate the unity and strength of Nigeria. Views of that nature are common among certain very influential Nigerian politicians – and among certain very influential politicians in every Sub-Saharan African country. Even many other prominent Nigerians who passionately reject the corruption, the authoritarianism, and the government-in-the-dark, that have become the established character of their country, have nothing to contribute to the Nigerian debate other than a belief that what the country needs is moral reformation in its leaders. They would not give their support to movements for the loosening of the federal strangle-hold on Nigeria, or for constitutionally empowering the various peoples of Nigeria to manage much of their affairs according to their cultures and ethical values in the context of a rational federal system. Rather, they would expend their energies and influence solely on cries for moral improvements in Nigerian leaders and politicians. Quite commonly, such prominent citizens elevate "corruption" to the status of root cause (rather than one of the symptoms) of the Nigerian problem, and they can be very skillful in denying that a change in the structure of Nigeria might be the solution to much of Nigeria's problems.

Such behavior and attitudes spring from the belief that Nigeria, and that all African countries, are complete and final as they are. And such views and attitudes are, to say the least, downright dangerous in the light of Africa's present situation – because they tend to engender a resistance to all questionings and to ideas and suggestions about the way forward for each African country and for Africa in general. To see how dangerous they can be, for instance, visit the opinions expressed by Nigeria's retired General Yakubu Gowon in a 2009 paper sent by him to a public seminar of the Arewa Consultative Forum, the primal organization of the Northern Nigerian political elite. In that paper, Gen. Gowon reserves the sharpest condemnations for all those who are clamoring for change in Nigeria, and who are demanding a restructuring of the Nigerian federation in such a way as to give increased autonomy to the ethnic nations of Nigeria. In his view, such persons are:[6]

a. elements *"who want to see the country balkanized into small territories to be headed by tribal leaders - - - made up of demagogues and other anarchists who will sooner take Nigeria back to the chaos of the 18th century";*

b. *those who desire the country's break-up into "geopolitical territories, whereby big ethnic groups may swallow up small ones without a challenge";*

c. *those who want "a new constitution that will allow them to keep 100% of the money derived from the sale of oil that is extracted within their territories".*

d. *misguided idealists and extremists who cannot be satisfied with anything.*

In short, Gen. Gowon sees no worth or merit whatsoever in the growing demands for change in the structure of the Nigerian federation, or in those advocating change. And that is because he is so absolutely satisfied that Nigeria is complete and good as it is – even though it is becoming more and more obvious to all, almost by the day, that the Nigerian federation will either radically restructure or continue to resist change until it implodes – and even though some of the worst inter-ethnic pogroms in Nigeria have been repeatedly exploding in his own home area. As far as he is concerned (and as he explicitly said in his paper under reference), the British came, pulled the nations that are now in Nigeria together into one country, and thereby delivered them all from the chaos and barbarism of their past! So, all the talk of Nigeria needing to be properly structured is wrong-headed – even perverse or criminal. Really, Gowon's viewing of Nigeria's problems in this way is a great pity – because Gen Gowon is one of the most respected, one of the most influential, Nigerians alive. He was military President of Nigeria for nine years (1966-75), and presided over Nigeria in the war to suppress Biafran secession. Also, although he presided, in his last years as military ruler, over a huge apparatus of corruption, most Nigerians concede that he was personally not corrupt. Today, he is the only former long-lasting military ruler of Nigeria that is not a multi-millionaire - and that gives him considerable credibility among the common people of Nigeria. That a Nigerian of his eminent standing should be so eminently ignorant and wrong about the realities of Nigeria is truly a disaster.

Unhappily, he has a lot of company among the rulers of Africa. Most influential Africans simply cannot, or will not, see a need for any change of approach to the affairs of their countries. To them, "nation building" means simply preserving each of their countries as an entity and in the structure bequeathed by the former colonial rulers. It was so from the moment the first Black African country became independent. It is so today. Leading Africans inherited, from European imperialists, countries that were very manifestly ethnically diverse, politically disunited and shaky – and in that light, very poorly structured. Rather than look carefully at their new country and ask how all groups in it could be reasonably happily included, instead of seeking structures and practices that could conduce to the fact and spirit of true unity in diversity, the new rulers of each country chose to employ the authoritarian institutions and traditions of European colonial rule to force all groups together. Accepting from the outgoing imperialists, or manufacturing, the "dominant" ethnic group in the politics, economy, military, and civil service of many countries, manipulating elections to sustain those purposes, employing bribes to recruit supporters and allies, and attempting to crush resolute dissidents with the power of the state – these were the ways in which the first rulers of each independent African state attempted to keep their country together. And, five decades later, it is still the way African leaders choose to "build" their countries.

Hardly any first ruler of an independent African country could reconcile himself to the possibility of his losing power to anybody through an election, or to constitutionally conceding some local autonomy to the restive nationalities of his country. In virtually every country, the new ruler came to see himself as the living guarantee of the "unity" and survival of his country, and believed that his most important duty was to show strength. Merely opposing him in an election could often be made to look like a crime.

In Ghana, Dr. Kwame Nkrumah, beloved by African nationalists all over Africa as the man who led the first Black African country to independence, and as the foremost oracle of a new Africa, responded more and more to the political difficulties

200

of his multi-nation country with policies that increased the powers of his central government, and that aimed to crush all elements of dissent. At the peak of the trend, he made Ghana a one-party state, and established laws ('preventive detention laws') that empowered his government to deal at will with dissidents (including, ultimately, some of his own original leading supporters). As the political cloud grew darker and darker around him, opposition to him in the Western world on account of his fervent African loyalty, his strength, and his later-day socialist orientation, acquired greatly increased opportunity to impact the politics of his country. Ultimately, he became a titan surrounded by a phalanx of very ardent young politicians, and withdrew increasingly into a fortified political powerhouse, out of touch with most of his countrymen. The final blow on him came from the Ghanaian military.

In Nigeria, the Hausa-Fulani leadership (first led by Sir Ahmadu Bello), being, on the whole, a minority empowered by the British, sought to retain power more securely and indefinitely over Nigeria by employing the power of the central government to engineer the disarray of the stronger nations, to plant their own ethnic members and loyalists in key positions in the Nigerian armed forces, to manufacture subordinate "allies" beyond their own Northern Region, to uphold such allies with enormous corruption and electoral fraud, and to use corruption to subvert and control important agencies of government. The whole edifice almost totally crashed soon after independence, but it has continued to live on and to employ the same old tactics (even in the hands of persons who, like Presidents Obasanjo and Jonathan, are not Fulani) – with the result that observers worldwide now fear that Nigeria may soon implode.

In the Ivory Coast, President Houphouet Boigny built himself into an imperial personage, the soul of his country, and its guarantee of survival and unity as one country – while continuing to preserve some semblance of democratic constitutions and elections. Twice, first as a college professor and later as a Nigerian Senator, this author served on groups that visited this great Ivorian in his hometown of Yamousoukro, where he had built, among other things, a cathedral and a palace (according to some, in imitation of Louis XIV of France). Even for a non-Ivorian, it was not difficult to see how much this very capable man was out of touch with the political realities of his country. After his death, his followers tried to keep his system going, together with its heritage of resentment in some regions of the country – with predictably painful outcomes for Ivory Coast .

In Kenya, the literate elite of the Kikuyu nation, led by Jomo Kenyatta, enjoyed at independence (in December 1963) the distinction of having provided most of the leadership in the anti-imperial struggle against the British. After independence, Kenyatta became the father of his new country and the symbol and guarantee of its unity. At the peak of his eminence, in fact, he was no longer just a candidate in the elections, he was the person certifying that his strongest electoral opponents did not qualify to even stand for election against him. Since his control had to be total, his country had to have a strong unitary government and only one political party. In reality, however, fears of "Kikuyu domination" were rising among the elite of the other nationalities of the country – and were already so rife that just before independence, the British had had to resort to a quasi-federal constitution for Kenya. Paying no attention to the fears that had generated the idea of a quasi-federation, the Kenyatta government of independent Kenya immediately launched into a big campaign for "national unity" – and, in less than one year, refashioned Kenya into a unitary, one-party, state, thus immensely intensifying the base for fears of the non-Kikuyu peoples of the country. Resentment grew about real or imagined discriminatory allocation of opportunities in favor of the Kikuyu.

When Kenyatta died, the ruling party's apparatus raised Daniel arap Moi (a Kalenjin) to succeed him. Moi immediately proceeded to take to new heights the Kenyatta use of authoritarianism to foster national unity. In the process, Moi attracted a lot of international attention for gross human rights abuses – including his repression of all dissent with the abrogation of all opposition political parties (on the grounds that multiple parties provided room for inter-ethnic conflicts), extra-judicial executions, tortures, disappearances of political activists, etc. But the myth of "national unity" enforced from the top soon began to unravel. Moi's own Kalenjin people, feeling politically empowered but otherwise underprivileged, led in the making of the inter-ethnic conflicts of 1991-4. And then, years later, came the much bigger

202

eruptions of 2007-8 whose vibrations are still very much alive as this is being written today.

In Uganda, Prime Minister Obote leaned more and more heavily on strong-arm measures and on the military in order to force the peoples of his country together. To him, the worst enemies of his country and government were the strongest kingdoms of the country – especially the Buganda kingdom, with its considerably well educated elite, strongly influential in the civil service and the army. Among some African nationalists and intellectuals in other parts of Africa, Obote enjoyed considerable popularity, because he was commonly perceived as a determined and sincere advocate of full independence and of "national unity" for his country. Unfortunately, his strong desire for Uganda's national unity meant, for him, only the emasculation of the internal forces that seemed to him to challenge the unity of the country – especially the prominence and nationalism of the Buganda people and kingdom. Having mostly got rid of the usually highly educated Baganda officers from the army, he leaned more and more on the support of the army. He also, like Nkrumah in Ghana, promoted socialism as an ideology of national unity – a direction that quickly earned him powerful enemies in the Western world, in the context of the Cold War. His military-backed authoritarianism reached a peak in his use of the military to suppress the Buganda kingdom in 1966, overrun its palace and confiscate valuables of the Bugandan monarchy, force the Kabaka to flee into exile, convert his palace into a military barrack, and abolish all the kingdoms. The confused conflicts that he thus provoked gave his enemies at home and abroad the opportunity to act together against him.

The man who ousted him, Idi Amin, first appeared to seek reconciliation in the country, and seemed to promise to restore the kingdoms. But he never went through on that promise. On the contrary, he soon followed in Obote's authoritarian steps; and then he took that style of government to hideous extremes, though against different enemies.

In spite of the manner of Yoweri Museveni's violent entry upon the leadership of Uganda in 1986, he came, in the years that followed, to appear as a likely departure from the general character of African leadership. Restoring the kingdoms, he embarked on

203

some popular political reforms. In fact, some people in the wider world began to see him as Africa's rising star – until the urge to unending power, corruption, and to repression as a tool of national unity, overtook him too. Disenchantment with his leadership reached a peak in 2006 when, against all good advice, he had the constitution amended, in order to enable him to put aside the limit on the number of presidential terms – in order, in effect, to enable him to rule indefinitely. His point-blank rejection of any sort of federal arrangement (or system of local devolutions) has gradually resulted in a conflict between him and Uganda's most powerful kingdom, the kingdom of Buganda. Like all previous rulers of Uganda, his response has been to try to disorganize and break up this proud kingdom with all the powers of the state of Uganda, but not only has he encountered stiff resistance from the majority of Baganda loyal to their kingdom, he has also found that some of the other peoples of Uganda might not remain quiet any longer.

In 2011, some influential elements in the Bugandan elite, resident at home and in Britain and America, finally opted to push for the secession of their kingdom from Uganda. In a 22-page document titled "Buganda Captive in Uganda" bearing the signatures of 6004 citizens, addressed to the United Nations and circulated to significant governments and leaders across the world, they made clear their objective of taking their Buganda kingdom out of Uganda.

But the attempt to secede from Uganda is no longer limited to Buganda. A powerful combination of leaders of the peoples of the north (the West Nile, Karamoja, Lango, Teso, and the Acholi sub-region) have also been pushing for a "Greater North" which would become a separate country out of Uganda.

In a speech in Busoba in February 2009, President Museveni said:

> "*I have heard people make noise, ebyaffe, ebyaffe – kingdoms, kingdoms! This is empty, a sign of backwardness, sectarianism and parochialism. Uganda cannot live under chiefdoms in the 21st century, but we must learn to think nationally - - - if we are to develop*".[7]

Really! It is very strange that any citizen of Uganda would see "ebyaffe, ebyaffe!" as a retrograde, backward-looking cry in this country. Most of these people lived in considerably civilized, orderly and proud ethnic kingdoms before the coming of the British. In independent Uganda, in contrast, they have continually suffered from instability, corrupt and oppressive governments, civil wars, and terrible insecurity. Is it nonsense if they say, in the light of their experiences, that they would be happier and make better progress if they are allowed to manage their affairs under the auspices of their various peoples and kingdoms in the context of Uganda? Is a Ugandan national constitution of that nature impossible to conceive? Why is it that the men who have ruled this country just cannot, or will not, see that they have been generally unable to move their country forward simply because they have not been successful in bringing (have not even tried to bring) their countrymen along with them?

In Zimbabwe, President Mugabe (hero of the country's liberation war and once adored at home and among African intellectuals as a symbol of unity for his country) has ruled for over thirty years. In 2008, because of the devastating effect of his increasingly erratic government on the economy of the country, even some of his own nationality dared to vote against him, and he was beaten at the polls. However, claiming that he had to continue to do his duty to his country, he launched massively into rallying the traditional ethnic support systems, refused to give up power, and continued to rule – even though in a power-sharing arrangement with his political opponents. To him, having to accept the power-sharing arrangement was a "humiliation".

We could go on and on. It was the same almost everywhere in the early years after independence. It is still so today. In virtually no country have the political leaders ever sincerely sought to include the citizenry in some effort to find (or some discussion of) an answer to the mighty problem of the diversity and the expectations of nations in their country. The same African leaders who have been contributing much to, and speaking most volubly about, ambitious peace-keeping programs under the auspices of the AU and the regional organizations have, at the same time, in their own countries, been busy creating or reinforcing conditions for conflicts, resisting change that could lead to open and democratic politics, suppressing and repressing the various peoples of their countries, and leading regimes that perpetrate corruption and serious abuses of human rights.

Involving the public in open and free discussion has never been considered as an option in any country, with the exception of the Union of South Africa, Tanzania and Botswana – and now, hopefully, Ghana.. In fact, wherever some idea or suggestion for solution of the great problem of African countries has emanated among the common people themselves, the response of the most influential leadership and dominant groups has invariably been to stamp it down. For instance, the idea of a National Sovereignty Conference emerged in about the late 1980's in some African countries. A National Sovereignty Conference, according to its proponents, is a conference of the accredited representatives of all peoples or nationalities (large or small) that are members of a country, for the purpose of taking a hard look together at the country to which they all belong. This would give every single nationality in a country an opportunity, for the first time, to express its views about the trends and future of the country of which it is a member. The proposal is that under the auspices of the government of a country, all the national groups in the country would be invited to formulate the conditions acceptable to them concerning the continuance and structure of their joint country. A national conference of representatives of all the national groups would then be convened. At the conference, each national delegation would be given the chance to present its people's position on ways of crafting a stable existence for the country to which they belong. The objective is that the conference would guide itself to the formulation of a body of consensus upon which all the nationalities can agree to continue to be members of the country. Such a body of consensus would then become the Binding Principle upon which a new national constitution, and all future public policy and governmental actions, would be based.

A National Sovereignty Conference, then, is an in-depth and fundamentalist approach aimed at eliminating some of the heritage of the forcible and chaotic agglomerating of each country by European imperialists, and at giving each country a legitimacy based upon a foundational agreement of all its component nationalities. The positive possibilities of this sort of approach are easily self-evident, even though, of course, the modalities for the organizing of a National Sovereignty Conference would need to be most carefully designed and managed. For instance, it was at such a conference that the leaders of Ethiopia decided, after the fall of the Mengitsu regime in 1991, to allow the separation of Eritrea from Ethiopia. Unfortunately, the rulers and the dominant nationalities have opposed it in most countries in which it has been strongly advocated – the ruling politicians out of the fear that it could rob them of their authoritarian power, and the dominant groups out of the fear that it could take away their dominance.

In Nigeria, a citizens' organization with popular support across much of the country arose in the 1990's to champion the demand for a Nigerian National Sovereignty Conference. This body (popularly known as PRONACO), in addition to popularizing its idea at home in Nigeria, sent delegations to take it to Nigerians living abroad. By the beginning of 2005, PRONACO had succeeded so well that many Nigerians began to hope that the convening a National Sovereignty Conference was a possibility before the end of the year. But the Nigerian Federal Government (as well as the influential Northern leadership) were opposed to a National Sovereignty Conference. Therefore, while PRONACO's arrangements gathered momentum, the Federal Government (led by President Obasanjo) suddenly called a conference – a Political Reform Conference – for the poorly disguised purpose of preempting a National Sovereignty Conference and promoting President Obasanjo's political ambition. President Obasanjo's Political Reform Conference turned out to be a meeting of political parties with, of course, Obasanjo's political party in the majority. Even so, some of the conferees presented position papers on behalf their nations. But since the conference was meant to achieve no real purpose other than to preempt a National Sovereignty Conference and pave the way for a third presidential term for President Obasanjo, nothing was ever heard again about the position papers presented in it. The momentum for a National Sovereignty Conference fizzled out. The idea has continued to enjoy popular support. Its promoters, strongly convinced that they have struck on an idea that can transform every Black African country and open up a new future of stability, peace and progress in Black Africa, have continued to push it, even though without the kind of strong and focused leadership that it had enjoyed up to

2005. In 2014, another Nigerian president, Goodluck Jonathan, reluctantly yielded to pressure and convened a National Conference. But since he apparently had no real interest in any change (and only gave a National Conference as part of his strategy for attracting popular support in order to keep surviving as president as long as possible), his National Conference developed into a sort of general gathering without a real orientation (in composition and in purpose).

In the Union of South Africa referred to above, in contrast to the manner in which things are done in the rest of Sub-Saharan Africa, Nelson Mandela has demonstrated the power of trusting the people to discuss their problems openly. Apartheid in this former British colony was a gross evil. Under its banner, the white citizens inflicted deep wounds on all the other peoples of their country. The common belief in Africa and much of the world was that only rivers of blood could ever wash away the wrongs of apartheid. But then, Nelson Mandela appeared on the scene, as president of his country. By showing very sincere and convincing respect for, and trust in, all of the peoples of his country, he opened up a culture of open and honest discussion, of owning up wrongs, and of forgiving and agreeing to move forward together. The results have been more than astounding. To the surprise of Africa and the world, the Union of South Africa is stable and orderly, runs decent elections, peacefully changes its rulers, respects its own laws, is able to give its attention to the issues of development, and may soon emerge as the economic leader in Africa. Roots and pockets of political difficulties are not wanting, of course, but this country has the great fortune of having the Mandela tradition of respect, trust and open discussion as sentinel over its political life. If it keeps that tradition alive and progressively enhanced, it may become the leader of Africa.

No, the way that things are being done in the rest of Black Africa is not working. And it does not look likely ever to work. In essence, what Africans are doing is letting the Europe of an era of arrogant power determine the future and destiny of African peoples. Europeans of that era came to Africa to further their own national and personal interests, and, in pursuit of such interests, arrogantly created largely irrational territorial agglomerations everywhere in Sub-Saharan Africa, and gave irrational internal structures to those territorial agglomerations. After the European colonialists left, all that Africans have done politically is affirm that those irrational territorial agglomerations and their irrational internal structures are final and sacrosanct as they are – thereby making Africans suffer abominably, and needlessly.

Conclusion

To summarize then, while African leaders of government, leaders of the most powerful political parties or groups in their countries, may in fact energetically push and promote dazzlingly ambitious Pan-African peace and security constructs for Africa, they have never shown themselves to be much concerned about changing the manner in which the individual countries led and ruled by them are structured, led and directed. The modern political elite of most independent Black African countries are not appropriately cognizant of the enormous political problems of the countries they inherited from European imperialists. Most do not, or would not, recognize that the existence of many nations in the country they rule is a problem worthy of very special and careful attention and management. Yes, they might admit, it was some largely ignorant and arrogant European foreign conquistador that put the country together as it is. But, they all seem to say by their actions that such arbitrary and chaotic actions and accidents are the stuff that creates countries in history – and that all that is needed is stout resolve of leadership to keep the inherited country together by any means (by force if necessary), and problems will iron themselves out in time. People who raise questions about the nature and structure of the country, about the impact of it on their own part of it, people who propose a closer look at their country – all are trouble makers, "enemies of national unity", "tribalists", "obstructionists", "balkanizers", "Pakistanists"! The job, the duty, of leadership is to silence the trouble makers – by drowning out their voice; and, if they persist, by launching the power of the state against them, or by buying them over with huge bribes from money stolen from the public treasury. If all this provokes political conflicts and turmoil in a particular country, then the Pan-African concert, the AU, assisted by international supporters and agencies, should move in to quell the trouble and restore peace. In no single

Black African country since independence has any ruler or ruling group ever said to his countrymen, or wondered aloud,, "Now that the European foreigner who forced us together into this country has left, should we not now ask ourselves if what he has left for us is the way we really want to live". In no single Black African country wracked by conflicts, mass killings, and horrendous political disasters, has any ruler or ruling group ever suggested that some sort of restructuring of the pattern of relationships among the nationalities inside their country might be something to consider seriously and to attempt as a solution. No. Essentially, what the dominant political leaders of each African country are doing in the politics of their country is re-conquering the peoples of their country over and over again. The huge personal fortunes that they almost invariably take away with them from public office are the spoils that a victor in war commonly feels entitled to loot from the vanquished.

Asking the people any questions, or stopping to answer their questions, is deemed as weakness on the part of leadership! This author was one of the makers of some of the students' protest demonstrations against some actions of the Nigerian Federal Government in the months after Nigeria's independence. As I remember this particular incident, we students were out in the streets peacefully protesting a proposed government action that threatened to distort our country very fundamentally and that was massively rejected across most of our country. While we students, joined by enormous crowds of people (estimated by various news media to be over 20,000), swarmed around, under a police tear-gas and baton blitz in the streets, a journalist who managed to get access to our Prime Minister asked him whether, in view of such popular rejection of the government's action by the people, he might consider dropping or modifying it. Our Prime Minister, according to the report that circulated among us later on our campuses, answered the journalist with the question: "Who are the people?" Even a British colonial governor, though he would have felt more contempt for us Nigerians in such a situation, would have been unlikely to put it in such stark words.

This pattern of behavior among Sub-Saharan African rulers of our time will long astound the world. People from a different civilization came to Africa and, in the process of using their better technology to acquire territorial possessions for themselves, ignored and trampled down Black African nations and culturally distinct entities all over, and, in a generally rough-shod manner, set up new countries to serve their own purposes. In a few decades, the strangers left, bequeathing the new countries to Africans. For the people of northern Africa (Egypt, Libya, Tunisia, Morocco, Algeria) who went through the same experience, the new situation was much more meaningfully structured and much easier to live with. Each had a national culture and language (Arabic), a unifying religion (Islam), and some national history. For Black Africa, the situation was very different. The new countries here were all characterized by rough boundaries that had no correlation to the culture, history, or even geography, of Black Africa and its peoples; by the combination together in each country of very many nations with different histories, cultures, languages, political traditions, ambitions and desires, etc.; and by internal structures that mostly tended to generate stress or even conflict from the first day (in many cases, even before the first day) of independence. And yet, in no single Black African country did any ruler or ruling group offer the suggestion, or show some deference to any suggestion, that the peoples who now found themselves thrown together in their new country might need to review, at least, the structure of their being together. On the contrary, in every country, the assumption by rulers and dominant groups has been that the country has come to stay as it is, and the quest has been for power and more power for those who rule. In some future time in our history, historians are very likely to expend much effort on probing the roots of this strange behavior.

But the counter-response has arisen, and is growing and being variously formulated in many Black African countries and circles. To some, it is the movement to complete Africa's independence. To very many Black African peoples, it is a quest for some autonomy, and for some freedom to respond in their own various ways to the challenges of development in the modern world. In every case, it is a steadily growing preparation towards change and transformation – and if the need should be forced to arise, towards upheavals and violent revolutions.

211

CHAPTER SEVEN

Trend In Our World

The predominant response of powerful and influential Africans to the very manifest realities of the countries that Africa inherited from European colonialism, then, has been unreasonable and unfortunate. Nobody can claim that these realities are difficult to see. They are not. Nigerians live in the midst of perpetual complaints about the impact of Nigeria on its many nations. It is impossible to read the Nigerian newspapers any one day without encountering such complaints. Millions of literate Nigerians, fleeing from conditions in their native land, live today in many countries around the world. In such countries, many of their various nationalities have exclusive national associations, descendants unions, and the like. – Yoruba Association of United States and Canada, Igbo Union of United States, Zumunta, and so on, and so forth. The most important preoccupation of every one of these associations and unions is the condition of its own nation back home in Nigeria – the impact on it of the trends of Nigeria's affairs. And whenever any of these many associations holds its conference or convention, discussions of its nation's fate in Nigeria, and some communiqué thereon, are the inevitable outcomes. At home in Nigeria too, exclusive associations and unions of various nations are a regular fact of life. It has always been so since Nigeria was created in 1914; it is more assertively and aggressively so today. In every other Sub-Saharan African country, the same, to a greater or lesser extent, is true. Even a casual surfing of this subject on the worldwide web will show countless websites of the nationalities of Black Africa, each website proclaiming the desire of a nationality for the liberation of its cultural energies for its progress and prosperity in the world.

What all these mean is that the nationalism of each of the many nations that constitute every Sub-Saharan African country is very much alive and growing more and more markedly assertive. It is impossible to miss that fact in any country. It is a major factor (often *the* major factor) in the making of political parties and in the voting in elections. Arguments over most major, non-elective, public appointments in every country commonly provoke a clash of nationalisms, and so do debates over government-provided development programs or projects. Even when peace appears to reign in a country, the nationalisms of its various nations are proclaiming their virility unceasingly. The rulers and dominant groups in African countries choose to ignore the message at the peril of the countries they lead. No sub-Saharan African country (with the exception of Somalia, Botswana and Lesotho) is a nation; each is an agglomeration of many nations. And those nations speak all the time. Ignoring their voices has been the underlying source of most of the ultimate outbursts, clashes, and horrors of Africa's political life.

It is true, of course, that there are very many well-meaning prominent Africans (politicians, business people, college professors, teachers, professionals, ministers, etc.) who may or may not belong to top leadership positions, who strongly hold the view that their countries will somehow wade through these times to some sort of stability, even if nobody did anything. Today's troubles of African countries, such people believe, are "teething problems"; over time, the teething problems will go away.

It is difficult for any African to dismiss such well-meaning hopes. But there is a serious problem: when one looks around the world, on every continent, one cannot find that such thoughts and hopes are supported or justified by the experiences and behavior of other peoples. There are, and there have been, many countries in our modern world similar to Sub-Saharan African countries, each in the sense of comprising many nations. More and more clearly in our times, the observable fact is that many nations that are parts of multi-nation countries don't want to be there, but are fretful about being there – and desire to be free to control their own affairs and their future. A brief survey of the countries being thus buffeted or even broken up on other continents other than Africa will be helpful at this point.

Global Summary

First, let us take the continent of Europe. Spain is one of the oldest of the modern nation states of Europe, that is, one nation which early evolved into one single state when the other nations of

Europe (the English, French, Germans, Italians, etc.) were still fragmented under various small kingdoms, dukedoms, etc. When the Spaniards became unified in the 15th century through the marriage of the rulers of the Spanish kingdoms of Aragon and Castile and the subsequent inclusion of the other smaller Spanish kingdoms, the modern nation state of Spain was born. However, Spain also came to include the territory of two smaller, non-Spanish, peoples — the Basques and the Catalans. The Basques are an ancient people, with their own language and national culture, living in the Pyrenees Mountains of northern Spain. The inclusion of the Basques in Spain has constituted a running sore on Spain's side in modern times. A Basque liberation movement arose in the late 19th century, and in 1959, ETA, a terrorist organization dedicated to the use of violent force to achieve Basque independence, was founded. ETA is one of the most sophisticated terrorist organizations in the world today. There are many other Basques, rich and influential people, who also want a separate Basque country, though they are opposed to the ETA's violent methods. The Basques nearly got their separate country in the course of the late 1930's, and today have considerable autonomy in Spain. But the goal of most Basque nationalists is not regional autonomy within Spain but a separate country of their own, and very few observers in the world seriously doubt today that they will indeed get it someday.

The homeland of the Catalans occupies the northeastern Spanish province known as Catalonia. The Catalans have not been as militant as the Basques, but they too have increasingly become emphatic in their demands for separation from Spain. In the 1930's and 1940's, the authoritarian governments of Spain clamped down on the Catalans and, among other things, prohibited the use of their native Catalan language. But before the end of the century, the Catalans had fully revived their language. As a result of their agitations for separation, Spain has granted them some sort of provincial autonomy, but by about 2009, most Catalans had become persuaded that what their little nation needs is full independence in a separate country of their own. In December 2009, without asking for the permission of the government of Spain (in fact, in defiance of some earlier court orders), the Catalans organized a referendum of their own on the issue of full independence, and nearly 95% of those who voted supported the proposition that Catalonia should separate from Spain. Though this referendum was not authorized by the government of Spain, it nevertheless has strongly affirmed the Catalan quest for a separate small country of Catalonia in the world.

The small state of Belgium, created in the early nineteenth century by the powers of Europe (the victors in the Napoleonic wars), comprises two peoples: the French-speaking Walloons of Wallonia, and the Flemish-speaking Flemings of Flanders. The political history of the country has always featured rivalry and conflicts between its two peoples. Constitutional arrangements granting local autonomy to each of the two peoples have not eased out the conflicts. Following a troubled national election in 2007, the country moved much closer to breaking up into two separate countries.

The same kind of troubled political life was characteristic of Czechoslovakia, a country which came into existence in 1918 and comprised two peoples – the Czechs and Slovaks. In the early 1990's, the Czechs and the Slovaks had the good sense and political courage to agree to separate peacefully into two countries (the Czech Republic and Slovakia).

In 1982 this author traveled fairly extensively in the Soviet Union, as a member of a Nigerian official delegation, at the invitation of the Soviet authorities. It was, in spite of the enormous coercive power of the Kremlin, quite easy to see the tension generated by the fact that the Soviet Union consisted of many nationalities. During two days in Uzbekistan, the splendid homeland of the Uzbek nation, our Soviet guides generously took us on tours of the Uzbek's main city of Tashkent and their old city of Samarkand. Even under the eyes of the Soviet officials who were guiding us, the Uzbeks did not seem to fear to exhibit hostile attitudes towards Russians. I came away convinced that, if the center of Soviet power ever weakened or stumbled, the many nationalities of the Soviet Union would separate into so many countries. I said as much to some foreign friends – American historians – who were visiting Africa and who stopped to visit me in Lagos a few days after my return from the Soviet Union. And that is what came to happen less than ten years later. To date, some twelve separate independent countries have been carved out of the

Soviet Union – Russia, Ukraine, Belarus, Moldavia, Georgia, Armenia, Azerbaijan, Kazakhstan, Uzbekistan, Turkmenistan, Kyrgyzstan, and Tajikistan. One small nation that did not manage to break free when these others did, the Chechens of Chechnya, have been fighting Russia since then in their determination to have their own independent Chechnya.

One of the new countries that recently separated from the Soviet Union – the small country of Georgia – happened to contain two small provinces, namely Abkhazia and South Ossetia, that were ethnically different from the majority ethnic Georgians. Under the Soviet system, these small peoples had been administered as parts of Georgia. As soon as Georgia became a separate country, the two immediately began to agitate for separation from Georgia, and for separate small countries of their own. In 2009, the two became separate countries, with the help of Russia.

Yugoslavia is undoubtedly Europe's best known example. The Austro-Hungarian Empire collapsed as a result of the First World War (1914-18), and the victors (Britain and France) carved from its former Balkan provinces a new country which came to be known as Yugoslavia. Yugoslavia consisted of many nationalities—Serbs, Croats, Slovenes, Macedonians, Albanians, etc., with the Serbs being the largest nationality. Yugoslavia never enjoyed political stability. In the years after the Second World War, the truth about the political troubles of the country was largely hidden from the rest of the world by the authoritarian leadership of its communist president, Joseph Tito. Even under Tito, however, ethnic-based agitations were a strong factor in Yugoslav politics. Once, in the academic year 1959-60, during one of this author's travels in Europe as a college student representing Nigeria in international students' conferences, Croatian students studying in Sweden invaded and seized the Yugoslav embassy in Stockholm, demanding that Croatia be carved, as an independent country, out of Yugoslavia. As soon as Tito died in 1980, Yugoslavia began to disintegrate. In 1991, following prolonged and unproductive negotiations, the Croats and the Slovenes declared the independence of the two separate countries of Croatia and Slovenia. The majority Serbs immediately mobilized in order to suppress the two, and some of the worst inter-ethnic atrocities in modern history ensued. The United Nations had to intervene to broker the dismantling of Yugoslavia. In the end, seven countries have been carved out of that country – Serbia, Slovenia, Croatia, Macedonia, Bosnia-Herzegovina, Montenegro, and Kosovo. Most of these countries are small. The smallest, Macedonia, had a population of only 684,000 at the time of its separation.

Britain (otherwise known as the United Kingdom) entered the 20th century as a union of four nations – the English of England, the Scotts of Scotland, the Irish of Ireland, and the Welsh of Wales. Since the beginning of the 20th century, as a result of separatist agitations by the Irish, Scotts and Welsh, Britain has been going through a process of breaking up. Strong Irish agitation resulted in 1921 in the creation of the separate and independent Republic of Ireland. A small Irish province (Northern Ireland) could not go with the rest of Ireland at that time, and that province has been the scene of violent agitations and terror campaigns since then. In the 1920's, both the Scotts and the Welsh founded nationalist movements and political parties to lead their separate struggles for separation. In fact, some Welsh nationalists employed some violence for some time. The result of the agitations is that Britain has gradually yielded ground, allowing the Scotts and the Welsh to have more and more autonomy to manage their own affairs. By the end of the century, each had a homeland government. Both have made it clear, however, that a homeland government inside Britain is short of their ultimate goal – and that what they want is complete independence. With the Scottish National Party gaining more and more strength in the elections to the Scottish home government since 2007, Scotland has gradually moved closer to separation and independence. In 2010, the Scottish National Party won an overall majority in the Scottish National Assembly and announced plans to hold a referendum in a few years on Scottish independence. In 1955, the Welsh proclaimed their city of Cardiff as the capital city of their future separate country, and soon after, they set up a commission to develop their Welsh language as the official language of their future country. Neither the government of Britain nor the English as the dominant nation in Britain has ever employed coercion to stop these Scottish and Welsh developments, even though those developments have progressively pointed in the direction of the breaking up of Britain.

Then, let us move to Asia. In the late nineteenth century, British imperialist agents created India as a British protectorate. Even as the peoples of India worked together for independence from Britain in the 1940s, it was obvious that they would not be able to stay long together as one country. At independence, the country broke into two, the mostly Muslim peoples of the far northern provinces becoming Pakistan. Later, Pakistan too split up—into Pakistan and Bangladesh. Even after that, agitations for secession from India have continued among some of its peoples, like the Kashmiri, the Sikhs and others.

In the seas south of India, the small island state of Sri Lanka (formerly known as Ceylon) is home to two peoples—the Tamils and the Sinhalese. Like India, Sri Lanka used to be part of the British Empire. Since independence, the two peoples of this small island have fought each other relentlessly. The Tamils want a separate small country of their own, and they have continued to fight the Sinhalese in a vicious and bloody civil war for that purpose. .

Indonesia has, since independence, been confronted by many separatist agitations. In this huge country of 210 million people, with some 300 old ethnic peoples and kingdoms, ethnic and religious agitations and conflicts are common. Of the unambiguous demands for separation, the most serious have been based in East Timor, Aceh, Riau, Ambom, Irian Jaya, and Madura. After 25 years of war against the powerful Indonesian military machine, East Timor achieved separation in 2002 and became an independent country in the world, with the name Democratic Republic of Timor-Leste. War has also been fierce in Aceh. In fact Aceh looked close to succeeding in obtaining its separation – until the great tsunami of 2004 came and inflicted mammoth destruction on the territory and its people.

In general, Indonesia's response to separatist agitations used to be to declare war and plunge into terrible fighting in order to suppress separatists. But the country seems to have become tired of these tough and expensive wars and, in recent times, it has been taking steps to modify its approach to the challenges of separatism. Indonesia is now engaged in trying a program of giving local autonomy to its provinces – the goal being to increase local control over government and over economic resources.

China, the world's largest country in population, is made up of many nations. Of these, the Han Chinese make up 93% of the population of the country, and about 55 other nations share the remaining 7%. More and more in these times, China's troubles from national separatist movements have been on the increase. The two leading nations actively demanding separation from China are the Tibetans of Tibet, and the Uighurs of Xinjiang. But there are other potential candidates – like Manchuria and Lower Mongolia..

Finally, we move to the Americas. The United States, though one of the largest countries in the world, does not have separatist nationalist problems because its immigrant national groups from various parts of the world are scattered and intermixed in the country, and none is settled uniquely in an area that it can call its homeland. Canada, though a country of immigrants too, is different. The French and the British established their separate colonies here in the 17th century. In the Seven Years War, (which Americans call the French and Indian Wars) 1756-63, the British and French fought each other in North America. British victory resulted in the cession to Britain of, among others, the French colonies in Canada. British-owned Canada thus came to consist of two different nationalities (the English and the French), each living in its own area of the country. Later, when Canada became an independent country, it began to experience difficulties from its being a multi-nation country. In the course of the 20th century, the French province, known as Quebec, began agitations for separation in order to form a separate country of its own. Some French Canadian nationalists even employed terrorist means for some time in their attempt to achieve separation. Today, such terrorism has been given up, but the struggle for separation has continued – and it has achieved important political and constitutional concessions.

Motivating Factors

In short, then, where two or more neighboring nationalities, each living in its own homeland, become amalgamated or unified together to form one country with one government, the dynamics of their political interactions in their common country have tended, especially in more modern times, to generate separatist nationalist agitations and inevitably some measure of instability.

A lot of well-meaning people in the world hold the view that the growth of education, or the growth of economic prosperity, will cure divisions and conflicts in multi-nation countries, and gradually eliminate desires by different nations in such countries for autonomy and separation. Certainly, it seems logical in theory, to assume that as the level of literacy and education rises higher and higher in nations living together in a country, or as the level of economic prosperity grows, they should be better and better able to live harmoniously together in that country and increasingly accept common membership of their country. However, experience in our world has not shown that to be the case in reality. On the contrary, what experience shows is that the more educated people in such countries have become, the more each component nation has tended to become aware of its distinctive character as a nation, to become proud of its cultural and historical heritage, to appreciate the differences between itself and the other nations in its country, and to desire to be in control of its own affairs and its own future. Also, the theoretical expectation that growing economic prosperity will make ethnic nationalist agitations for separation and autonomy in a multi-nation country go away is not supported by most observable facts. Throughout the 20th century, the United Kingdom (Britain) has been one of the richest, strongest, and proudest countries in our world, but that has not stopped the Irish, Scots and Welsh from agitating for separation from Britain in order to have independent countries of their own. Spain is a very rich country, and the ethnic Basques and ethnic Catalans are among the richest in Spain – and that has not prevented Basque and Catalan demands for separate countries of their own. The Chinese economy is the fastest growing economy in the world at the beginning of the 21st century, and that does not seem to be any consideration at all with the peoples that seek separation from China. The Indian economy is also one of the fastest growing economies in the Third World – and that is not stopping Kashmiri separatism or Sikh demands for autonomy.

With regards to economic factors in the motivation of national separatist desires, the picture that emerges appears to be as follows: Prosperity or fast economic growth in a multi-nation country does not necessarily prevent national separatist demands and agitations in that country. But poverty or slow economic growth in a multi-nation country does strongly tend to become a good motivation and argument for national separatist movements. The belief is almost impossible to counter that when a nation is free and independent to manage its own affairs, it has a better chance of making political, economic, social and cultural progress – a better chance than when it is one of many nations in one country. It is no use for opponents of national separation to argue that the progress and prosperity may not necessarily follow the separation. The proponents of national separation know that the initial years after national separation may be rough (like the experiences of the former Soviet republics in their first years after separation from the Soviet Union), but it is impossible to question the optimism of the longer prospect. History does seem to justify that optimism unambiguously – especially the history of the European nations that evolved into nation states at the beginning of modern times (Spain, Portugal, England, France, etc.), of Germany and Italy that later evolved into nation states, and of Japan in our times, and others. In every case, when the people concerned became a unified, separate and autonomous country, that development generated a national energy that produced a surge of cultural, economic, political, and social growth.

Here are a few notable examples of such growth. The modern history of Europe began in about the 15th century when each of the European ethnic nations began to crystallize and become a country on its own (the countries that we know today) – first the Portuguese in Portugal and the Spaniards in Spain, then the English in England, the French in France, the Dutch in Holland, the Swedes in Sweden, the Russians in Russia, etc. The immediate effect of all these transformations was that each ethnic nation in its own new country became strong quickly, able to utilize available and emerging technologies to advance its wealth and power. For instance, employing advancing ideas and new technologies in ship-building and long-distance sea navigation, some of these new countries sponsored explorations of the coasts of Africa, Asia and the Americas, launched huge trading enterprises to the newly discovered lands, established colonies in the Americas, and transported Africans across the Atlantic to provide cheap labor to their American colonies. With all these, each of the new countries of Europe became very rich and

221

powerful, and Europe shot far ahead of the rest of the world in wealth, technology, and power.

Of the nationalities of Europe however, some, notably Italy and Germany, remained divided into many small kingdoms, some of which were ruled by powerful neighbors. However, a strong Italian nationalist movement arose, and in the year1861 it achieved the unification and freedom of all Italians to form one single country of their own – and thus the entry of Italy into the modern world as one autonomous independent country. The Germans followed suit, and in 1871 unified their country and called it the German Reich (that is the German Empire). Both Italy and the German Reich quickly joined the ranks of the rich and powerful countries of Europe. In fact, by investing heavily in education (especially technological education), Germany quickly became the richest and most powerful country in Europe. In the last years of the 19th century, many of the European countries further expanded their wealth and power in the world by carving out empires for themselves in Africa and Asia.

While the European countries were thus busy carving up Africa and Asia in the late 19th century, one ethnic nation in eastern Asia, the Japanese, decided to emulate them. First, the Japanese forcibly ended the division of their country into small semi-autonomous domains, and unified their country. Then they created a national constitution, and then they began to invest heavily in education and technology. Exactly what had happened in the case of the European nations then happened in the case of Japan. Japan quickly became a strong country economically and technologically. By as early as 1905, Japan commanded the strength to defeat a major European country, Russia, in a war.

A nation living in its own ethnically homogenous country, where it does not have to contend or argue with any other nation or culture, can command a big advantage to chart its own path and to grow and prosper – if it uses its advantages constructively and sensibly and the objective conditions are reasonably favorable. In contrast, endless contentions in a multi-nation country among different component nations, each with its own culturally determined group behavior, ambitions, expectations, goals, etc., unquestionably can command the power to slow down socio-economic growth in that country and generate confused and blurred visions of the road ahead, even if the objective conditions (such as natural resources) are favorable.

The fundamental and basic power behind the expanding movements of national separatism in the multi-nation countries in our world, then, is the elemental force of nationalism - the strong feeling of group self-love and group pride in a nation whether large or small, an ethno-linguistic group identified by its own culture and its homeland territory in which it lived in its history and in which it still lives, recognizing and accepting itself as one group. For such a nation, large or small, having to live with other nations in a country, sharing the sovereignty of one country with other similar nations, or even having to accept any sovereignty above its own national sovereignty, has never been easy in human history. Actions of the most powerful nations in our times have ignored that vital fact and produced many countries in which many weak nations were combined together with one another or subsumed under more powerful nations - such as the creation of Belgium in 1831 by the Concert of Europe, the creation of Yugoslavia, Czechoslovakia, etc., by the victors of the First World War, the inclusion of many small nations with Russia in the Soviet Union, and the creation of many multi-nation countries in Asia and Africa by late 19th century European imperialism. In the course of the 20th century, nations included in these arrangements, and even nations so involved in earlier periods of history (like the Irish, Scotts and Welsh in Britain, the Basques and Catalans in Spain, the French Canadians in Canada, etc.) have increasingly sought to free themselves in order to establish their own autonomous and separate countries.

As earlier pointed out, the general growth of literacy and education in the modern world has served, and is serving, as a dynamic stimulus to the growth of the phenomenon of nationalism and demand for national autonomy in nations that are parts of larger countries. Education does not only enhance national group knowledge and pride, it also tends to accentuate the desire for economic, social and political development, progress and modernization. It accentuates the demand for increasing levels of subsistence goods (the provision of basic material needs) as well as increasing levels of security-of-persons provisions (guarantees of human rights, open political system, equality before the law, protection by the law, equality of access to opportunities, etc.). Education tends to increase intolerance and resentment about lack of development, or slow development, in the provision of these needs.

Especially in the less developed regions of the world, a country's combination of diverse nations has tended to contribute significantly to its slow socio-economic development. As Gerald Scully points out in a report titled "Multiculturalism and Economic Growth" (Policy Report number 196 for the National Center for Policy Analysis, Dallas, Texas), [1]

"Culture standardizes relationships by allowing people to make reasonably confident assumptions about the reactions of those with whom they interact. - - Even if different groups live together peacefully (in the same country), the lack of a common language and common norms reduces cooperation and increases the costs of transacting."

And the consequence of that is usually the enhancement of inefficiency and waste in the economic system – resulting in slow development and in poverty.

Stephen Lampe in *Building Future Societies* argues that development finds a fertile ground in an atmosphere of homogeneity:

"Moreover, when it is said that development should take into account the culture and conditions of a people, it is really like saying that development must respect the Law of Homogeneity. The more closely development projects reflect the circumstances of a people, the more the projects can be said to have conformed to the Law of Homogeneity; and the more sustainable such projects are likely to be". [2]

Also, the growth of every culture has its own trajectory – the direction in which its customs, laws, economy, political traditions, and its system of rewards, are growing. When the diverse cultures of diverse nations cohabit and compete in a country, especially an underdeveloped country, confusion and inefficiency are usually the consequences. Furthermore, the common experience is that a dominant nation in a multi-nation country (whether the dominance is numerical or political), is prone to structure economic and political opportunities to the benefit of

224

itself and its members – with the usual result of conflict, economic inefficiency, and increased chances of poverty for the country. A report by Japan's Institute of Comprehensive Studies asserts that without a strong national spirit and confident identity, a country cannot efficiently take advantage of development assets in the world and rise to high levels of development.

In the less developed multi-nation countries of the world, one of the strongest reasons advanced by national separatist movements is that the multiplicity of nations in their country, the ethnic conflicts, and the distortions caused by the unfair behavior of dominant groups, make it impossible to achieve an acceptable pace of economic growth. Two Japanese economists who have studied the Japanese development model in the years after the Second World War, Yujiro Hayami and Yoshihisa Godo, assert that the development efforts of a culturally homogenous country are likely to be more productive than the development efforts of a culturally heterogeneous country – that the more development efforts, assimilation of technology, and transformation of institutions, are correlated to the culture of a people, the greater are the chances of success.[3]

Furthermore, experience in most countries indicates that a country, especially an underdeveloped country, comprising diverse nations, is less likely to adopt institutions of freedom, or to run them sincerely and with integrity. In such a country, the endless jostling of the component nations for advantage, and the maneuvers of the dominant nation to sustain its dominance and allocate the most advantages to its members – all these usually tend to result in distortions of the political process, the manipulation of elections, the falsification of vital records, the appointment of poorly trained and ill-equipped ethnic national favorites to vital public jobs (even when more educated and better trained citizens may be available), the padding of important institutions (like the courts, the police, the military, the regulatory agencies, etc.) with persons dedicated to ethnic-sectional missions, discrimination in the allocation of public appointments and economic opportunities, and so on. All these detract from human freedom and dignity. In the report earlier referred to, Gerald Scully opines that "a lack of personal freedom is correlated with the degree of cultural heterogeneity in many non-Western societies".

225

National heterogeneity in a country also fosters inefficiency in the political and economic systems in some other ways. There is no question that economic freedom and rule of law are fundamental requirements for the achievement of high levels of economic growth in the modern world. According again to Scully, scholars are coming more and more to the recognition

"that the key to economic transformation of the Third World is to move toward freer institutions, and that cultural heterogeneity is the major barrier to such transformation".[4]

According to statements made by a veteran Nigerian journalist, Oluremi Oyeyemi, in an interview with a newspaper in New York in March 2010, the above are in line with conclusions that are derivable from some published United Nations data on human development. The data, Oyeyemi said, show that the top 25 countries with the highest indices of human development in the world, are all characterized by significant homogeneity in ethnicity, language and religion – or, at least, two of these.[5]

For all these many reasons or combinations of them, and because more and more citizens of all countries are becoming more knowledgeable about these facts, countries comprising diverse ethnic nations are in trouble in the world. On all continents, the nations that are parts of such countries are agitating, challenging in some way the continued existence of the countries to which they belong, or demanding some sort of autonomy or even the right to establish independent countries of their own. The poorer the quality of the governance of a multi-nation country, the greater the chances of ethnic national conflicts in it – and the greater the chances of secessions from it and even of its total break up. In the light of these worldwide realities, hopes that, without some serious change in approaches to the affairs of Black African countries, the turbulence in them will somehow go away, are mostly pipe dreams.

CHAPTER EIGHT

The Coming Challenges

In the light of the realities described in the previous chapters – and in the light of the growing trends in the contemporary political history of our world – those well-meaning Africans who think or hope that the turmoil in Africa, or in any one African country, will somehow go away on its own, need to think again. If anything, much of the turmoil in many Sub-Saharan African countries is more likely to grow more clearly defined and more pointedly channeled along lines of ethnic national autonomies and separations and ethnic boundary adjustment demands, until internal nationalist movements become so many and so powerful as to constitute crushing burdens on many countries of Sub-Saharan Africa. That appears to be the line of Sub-Saharan Africa's coming revolutions. As has happened in recent times in Tunisia and Egypt, the popular uprisings in these revolutions in tropical African countries will most probably be sparked off by mass rejection of repression, corruption and grinding poverty – and then very probably develop more deeply fundamental political goals.

The trend towards such an end is quite easily observable already among our nationalities in Black Africa. Certainly, each of our nationalities was one nationality long before the 20th century, but that is not to say that every one was conscious of itself as one nationality, or experienced definite national consciousness. For most, national consciousness began to grow as a result of various influences from roughly the late 19th century. Christian missionary influence, especially the translation and presentation of Christian literature and Christian teachings in the languages of different nationalities, served as a powerful influence on the generation of national consciousness. Then the growth of Western education powerfully reinforced the development, especially by stimulating the studies of national histories and cultures as well as the rise of national cultural movements. And then political experiences in the inter-relationships of nationalities with one another in the new countries created by European colonialism greatly stimulated the development. By the end of the 20th century, national consciousness had become a clear reality in the life of most of tropical African nationalities large or small. With the further expansion of education, and with increasing contacts with the wider world, national consciousness has grown stronger and stronger among all our nationalities. By the opening of the 21st century, Sub-Saharan Africa had reached the point where national consciousness, national pride, national desires of many nationalities to protect their unique interests, and even to control their own lives and their own futures in the world, are powerful factors. Not only have these developments become factors demanding attention in each of our countries, they have also begun to feed on the ethnic nationalist movements in the wider world. Many tropical African nationalist movements are already notable players in international organizations dedicated to the defense of the interests of indigenous nations.

In these trends, much of the character of tropical Africa's political future has already taken root. It hardly needs to be said that at least some of today's boundaries of countries in Sub-Saharan Africa cannot stand for ever or even for long. What sort of settlement or arrangement can, for instance, make the Somali people permanently accept their fragmentation across so many borders – with most in Somalia and the rest in all the countries that are Somalia's neighbors? Are there any other people in our world who are known to live happily with such a situation? It seems fairly certain that if Somalia survives its current travails and re-establishes itself as a unified and stable country, it will still have no other option, in terms of its borders, than to keep seeking solutions. What the nature of its search for solutions will be will, of course, depend on factors that we cannot say today, but it must not be forgotten that intensive and long-standing border disputes of this nature are prone to causing wars in the world.

Other African peoples may not have as acute a border problem as the Somali people do, but for very many, the problem is real enough. Trends observable in the behavior of nationalities in our world, as well as on our sub-continent, point to the probability that as the peoples of Black Africa become more educated, more exposed, and more informed as peoples, our nationalist demands and expectations are certain to increase. Even after more than a century of our present national boundaries, many still have not much of a hold on the lives of our peoples. In many parts of our sub-continent, people move from both sides of many boundaries as if the boundaries do not exist. In some cases, some of such movements seem to be becoming formalized. For instance, trade between the Yoruba on both sides of the Nigeria-Benin border has grown steadily since independence, and so too have cultural interactions. More and more frequently, important Yoruba persons in the two countries are establishing contacts, exchanging visits, and inviting one another to important events. And, as would be remembered, between the Bakongo people of the different countries of west-central Africa, such interrelations have been even much stronger – and have generated various political developments across national borders. All these raise a very important question: How will future generations of very many African peoples relate to their being sliced and spliced among neighboring countries? And what does this mean for the future of Sub-Saharan Africa?

The other kind of probability promises to be even more destabilizing and much more challenging. As African countries are now composed (each made up of many nationalities), and given the kinds of leadership these countries have almost universally had, the divisive and conflict-prone patterns of politics that they have generated, and the poor quality of life they offer to their citizens, the probability is very strong indeed that, in not too distant a future, many of them would begin to be confronted by demands for separation or secession by some of their component nationalities. That means that, not very far in the future, Sub-Saharan Africa could face serious pressures for a redrawing of its political map. In a world in which increasing numbers of small peoples on other continents are rising to demand separate independent countries of their own (many of them successfully), Sub-Saharan Africa cannot realistically expect all its own peoples to continue to endure the conflicts, the hostilities, the undemocratic politics, the corruption, the repression, and the consequent slow development and poverty, in the countries to which they now belong, without many of them desiring to seek a chance to try something different in smaller and ethnically more compact countries of their own. The potential for that is very strong, and the instances of that type of desire are already quite many. And the universal experience is that once political separatist tempers are born in an ethnic nation, they never seem to go away. In Nigeria, Angola, Congo Democratic Republic, Chad, Central African Republic, etc., not merely have banners of secession once raised continued to flutter in the horizon, new and potentially more assertive ones are raising their heads. In countries like Uganda, Mali, Senegal, and others, secessionist nationalist movements are growing. The success of the peoples of Southern Sudan to wrest their separation from the larger country of Sudan could become one of the most infectious developments in Sub-Saharan Africa's post-independence history.

These developments will, of course, be different from country to country. Probably, some countries that are small in territory and population, each containing many small nationalities, may be spared the more powerful and more assertive secessionist agitations and movements – because the sheer smallness of each of their many component ethnic nations may discourage their ethnic nationalist elites from pursuing dreams of separate statehood. But, even in such cases, no one can really tell what to expect. Even the smallest nationality can rise and develop great ambitions about itself and its future.[1] The elites of the Baganda of Uganda and the Ijaw of Nigeria do not seem to be bothered that separate countries of theirs would be very small; and the Baganda do not seem to be bothered that, if they separate from Uganda, their Buganda would be a small land-locked country. As for our larger ethnic nations, the rise of such ambitions is much more probable. Judging from the tempers that have already been generated among many of these larger nationalities, and the confidence that naturally comes from their having sizeable populations, the countries that now contain them (notably Nigeria) seem very likely to be heading towards a spate of separatist and secessionist politics in the near future.

Growth of Nationalist Upsurge.

Growing nationalist demands, then, are becoming manifest factors in the political life of Sub-Saharan Africa at this beginning of the 21st century. More and more Africans, and more and more of African voices of dissent, are insisting that what was achieved at independence in every Black African country was an incomplete independence - a half-way liberation. More and more people are speaking up to assert that their peoples are forced to live under some illegitimate sovereignty, since they have never consented to their being included in the countries wherein the colonial authorities had included them, or ever contributed to any discussion of the structure of their countries. That point is eloquently made in an article published in some Nigerian newspapers in March 2010, written by Alfred Ilenre, Secretary-General of the Ethnic Minority and Indigenous Rights Organization of Africa (EMIROAF), and titled "Bane of Uncompleted Decolonization". Among other things, Ilenre wrote as follows:

"Throughout the 30 years of debate, advocacy and lobby for the adoption of the Draft Declaration on the Rights of Indigenous Peoples at the floor of the UN in Geneva and New York, it became apparent that what is common to the whole world is diversity and not unity made possible by conquest or assimilation. Nigeria is trapped in the web of the malady of an uncompleted decolonization process.".[2]

A statement issued on African Liberation Day, May 25, 2010, by the Nigerian Yoruba organization, Action Committee for Restoration of Odua Sovereignty (ACROS) describes the turmoil that has been going on in Sub-Saharan African countries since independence as "a war of all against all or one of a few against the others". It contends that "Hegemony of one over others or the struggle of others against that hegemony has concentrated the attention of most African states". And then it explains:

The reason is very clear – these various peoples and nationalities that were forced together by the European colonialists were neither consulted about the political contraptions that were being put in place by their alien overlords nor were their desire for the fake unions ever consolidated by the neo-colonial rulers that took over at independence. The result has been ruinous for virtually everybody. Models of development that sprang up in parts of Africa e.g. Western Nigeria – 1952–1966 - were quickly trashed by the contradictions of this unresolved NATIONAL QUESTION. Murderous struggles for power at the center by hegemonic power blocks took the place of Good Governance, self-reliance and development.[3]

Successful peace-making and peace-keeping in African countries by African and international agencies may suppress the current types of turmoil, but it cannot remove the roots of dynamic instability – and that means that other types of turmoil will surface sooner or later. Kenya and Zimbabwe recently brought massive violence and blood-letting to an end with "power-sharing" agreements among leading political groups, but no serious observer believes that that is the end of their political troubles and conflicts. In Angola, Rwanda, Sierra Leone, Ivory Coast, etc., civil wars were recently terminated, but unless those countries use the fragile peace arrangements thus negotiated for seriously rational political restructuring, the conditions that produced the civil wars will persist – and generate some other types of troubles sooner or later.

In Nigeria, the voices of the future are already being heard. For years, as would be remembered, the peoples of the Niger Delta have been in revolt against Nigeria. The Delta revolt escalated to a very high level of sophistication with the entry of the renowned Nigerian writer and television producer, Ken Saro-Wiwa, into it in the 1990s. Son of a chief of the Ogoni people, one of the peoples of the Delta, Saro-Wiwa became leader of an Ogoni movement (Movement for the Survival of the Ogoni People, MOSOP), dedicated to the protection of the homeland of the Ogoni against environmental degradations caused by oil mining operations.- a struggle which ultimately led him into collision with the Nigerian federal government. To expand the struggle of the Delta peoples into a wider struggle for the rights of minority peoples of all of Black Africa, he founded a body with the name Ethnic Minorities and Indigenous Rights Organization of Africa (EMIROAF). In 1995, the Nigerian military government moved forcefully against him, had him and some of his people arrested, tried by a military tribunal and, against protests from the international community, had him executed.

His execution provoked widespread condemnations of Nigeria in the world, and a three-year suspension of Nigeria from the Commonwealth of Nations. At home, it stiffened the Delta resistance. The revolt became decidedly secessionist, and its strategy and weaponry more and more advanced. In 2007, persons claiming to speak on behalf of the culturally related peoples of the

232

Delta (the peoples of the six Nigerian states of Rivers, Cross Rivers, Bayelsa, Delta, Akwa-Ibom, and Edo) addressed a letter to the Secretary-general of the United Nations Organization, claiming to convey the joint desire of these peoples to break off from Nigeria and form a separate, autonomous, independent country. In that letter, the writers repeatedly referred to the boundary around Nigeria as an "evil line". The letter is a forceful indication of what many educated citizens of the nations of the Delta region of Nigeria think. It is very significant that the letter asserted the important principle which is becoming a banner of the counter-response all over Black Africa – namely, negotiation by the peoples in a country of their relationships within the country, and adherence of all to the terms of such an agreement. The letter points out that Nigeria is a country bound forcibly together, without any agreement among its many peoples. It also assures the world that a new Delta country would be underpinned by a solemn agreement among its peoples, and that its peoples would be peacefully and productively bound together by common respect for their mutual agreement. In Uganda, the proponents of a Greater North country out of Uganda are speaking exactly the same kind of language.

The Igbo attempt to secede from Nigeria and form a separate country named Biafra failed in the civil war of 1967-70, but strong Biafran sentiments have remained, and have resurfaced strongly since the late 1990s. Tapping into that, a movement of educated Igbo youths, with the defiant name of Movement for the Actualization of the Sovereign State of Biafra (MASSOB), emerged about the year 2000, and has grown phenomenally in confidence and influence among the Igbo people since then. In June or July 2009, MASSOB defiantly published the information that it had created a new official passport for the citizens of Biafra to travel with in the world. Many months earlier, Nigeria woke up one morning to the news that MASSOB had planted Biafran flags along hundreds of miles of public roads in the Igbo homeland in Eastern Nigeria. In more recent years, other Igbo youths have founded another movement, Biafra Zionist Movement, which is prone to more radical nationalist agitations and protests. Many Igbo intellectuals and professionals resident abroad have also created a Biafra Foundation. An introductory posting on the international site of the Biafra Foundation states as follows:[4]

"Nothing could be more preposterous, more delusional than for anyone, any state, any military power, or even superpower to believe that it has the recipe, the template for keeping together willy-nilly large groups of people that have major cultural, philosophical, social, linguistic, and other differences. This becomes even more poignant when there is abundant evidence of long standing hatred, paranoia, serious dislike, and deep seated suspicion of one group towards the other whether these reactions are mutual or visible only on one side".

Among the Yoruba people of southwestern Nigeria (another of Nigeria's three largest nations), the number is rapidly growing of Yoruba citizens who think that the Yoruba nation needs to opt for an independent country of its own – that remaining as part of Nigeria hurts the interests, the ethical strength, the culture, and the integrity of the Yoruba nation. Yoruba youths have created tens of "self-determination groups", all dedicated to the goal of self-determination or independence for their Yoruba nation. A Yoruba Diaspora intellectual body with the name Oodua Foundation, founded in 2006, has become a major force in the Yoruba independence movement. I one of its many writings and manifestoes, Oodua Foundation writes as follows: [5]

"We need our own nation-state or country. We are a nation – and a large and prestigious nation among the nations of the earth, a nation with a great history and proud heritage. - - - European imperialists came at a time of our technological weakness, despised and ignored our distinct nationhood, and consigned us wherever they chose. Now, times have changed - - -."

Even many Yoruba intellectuals who may not have come to that kind of definite position have been speaking out increasingly in ways that distance the Yoruba as a people from the moral squalor characteristic of Nigeria's public life, and demanding a radical restructuring of Nigeria in order to enable every Nigerian people to assert its own culture and ethics in the management of its own affairs. Characteristic of these statements are the following sentiments expressed by a Yoruba professor of philosophy, Dr. Segun Gbadegesin of Howard University, Washington DC:[6]

"Faithful to the vision of the founding fathers and mothers of the Yoruba nation who dream of a prosperous community of men and women, and worked hard to actualize their dreams at various stages in the life of the nation, we envision a nation that sustains the principles of welfare liberalism, the rule of law and its democratic values, a nation which memorializes its vibrant culture and promotes its values in the homeland and the Diaspora, a prosperous economy that exploits its natural resources through the instrumentality of its human resources that have been fully developed in the crucible of an educational system that caters for all children and adults.

The simple answer to the question "what do the Yoruba want" is this: The Yoruba want a Nigerian State which respects its multi-national character and gives adequate recognition to the inviolability of its federating nationalities, no matter how small or big, a Nigerian State that promotes equal justice for all its citizens and makes a sacred commitment to the secularity of its character. - - - The Yoruba have always wanted a Nigeria that practices and is committed to the principles of true federalism"

Another eminent Yoruba leader, Dr. Lateef Adegbite, Secretary-general of the Nigerian Supreme Council of Islamic Affairs, said:

"The Yoruba have always demanded the highest standards of governance from their rulers since the ancient times, and have also insisted that justice, due process, equity, non-discrimination, integrity, transparency, loyalty and humaneness be adhered to by those who run the government".[7]

A Yoruba Position Paper to Obasanjo's National Political Reform Conference in 2005, included the following:

"The Yoruba - - - - have consistently sought a democratic process built around such fundamental values as follows: sovereignty of the people, respect for human rights, equal political, economic and social

opportunities for all citizens; equity, justice, and fair play as ethical basis of politics and national unity; transparency and accountability as the basis of governance".

Dr. Wale Adebanwi, a professor of Political Science, wrote:

"The fundaments of Yoruba politics remain: A liberal, democratic state governed by competent, cerebral leaders, founded on social justice, equity, equality, enlightenment, and freedom".[8]

Typically, the authorities of Nigeria respond to all the above manifestations of dissent and resentment with confrontation and coercion. The earliest signs of resentment in the Niger Delta were dealt with in this way in the years soon after independence. In the 1990's, the coercion reached a peak with the executions of significant citizens of the Delta. And the result is that the Delta situation has escalated to a stubborn civil war. In order to crush MASSOB, federal law enforcement authorities have arrested and detained MASSOB leaders time and again; even the Nigerian army has been sent against some Igbo villages. Members of the Biafran Zionist Movement have experienced arrests and detentions. In 2005, leaders of Odua Peoples Congress (OPC, one of the largest Yoruba self-determination groups) were arrested and charged with treason – although the case quickly fizzled out, obviously for lack of substance. In 2008, a group of young Yoruba intellectuals held an open seminar, organized by a Yoruba self-determination group named Atayese, at the Obafemi Awolowo University in Western Nigeria on the future of the Yoruba nation. Days later, the Nigerian secret service agency, the SSS, invited the organizers of the seminar for questioning – on allegations that they were advocating that the Yoruba nation should break off from Nigeria. The effect of these kinds of response has been to harden dissent and reinforce the probability of Nigeria's dissolution.

Piece by piece, from various directions, the jigsaw pieces of that probability are assembling. A 2004 assessment by the United States Central Intelligence Agency (CIA) predicted that Nigeria could break up within fifteen years – an assessment that agreed with the opinions of many other informed observers in the world. The author of a well-researched book written on Nigeria at about the same time titled it *This House Has Fallen*. Richard

Dowden in his impressive new book on Africa (published in 2009), titles his chapter on Nigeria with the words: "Look out world: Nigeria" – as if he is alerting the world to a Nigerian mega-bomb that is about to detonate and blow up the earth. Dowden then goes on as follows:[9]

"Nigeria has a terrible reputation. Tell someone that you are going to Nigeria and if they haven't been there themselves, they offer sympathy. Tell anyone who has been to Nigeria and they laugh. Then they offer sympathy. No tourists go there. Only companies rich enough to keep their staff removed from the realities of Nigerian life do business there. And big companies rarely mention Nigeria in their annual reports for fear of what it will do to their share price. Journalists treat it like a war zone. Diplomats regard it as a punishment posting."

Dowden adds further down the chapter that, in fact, Nigeria's popular image falls short of the reality – and that Nigeria is a failed state that somehow manages to continue standing. Also, many foreign observers have marveled at the unbelievable capacity of many highly educated Nigerians to absorb endless filth and mess from their rulers and do nothing about it, and even keep smiling – partly because some harbor a strange hope that some bounty will somehow, some day, come to them personally from the filth and mess, but mostly because most have simply gone beyond caring. After witnessing this pathetic tendency in many intelligent and well educated Nigerians, observers can only lose hope in the possibility of revival or change in Nigeria – can only surrender to the sad probability that only a mammoth upheaval will ever solve the Nigerian problem. In January 2010, in an event in honor of the Nigerian writer, Chinua Achebe, Ambassador Princeton Lyman, a former United States ambassador to Nigeria, delivered a lover's rebuke to Nigeria, warning that Nigeria, in spite of its large population, petroleum wealth, and past contributions to peace in West Africa, was seriously becoming irrelevant in the world. And the predominant attitude of the world's most influential authorities concerning Nigeria has been demonstrated powerfully in the fact that, within five years, two American presidents (one of them a man of Black African descent, President Obama), visited Africa, and both pointedly excluded Nigeria (home of about one-fourth of all Black Africans) from their itineraries.

Among Nigerians themselves, the warnings about the impending dissolution of Nigeria have become a constant, unrelenting, outcry. The following are typical of such warnings: The most notable of the last survivors of Nigeria's nationalists of the 1950's, Chief Anthony Enahoro, said,

> "*if we desire to create a viable federal structure and warm relationships among our nationalities, we have to design a formula under which we can live equitably together and the formula must provide for the recognition of the existence and corporate integrity of the nationalities. The only thing keeping Nigeria together at present is force*"[10]

The Nobel Prize Laureate, Wole Soyinka, perhaps Nigeria's best known citizen worldwide, and an intrepid crusader for good governance in his country, said,

> "*if nothing happens, I cannot guarantee what recourse the people will take. - - - I don't rule out Nigeria breaking up. That is what happens to a failed state*".[11]

Another prominent Nigerian, Kole Omotosho, said:

> "*There is no need for a national conference because those who benefit from the rot that exists will not allow it. Each constituent part of what is Nigeria must first and foremost declare its independence from the failed state of Nigeria. Then those who are interested in forming a new modern state - - - can then go ahead and form such a state with due consideration for rules, regulations and proper procedures. Everything else is simply postponement of the inevitable*"[12]

And finally (to cut it short here), Dr. Bolaji Akinyemi, Professor of Political Science and former Nigerian Minister of Foreign Affairs, made the following sobering remarks in an interview with the news media on December 9, 2010:

> "*There is no head of state of this country – and probably I should say there is no prominent Nigerian of note – who believes that Nigeria will survive. None! - - - They don't believe that Nigeria will survive and, therefore, what*

*we all seek to protect and advance are sectional interests
and personal interests masquerading as national interests.
- - - They don't believe that, really, Nigeria will survive
as Nigeria.*[13]

In Uganda, very influential voices among the Buganda people
have, for decades, been leaning more and more in the direction of
support for secession, and the carving out of an independent
Buganda. In an article published on February 20, 2010, a
Bugandan citizen, Moses Kalanzi, powerfully defended the
Buganda kingdom against the persistent pressures on it by
Ugandan governments. Buganda, he said, was by no means a small
kingdom – and was at least comparable in size and population to
countries such as Estonia, Latvia, and the Republic of Ireland, all
of which were recently separated from larger countries in the
modern world. Buganda's ancient institutions, he added, had
adapted creditably to modern conditions and had remained intact,
and the kingdom's language, common identity, and loyalty to
cultural institutions, were those of a respectable nation in the
world. Since the creation of countries like Ireland, Estonia and
Latvia is commonly lauded as a triumph of nationalism and self-
determination, it was illogical to treat the nationalism of Buganda
as reactionary and tribal. As for Uganda, he contended, "there is
nothing like a Ugandan nation" – except only as far as 19th century
Turkey, consisting of various nations, was loosely known as a
nation. And since the government of Uganda had for decades
supported the secession of the peoples of South Sudan from the
Republic of Sudan, what sense was there in the Ugandan
governments' intense hostility to Bugandan nationalism?[14]

It is worth repeating that in February 2011, representatives of
the kingdom of Buganda submitted to the Secretary-General of the
United Nations a strong petition demanding the right of Buganda
to secede from Uganda, and that some other peoples of Uganda are
doing the same openly and loudly. It must be remembered too that
various peoples in many other Black African countries are doing
the same – in the Congo Democratic Republic, in Angola, in
Nigeria, in Chad, in Senegal, in Mali, etc.

How will our countries handle these?

The choice is entirely in our hands – either to work towards reordering our sub-continent sensibly and peacefully, or to continue in the accustomed ways in which our group lives were programmed by colonialism, until our countries plunge into serious upheavals. To tread the sensible and peaceful route, what will be needed of leadership and the political system will be more or less the same in all countries. Each country will need to respond to its peoples, large or small, with respect. Each will also need to create an atmosphere of open and free debate and discussion. In the final analysis, even though every country commands some capacity to coerce, keeping any country together by force is not an easy task – especially for a poor country – in today's world. As the example of Yugoslavia teaches, a people that want absolutely to separate from a poor country will, in the end, do so. And as Indonesia is now showing, a policy of tough military responses to a series of secessionist movements is wasteful and debilitating; negotiating and conceding local autonomies is infinitely preferable. Britain's readiness to grant "devolution" (that is, local autonomies) to Scotland and Wales has tended to mollify many Scottish and Welsh nationalists, effectively eliminated violence in their nationalist movements, and contained their nationalist agitations in the confines of regular British politics. Britain's type of response – consisting of democratic debates and devolution – holds out a very valuable lesson to all Black African countries.[15]

But even with the best of approaches, some African borders seem to be certain to get adjusted, and some African peoples seem to be very likely to break off from the countries they presently belong to and become autonomous and independent countries on their own. For instance, at this point, over fifty years after Nigeria's independence, and over fifty years of a convoluted pattern of relationships and politics, it has become virtually impossible, according to the assessment by many leading Nigerians, to imagine a country like Nigeria remaining intact for much longer within its present borders. But careful approaches consisting of open and democratic debate and courageous concessions to nationalist demands in every country can save Sub-

Saharan Africa from plunging wholesale into an era of secessionist and border conflagrations.

The great question then is: How is Sub-Saharan Africa likely to face the challenges when they arise? Unhappily, the prospects do not look good. The quality of politics and governance in most of our countries is such as to turn such challenges into devastating turmoil. Contemporary African governments and leaders are not used to generating or promoting, or even tolerating, discussion, and are generally disinclined to seek consensus or compromise. The roots of their generally disastrous responses and approaches to the duties, problems, and challenges of governance in our countries have been amply described in an earlier chapter. It is painful to watch how long and intensely many of the best minds of Nigeria have offered suggestions, proposals and even entreaties, to the rulers of their country for some serious discussion of their county's very serious problems of ethnic diversity – all without any constructive response. It is shocking that anybody who claims to rule a country like Uganda can feel comfortable with ignoring, and even deriding, the voices of sizeable majorities of citizens in many parts of that country, including large numbers of the educated citizens of the country, one of the most literate countries in Africa. In Zimbabwe, it is futile hoping that Mugabe's departure (which, because of his age, may come soon) will change anything much; the stronger probability is that his successors will rule as he has done. In most African countries, in fact, the quality of politics and governance has steadily gone worse, not better; and political leaders have tended to become more defiantly confident in rigging the elections, in rejecting discussion, and in amassing huge unearned fortunes from the public coffers.

More and more too, when outsiders raise a voice against the horrors of politics in Africa these days, African politicians have developed the stock response that such outsiders are merely trying to give Africa a bad image. Not only the international news media have been so routinely accused, even more obviously objective functionaries and agencies in the international community have been also. Following the worldwide outcry against the violent rigging of the Nigerian elections in 2007, an outcry that was led by international observers who were eye witness observers of the election criminalities, many influential Nigerian politicians countered with the response that election rigging is not an exclusive Nigerian, or African, phenomenon, but a phenomenon common to all countries. Many prominent Nigerian citizens who had a stake in the corruption in their country took turns to repeat this nonsense for quite a time, and to claim with glee that even Americans had rigged the 2000 American presidential election. The AU's denunciation of the International Court's warrant of arrest for Sudan's president over his alleged war crimes or crimes against humanity in Darfur represents the high water mark of this stock response by African rulers to the outrage being increasingly voiced by the rest of the world.

The obvious implication of this kind of response is that African leaders are determined to hold on to their freedom to brutalize their countries and their peoples. They may, on the African Union stage, make the most eloquent statements about the rights of man and of peoples, but in their own countries, they choose to learn nothing and forget nothing.

Even on the African Union stage, their actions are by no means easy to correlate with their stated intentions. Already, it is significant that the AU peace and security apparatus has exhibited the most vigilance and effectiveness in trying to banish coups against rulers – much more than it has done in any other sphere. The few countries (like Niger, Guinea and Madagascar) where coups have toppled rulers in recent years have been punished with suspension from AU membership and privileges. But the same levels of vigilance and effectiveness were not exhibited by the AU apparatus when the Nigerian rulers blatantly and violently rigged the Nigerian elections of 2003 and 2007, when Mugabe refused to surrender power after losing the Zimbabwe national election of 2008, and when the Kenyan elections were rigged in 2008. It is instructive that when each of these acts of outrage were being perpetrated, the AU instruments prohibiting and denouncing them existed – the charters and conventions inherited from the OAU (the African Charter of Human and Peoples Rights), and those that the AU itself has created (the African Peer Review Mechanism; African Court of Human and Peoples Rights; African Union Convention on Preventing and Combating Corruption; African Charter on Democracy, Elections and Governance).

The architects of the philosophy and instruments of the AU grandly proclaim the AU's right and responsibility to protect all Africans and African peoples, but it is not the AU but non-African agencies and interests that have stepped forth when Africans have needed to be protected against their own rulers. The example of the International Court's action against President Omar Bashir of Sudan has been mentioned above. Another notable instance is the European Union's sanctions against Mugabe. As would be remembered also, in the other region of Africa, the Maghreb, it was outside forces (the United Nations, the European Union, NATO and the United States) that rose up to offer some cover to Libyan youths against the armed forces of their country. At least until this moment, it has been mostly from the wider world beyond Africa that such steps have been reliably taken to protect African lives and human rights. In fact, judging from the AU'S denunciation of the International Court over the Bashir case, the prospect seems to be that African leaders, jointly, will more and more resist the wider world in these matters. And the battle cry for such a resistance is easy to drum up and be given some plausibility among many Africans – namely, defense of Africa's independence.

For Sub-Saharan Africa to be able to cope peacefully with the challenges of the future, challenges that seem inevitable in view of the composition and structure, and the generally conflict-prone politics, of its countries, and in view of intensifying tendencies in ethnic nationalism in the world, Sub-Saharan Africa needs that each of its countries should clean up its politics and governance. Peace-keeping and security arrangements by the AU will not do. It has to be a whole package of profound changes – a consciously sought, deliberate, painstaking, restructuring of the responses of Black Africans, Black African political elites, Black African intelligentsia, and the masses of Black African peoples, to the types of conditions that Black Africa now has in its countries. The crucial battle front in such a war of change has to be in the domestic politics and life of each country. In our world, countries where the citizens are sovereign and free, where governments are servants of the people, and where free institutions enjoy the support of the leaders and the people to run with integrity, have the better chances of resolving, or at least containing, their problems peacefully – and of therefore succeeding and prospering.

Countries that lack those attributes live in increased danger of tensions and conflicts and even disintegration.

Some African pundits will respond here that many Sub-Saharan African countries have improved the quality of their politics and governance by writing much of democratic clauses into their constitutions. Yes, they have indeed. But very laudable democratic statements in the constitutions of these countries have never sufficed to alter the tone of their political lives. It does not matter that we, in every country of Black Africa, have written democratic systems and free institutions into our national constitutions. What matters is that we have been running some of the world's most authoritarian and most corrupt governments – employing coercion to hold on to power, and to hold disparate peoples together willy-nilly, exploiting public office to accumulate huge unearned personal fortunes, systematically rigging elections, falsifying national statistics and records, creating overblown secrete police institutions awash in money, manipulating and distorting judiciaries, stalking and trying to squelch "dissidents" (citizens who dare to speak out), especially "dissidents" from among "suspect" ethnic nations within our countries.

Africans in every Sub-Saharan African country need desperately to effect a radical turn away from these destructive paths. Otherwise, if (or rather, when) the great tests shall arise (like demands for border redefinitions or for ethnic separations), many African countries may plunge into conceivably much bigger and more destructive turmoil than has hitherto been seen in Africa.

Also, in such circumstances, even the grand and ambitious AU peace and security structure will face the probability of floundering and failing. It may even degenerate into a structure that polices Africa for the enforcement of the wills of corrupt and self-perpetuating regimes, rulers, strong men, and so-called dominant groups. Given the well-established tendencies in African politics, it seems probable that the AU arrangements may actively discourage coups (one type of unconstitutional, illegal and criminal change of government), while having no measurable influence on rulers' electoral manipulations and rigging of elections (another, and more common, type of illegal and criminal seizure of government). The AU apparatus may peace-keep to shut down a people causing "trouble" over their desire to be unified with their ethnic kinsmen beyond their present country's border, or even to separate and have an independent country of their own – but appears unlikely to be able or disposed to get the government of any country to respect such a people and to ascertain and respond to their desires, or to ensure that they are free to express themselves, or to protect them against military occupation of their territory. In the same way, the AU apparatus may peace-keep and shut up a pitifully marginalized and neglected people that are in revolt to get some justice, but not able or disposed to get the government of any country to do justice to any aggrieved peoples. It may restrain some of the more violent conflicts, ethnic cleansing, genocide, etc., in African countries, but is unlikely to have any serious impact on the culture of graft and corruption among the rulers and the influential citizens of any country. It therefore is not likely to impact the do-or-die strife for power and for the accumulation of great unearned fortunes among the African political elite – itself a major factor in political violence, employment of armed thugs in politics, political assassinations, the sudden fracturing of political parties and governments, the criminal viciousness that often marks African election campaigns and elections, the frequently seen competition among opposing African political parties to rig their country's election and, in some cases, the escalation of political rivalries into civil wars or inter-ethnic pogroms.

A culture of strong-man rulers, of self-ordained titans who presume to command exceptionality in wisdom and leadership capabilities, has since independence been a curse on Africa, and can only be a curse as long as it lasts in any African country. The concept of a "dominant ethnic group", ordained by European colonial administrators to be rulers of their country, has since independence poisoned the political life of many an African country, and can only continue to poison and destroy wherever it holds out. Any design presuming to be a substitute for the sovereignty of all the people of an African country, for the supremacy of law, for the equality of all citizens before the law, for transparent and verifiable processes of government, is a path to death and ruin. Politically, European imperialism strapped an awful destiny on Black Africa; only a full and unstrained exercise of the sovereignty of Africans themselves can throw off that destiny. No strong man or ordained group can do it for them. If an African country will, or will not, survive intact as it is, that can only be the ultimate decision of its component peoples; no strong man or ordained group can force the peoples of any country together forever.

In summary, the rulers and peoples and citizens of each Sub-Saharan African country need, together, to opt for and seek a sincerely democratic political, economic and social life, and a return to the African culture of compromise, consensus and inclusiveness. The European imperialist came to Africa to conquer and dominate; the African ruler should not be out to do the same.

How all these will be accomplished in the political life of each country will, in the nature of things, vary from country to country. However, the constitutional and political mechanisms and goals that have been the source of instability and conflict in each country, and that need to be attended to, can be listed as follows:

- *the winner-take-all, dominant-group, and power-man mentalities that were bred into the political system of each country from its colonial beginnings; and a turning away from the African traditions of compromise, inclusiveness, and consensus.*
- *the staunch refusal to acknowledge and carefully respect the identity, peculiarities, strengths, pride and unique needs of every nation or people in a country, irrespective of their size and present level of cultural attainments;*
- *the resistance to a culture of open participatory politics and of government in the sunshine, structured and guarded by law;*
- *the refusal to acknowledge that power belongs to the people, irrespective of whether the people seem knowledgeable or ignorant, or whether they seem friendly or hostile, or whether they are rich or poor; a culture in which the government fears the people and acknowledges its role as servant of the people in all things;*
- *the resistance to a culture, created and upheld by law, of free, peaceful and open discussions by the citizens of every country, of all aspects of the affairs, structure and existence of their country – even if some evince nationalist, separatist or secessionist attitudes;*

- *the rejection of a culture of human rights and civil rights, created and upheld by law, and enforceable through criminal prosecution and civil litigation;*
- *resistance to conscious elevation of law to sovereignty in society, and to uncompromising equality of all citizens before the law;*
- *the resistance to a tradition of independent, respectable, and consciously respected, judiciary, independent law-enforcement agencies, and regulatory agencies – all of which, by law, by practice, and by the uncompromising resolve of the people and their government, stand beyond the realms of politics and beyond the effects of political and special influences;*
- *the lack of a tradition of citizens' independent organizations that, under the law, watch over aspects of the affairs of their country.*
- *The refusal to enact or respect laws upholding the freedom of the news media, protecting the news media from interferences or molestations by government, and prohibiting government ownership of news media institutions.*

Concerning the northern African belt where the Arab and Black African peoples meet, the AU has been hesitant to generate and promote open and sincere discussions of differences – towards the ends of achieving sustainable solutions. The recent separation of South Sudan from the Republic of Sudan will probably open a new chapter of Afro-Arab discussion and relations here; but that remains to be seen.

Possible Benefits of a Return to African Political Traditions

The previous paragraph mentions the need to return to African traditions of compromise, consensus and inclusiveness. In more than fifty years of the existence of African countries as independent countries, it has been almost entirely unheard of to mention such principles as part of the African heritage, or as part of modern Africa's needs. Yet, these principles were very foundational to the way many Black African peoples organized and held their state systems together before the coming of European imperialism.[16]

For instance, in every kingdom of the large Yoruba nation (now of Nigeria, Benin and Togo Republics), though the king (or Oba) was the supreme ruler and symbol of his kingdom, he was a constitutional monarch who exercised authority only within a system of council of chiefs, and who was strictly prohibited from exercising any kind of personal power beyond that system. The Oba also lived under very powerful rules that demanded of him that he should respect the quarter chiefs and other high chiefs, the priesthood, the lineages, and certain great rituals and totems. Though he was spoken of as "owner of the land", almost all the land belonged to the lineages – in the cities the plots of land on which their lineage compounds stood, beyond the city walls their farmlands. The king's government could not touch a lineage's compound for any reason whatsoever, and could not do anything to part of a lineage's farmland without the express consent of the lineage. Beyond the capital town of each kingdom, the kingdom consisted of many small towns and villages owing allegiance to the Oba. However, the leader of each such small town or village was generally independent in the day-to-day management of his community, where he exercised authority in a conciliar system exactly like that of the Oba. Such a subordinate ruler acknowledged the Oba as overlord, brought him gifts and dues at certain annual festivals, and might send men to fight for the Oba during a war or to work with the men of the Oba's town in repair works on the Oba's palace or town wall. But rigid levies by the Oba on the rulers of his subordinate communities were never part of the Yoruba system, and intrusions by the Oba in their day-to-day affairs were beyond the norm. The smaller rulers paid homage to the Oba, and the Oba was required to hold them in very careful respect. The system was one of mutual honor.

In the powerful Ashanti kingdom, the golden stool was symbol of the oneness of the state, and the Asantihene (king) who sat on it was the sacred ruler of all; but the leadership of each clan in the state was respected by the king as rulers of their clans. In the Buganda kingdom, the Kabaka (king) was ruler and symbol of the oneness and power of the kingdom, but the traditions and practices made him pay the most conscientious respect to the local chiefs. Holly Elisabeth Hanson's book on the structure of the Buganda kingdom describes how the Baganda ruling classes knit their kingdom together like a family. In the Basuto kingdom which crystallized in the early 19th century, the traditional Bantu system of supreme king and largely autonomous local chieftains accounted for the cohesion and power of the kingdom. Much the same traditions characterized the pre-19th century system of the Hausa kingdoms, one of Africa's largest peoples. In the early 19th century, the Fulani jihad forcibly imposed on the Hausa people a radically Islamic regime, with local Emirates owing allegiance to a Sultan. After the new Sultanate government had settled down, it too was characterized by a carefully balanced system of devolution between the Sultanate establishment and the Emirate establishments.

Compromise, consensus, inclusiveness, balance – these were the soul of probably most of Black Africa's political systems. They were fundamental to Africa's concept of democratic political life. Returning to them, in the context of a modern democratic system in our time, may bequeath a lot of stability to modern African political life.

To illustrate the positive possibilities of African traditions of consensus and inclusiveness, note the record of the Mandela presidency in the Union of South Africa. Of Africa's prominent persons who fought for their peoples against white domination and oppression in the middle of the 20th century, none suffered more than Mandela. After he came out of 27 years of imprisonment and became president of his country, if he had started to spit fire and hurl brimstones against the white people of his country, countless millions of angry young Africans all over Africa would have hailed him. But he let the authentic African ethos in his cultural consciousness triumph – the spirit that had empowered a Moshoeshoe to knit together fragments of peoples and to create a new strong people and state in very inauspicious circumstances in the 19th century.

Review also the recent, less known, story of political change in the small country of Lesotho in southern Africa. Lesotho became independent in 1966 and, as would be remembered, adopted a Westminster parliamentary system of government, with the Lesotho king as Head of State, and an elected parliament (elected on the basis of popular voting for candidates of political parties) that appointed a Prime Minister or Head of Government. In its first post-independence election in 1970, and in every election thereafter, this poor country ran into serious political troubles, even though a party always won election with a commanding majority. Reactions to the elections by losing parties grew more and more intense, until violence resulted, even featuring some home-grown terrorism. A climax finally came with the election of 1998. Even though local and international observers adjudged this election to be reasonably free and fair, the losing parties started large-scale violent protests – until the Prime Minister, fearing a coup, called for the help of the SADC. But the coming of the SADC peace-keeping troops sparked even greater and enormously more destructive violence lasting for months. At last, in thoughtful and constructive response, the country set up an Interim Political Authority (IPA) and charged it with reviewing the electoral system. After a careful review of the whole situation, the IPA proposed a proportional electoral system that would ensure that all parties, including those that lost at elections, would be represented in the parliament. To the existing 80 elected Assembly seats in the parliament, the new system added 40 seats to be filled on a proportional basis. The first elections were held under this system in May 2002. The party that had won in 1998 still won, with 54 percent of the popular votes; but the new proportional system ensured that opposition political parties were accorded significant numbers of seats, and this gave Lesotho its first peaceful election since independence. To be sure, the story of Lesotho is a story of one tiny country. Nevertheless, it shows what is possible when the people of a country stop, take a careful look at the affairs of their country together and, in the collective interest of their country, work out a system based on give and take – compromise, inclusiveness, consensus, balance.

For an illustration of the opposite to compromise and consensus, let us turn to the political history of Nigeria. The British, before departing from Nigeria, engineered the political dominance of one Region (the Northern Region), over the affairs of a Nigerian federation consisting of three Regions (East, West, North). Ultimately, the most damaging consequence of this was that the politically dominant group in this dominant Region developed a rigidity of posture in Nigerian affairs – a rigidity and stone-walling that made compromise and consensus, and even open discussion, impossible – and a striving towards maximizing the control of the central authority over all things.[17]

That led to conflict and near collapse in less than two years after independence; but even then, the thrust did not alter. And since the 1970's it has been further facilitated by three important developments – the seizure of government by a series of Northern military officers and their rule over the country for decades, the breaking of Nigeria into smaller states, and the growth of petroleum to the position of mainstay of the Nigerian economy. The Northern military rulers turned the federal government into the commander of the states of the Nigerian federation. Being all Northerners, the military rulers enhanced Northern domination in all ways possible. Moreover, with the creation of a few states by the military government in 1967, the creation of more states became generally attractive, and the military rulers seized upon that to enhance their power – by creating more and more states, mostly without any particular rationale. Even the larger nations were split up in order to create more states. Ultimately, Nigeria arrived at 36 states, but the federal establishment has continued to envisage more and more. Nigeria's central authority has usually seized on this development to increase its own scope continually, to diminish the competence of the small states continually, and to seize the development assets earlier built up by the original three Regions (on the grounds that the small states are too small to command the strength and resources to hold such assets).

Also, as collector of the royalties and rents generated by the petroleum industry (today assessed at over 80% of Nigeria's national revenue), the federal authority became Nigeria's big boss, able to depress the states to nearly the status of beggar entities. Even financial resources generated in the states were "centralized" and put under the control of the federal authority. The Northern holders of federal power became further entrenched and further emboldened. The Nigerian federation ceased essentially to be a federation and became a camouflaged unitary system controlled and perpetually manipulated by the dominant political elite of the original Northern Region. When others from other parts of Nigeria happened to have control of the federal center, they found its excess of resources and power so alluring that they just kept it intact or expanding. In the circumstance, many thoughtful Nigerians came to the painful conclusion that the only way to effect any beneficial change is to break up Nigeria – or to find some way to pull their own nationality out of Nigeria.

In such circumstances, any chance that the voices of all of Nigeria's peoples and citizens could mold their country has vanished. Seeking the favor of the central authority, the great dispenser of funds, has become the insidious influence molding and directing Nigeria's politics. In each small state, the group that claims connection to the holders of central power insists that only it can run the affairs of its state – and it will do anything to seize and keep control (including, of course, the rigging of elections with the help of the power and people from the center, and the agencies of the federal government). There is no possibility of any meeting of minds here. For the ambitious Nigerian, the options are clear – take the personally profitable step of attaching oneself to the conduits to Nigeria's center (and thus turn against one's own people and the ethics of one's own culture, but position oneself to share in the funds that are sent from the center ostensibly for one's State Government or Local Government), or fight back to defend and protect one's people and home area against the rampage (and thus live with the risk of being killed in the process), or (as many are now doing) just turn one's back, shrug one's shoulders, and walk away from the whole mess. Over time, more and more Nigerians have come to the painful conclusion that the only way to effect any beneficial change is to break up Nigeria – or to find some way to pull their own nationality out of Nigeria.

Touching of minds and working out some consensus in Nigeria would have worked totally differently – and might have given Black Africa a country ranking among the leading powers of the world. It might have preserved the Regional autonomies of 1960 (even if the number of Regions was increased), pulled out the more extreme barbs of federal power, slightly adjusted the North-West boundary along ethnic lines, and created one Region for the combination of the small ethnic groups in each of the three Regions (perhaps two for the small ethnic groups in the huge Northern Region). All of that is now history of course – and now largely impossible. Another later line of consensus might have taken seriously the idea of a National Sovereignty Conference when it arose in the 1990s, fine-tuned its modalities, and thereby given the country a new running chance. But these are only two of undoubtedly many instances when Nigeria might have turned its history around. As these words are being written in the 54th year of Nigeria's existence as an independent country, developments in Nigeria point strongly to the probability that it may already be too late to persuade at least some Nigerian peoples that Nigeria should be their home for much longer.

In general, Black African elites have been averse to a realization that, as far as the countries they inherited from colonialism are concerned, they have a peculiar problem in the world. Many of their countries are, as now composed, structured and run, essentially unworkable. During the first years after independence, when only the preludes to the inevitable disasters were playing out, the governments of Africa's countries felt that a body like the Organization of African Unity would do to provide an all-African response to the African political experience. But then the much bigger disasters came – and the conviction grew that the OAU would not do, and that a stronger and more comprehensive and more proactive African response, the African Union, was needed. Unless very fundamental changes are effected in the politics and lives of individual Sub-Saharan African countries, the AU too will, in due time, fall flat, or degenerate into an arrangement for shoring up the rulers of Africa against the peoples of Africa. There are many informed Africans who fear that such a continental power, more easily mobilized, may be what is desired by those African leaders who have been pushing for a unification of Africa into one country with an African army.

CHAPTER NINE

Way Forward

In its ultimate essence, this book is dedicated to the desire, the hope, and the confidence, that Black Africa can overcome its present pitfalls and move forward in the world. Each Black African country in which positive steps have been taken to achieve some political stability is proof that Black African peoples can rise above the terrible disruption and disorientation inflicted by foreign conquest and imperialism, settle down, and chart paths towards progress and prosperity. In the previous chapter, we emphasized that, for Africa to be able to move forward in this world and take adequate advantage of the development resources increasingly available to all mankind today, "the peoples and citizens of each African country need, together, to opt for and seek a sincerely democratic political, economic and social life, and a return to the African culture of compromise, consensus and inclusiveness". We then listed some of the specific constitutional and political failings that have made it impossible for African countries to accomplish some leap into the new society of law, freedom, sanctity of life, and respect for human rights, etc. Without recognizing, acknowledging, and handling, these facts and the truth, it is impossible to achieve healing, clarity and progress. In the present chapter, we will explore the steps towards needed "restructuring".

The Kenyan scholar, Ali Mazrui, who has served in the fore-front of African scholarship for decades, has, among many other African subjects, made very significant contributions to the discussions of Africa's conflicts and wars, and offered important insights and suggestions on how Africa can settle down, achieve stability, and prosper. He concludes one of his contributions as follows:

"As a final warning, let me stress the importance of moving with speed towards political reform in Africa. - - - Africa is a continent of immense potential. It is our obligation to move swiftly to resolve its problems and make sure that its people are given the chance to enjoy the blessings of peace and prosperity. Black Africa has lost too much ground.[1]*".*

In the roughly half a century since independence, Black Africa has steadily fallen back in the human struggle for the better life, for liberty from the rigors of nature, and for comfort and happiness. The important question is not whether Black Africa has seen some improvements – yes, it has. The important question is how those improvements compare with improvements in the rest of the contemporary world. The past half century has been one of the most pulsating periods in the history of mankind – a period in which technology has constantly exploded, creating at an ever accelerating pace the tools for human progress and prosperity. Throughout most of it, most of Africa has ruled itself – and allowed the confusions, turbulences and self-inflicted agonies of its politics to inhibit its readiness and ability to run with the rest of the world.

Ali Mazrui is right. Africa must henceforth move "with speed - - - swiftly". If Africa does anything less than that, the probable outcome may go beyond the worst that the human mind can fathom. For one thing, the continual images of Africa as a land of crooked politics and rogue politicians, of disorder and lawlessness, of incomparable corruption, poverty, and dissoluteness, of masses of forcibly orphaned and abandoned children and destitute mothers, of self-inflicted mass death and ruin, etc., all in a world of growing wealth, beauty and even elegance, is doing a great havoc to the collective psychology of a whole generation of Africans. It is well known to us African immigrants in other lands outside of Africa that our children appear much less likely to own up to their school friends the original source of their families. Even when the parents dutifully speak their native language to their children, the children are much less likely than immigrant children from non-African sources to want to learn their parents' language. African-Americans, the earlier people of African descent in the Americas, deserve to get some pride and spiritual boost from the continent of their origin, and those seemed to be on the way in the 1960s as country after country in Black Africa became independent. But steadily since then, what Black Africa has given to its descendants in the Americas is, largely, embarrassment and even dismay. In short, the soul of a whole race of people in Africa is suffering and shriveling, while their rulers continue to disrupt and destroy their countries, to grab and hold personal power and amass unearned wealth, to promote some dream of ethnic dominance, and to subdue the ancient nations in their various countries.

In the obverse, however, even in this wrack and ruin, African people are, slowly but surely, getting more educated, more and more exposed, and better and better informed about conditions in other lands. And that is very rapidly intensifying the discontentment of the peoples of the continent – especially of the younger generation, in this continent where the youth constitute the overwhelming majority. For now, out of terror of, or discontentment with, conditions in their native countries, educated Africans (mostly of the younger generation) are fleeing in droves – to other countries where they know life is better, fleeing to America, Europe, Australia, Canada, etc. The makers of the policies of African countries will do Africa and the world a great service by recognizing that this flight may stall someday (whether by escalation in the already noticeable rejection of the African stream in some countries around the world, or by some willful rejection of flight by educated Africans themselves), and that when the stall eventuates, Africa (and the world) will have a cataclysmic account to deal with. For yet another, Africa is, as earlier explained, in danger of serious new types of turmoil resulting from demands for border adjustments or ethnic separations or secessions on the continent. In the quest for transformation, order and progress, therefore, Africa cannot afford merely to walk; she must run with deliberate haste and urgency.

For the swift race to transformation, order, progress and prosperity in Africa, Ali Mazrui in his writings suggests various steps and measures. First he suggests that Africans, in their present countries, should cultivate tolerance – "the ability to accept difference". Secondly, he suggests that Africans should explore the virtue of "decentralization" or "pluralization" of power in their countries – a process of conscious, systematic and appropriate delegating of power from the center to the peripheries. Such pluralization of power can be achieved, he proposes, in a number of ways. One way is to institutionalize multi-party political systems by the national constitutions – and make one-party systems unconstitutional. Another is to explore the use of federal constitutions. Another is to nurture a capitalist economy and society, resulting in the diffusion of power and influence to various sectors - the political sector, the business sector, the news media, the professions, etc. And yet another is to take steps in every country to enhance the role and participation of women in the political process – some measure similar to what a strong movement has been promoting in India, to have one-third of the legislature reserved for women. This should also include, he adds, increasing the representation of women in the executive arms of government as well as in the military. Finally, Ali Mazrui suggests that measures be taken to reduce the rivalry between civilians and the military in the political life of African countries. One way to do this, he proposes, is to constitutionally give the military a role in the regular governance of each country – some assigned share and representation for the military in the legislature, and some specified position (like that of vice-president) in the executive arm of government. With regards to Pan-African inputs into the quest for transformation, stability and progress in African countries, Ali Mazrui proposes measures and institutions not too dissimilar from the structures and roles now given to the African Union. Furthermore, in those cases in which total state failure or collapse has occurred, Ali Mazrui asks whether unilateral intervention by a stable neighbor might not be a good idea for Africa to explore – something like the Tanzanian military invasion of Idi Amin's Uganda in 1979. Thus, would it have helped if Yoweri Museveni's Uganda had intervened forcefully in Rwanda in April 1994, the way that Julius Nyerere's Tanzania had intervened in Uganda in 1979? In the same vein, he asks, would not a short-term merger of Rwanda and Burundi with Tanzania in 1994 have helped the situation?

Without doubt, readers will have different reactions to Ali Mazrui's suggestions, proposals, and posers. There might even be some who would be strongly critical of particular aspects of them. But agreeing or not agreeing with him is not the important issue. The important thing is that the concerns and suggestions voiced by him highlight the awful political predicament of African countries and peoples in our times, and the enormous need for serious search for ways to guide Africa towards stability, progress and prosperity. In the final analysis, the vital demand of the moment is that Africans should stop, take an objective look at their countries, and hurry to embark on transformation. As hitherto constituted, led and managed, many of the countries of Black Africa can have no peaceful future ahead of them. But that can change. It can change – and change quickly – if Africans will abandon the preconceptions, assumptions, and unrealistic expectations that have hitherto ruled over the affairs of their countries, and respond rationally and objectively to the facts and realities in the life of each of their countries. No matter how small, no African people or nationality will melt away or be swallowed up by some neighbor. No matter how small, each African people is a factor of great importance in the world, and needs to be related to as such. The only viable vehicle of transformation, of guiding Africans on the path of order, stability and progress, is sincere and open dialogue, plus a sincere willingness to make our societies work – to bow to the imperious reality that each of our countries is a plurality and that the strong and centralized unity that we have been seeking in each of our is near impossible to achieve.

Those who think that their own nation, appearing to be dominant among the nations in its country today, will dominate all the other nations of that country forever, are suffering from a dangerous delusion. Their ethnic ambition is anachronistic, unrealistic, and dangerous – dangerous because it bars the path to dialogue and consensus, and to stability, peace and progress. Resolute hold by an authoritarian political apparatus on the affairs of any country is unrealistic and dangerous. A Rwanda or Burundi firmly ruled by a small Tutsi minority or exclusively by a large Hutu majority, a Nigeria perpetually manipulated and crooked up in order to sustain a Fulani or Yoruba or Igbo or any other ethnic group's domination, a Congo Democratic Republic, an Angola, a Chad Republic, a Central African Republic, any country of Sub-Saharan Africa, whose people are held together and held down by some authoritarian and corrupt leadership and apparatus, risks never having peace, stability or progress. By being realistic and sincere, Africans can find together ways to change all of these prospects.

Through being realistic and sincere also, Africans are very likely to be guided to constructively creative paths for restructuring their continent and countries. In all of our countries, it is reasonable to expect that a consensus to decentralize or pluralize power in some way will dilute tension, give each nationality some breathing space, and promote harmony and a bonding together of the many nationalities of each country. In most of our countries too, a mutually sincere quest for power decentralization or pluralization is likely to recommend a federal arrangement. It is usually thought that a federal arrangement is suitable for only our larger countries, but that is not so. Even the smallest of our multi-nation countries may, as an outcome of sober and sincere dialogue, find a federal solution very advantageous. In essence, federalism represents acceptance and tolerance of, and respect for, difference – a healthy willingness and readiness of the people of a country to let each different nationality, or other component entity, run its own affairs in its own way and along its own culture and ethical character – all in the context of their one encompassing country.

Examples to Emulate

There are many multi-nation countries in our world that we Africans need to look to for examples to emulate. One such country, the United Kingdom, has been earlier touched upon. The British policy of "Devolution", which has granted to each of Scotland and Wales much national autonomy and a national legislature and government, is an example of constructive statesmanship worthy of emulation. It ensures, as earlier pointed out, that the debate over separation remains contained within the normal spectrum of United Kingdom's politics. It also ensures that even if Scotland and Wales go on ultimately to separate from the United Kingdom, such steps will be taken in peace and without disruption. Another such country, Indonesia, has also been touched upon. By shifting from a policy of wars and military occupations against provincial secessionist movements, to one of granting local autonomies, Indonesia is giving itself a chance to handle, or perhaps resolve, its secessionist difficulties in more constructive, more peaceful, and less expensive ways.

Yet another such country is the small country of Switzerland in central Europe. Switzerland has a population of only 7.5 million and territory of just 16,000 square miles. Similar to most small countries of Sub-Saharan Africa, Switzerland is a land of much diversity. Language varies from region to region –

with a total of four main languages (German, French, Italian and Romance). Geographically, its Alpine topography makes it a land of hills, valleys, lakes, and well defined regions. And historically, the peoples of its various regions came under different cultural influences in their history – some under German influence, others under French, or Austrian, or Italian, influence. Finally, Switzerland is also a land of religious diversity. A Roman Catholic country in the European Middle Ages, Switzerland experienced a lot of religious changes in the course of the Protestant Reformation at the end of the Middle Ages, with some of the most powerful protestant churches having their origins and bases in different towns of the country, while the rural areas remained mostly Roman Catholic. In modern times, because of Switzerland's reputation for freedom, it has been the destination of large numbers of Muslim, Buddhist and Hindu immigrants. In this country, people enjoy freedom to practice their religion in an atmosphere of tolerance, respect and restraint. Switzerland's diverse cantons came together gradually, until their loosely joined confederacy was granted recognition in Europe in 1648. In later times, parts of the confederacy were occupied by powerful neighbors, but in 1815, the leading countries of Europe, meeting at the Congress of Vienna (to settle the affairs of Europe after the defeat of Napoleon) confirmed Switzerland's independence and granted it the status of neutrality. But it was not until 1848 that the country finally became a proper country with a national constitution.

The modern constitution of Switzerland is a product of very splendid respect for all the country's linguistic, geographical, cultural, religious, and historical diversity. That respect for the country's diversity is born out of a fundamental and realistic deference to differences. All the Swiss people acknowledge that their country is not a nation, but that it is a *Wilensnation*, a 'nation by will' or a 'nation by consent' (the consent of all its component groups large and small). The Swiss federation has twenty-six states (called cantons). Some cantons are fairly large and some very small. For instance, one of the largest has a population of slightly over one million, while one of the smallest has only a little over 15,000 inhabitants. Yet each canton, according to its strength, has its own legislature, its own government, its own legal system, its own court system. Each enjoys much administrative freedom, controls its own education and social services, and has its own police force. Each even has its own unique decision-making tradition. Most take legislative decisions through their elected legislatures, but some have a system whereby the general citizenry gather in a popular assembly at certain times in the year to vote on the affairs of their canton. The federal government, made up of an elected legislature and a small (seven-member) executive council appointed by the legislature, is responsible mostly for foreign policy and security. Over and above this constitutional structure, Switzerland has perhaps the best record of human rights and freedom in the world. Through its system of "direct democracy", any ordinary citizen can exercise the right of "initiative" to challenge an act of government or to propose a law, and cause a national referendum to be conducted on his proposal – with the result that Switzerland frequently holds referendums. All of these make this small country one of the most successful countries in the world – with exceptional social harmony and political stability, one of the most stable economies and soundest currencies in the world, famous financial and banking services, and a great role in worldwide charitable and humanitarian initiatives.

Switzerland is about the size and population of the smallest countries of sub-Saharan Africa. What Switzerland has, every African country, made up of a diversity of ethnic nations, cultures and religions, can have. It is just a matter of responding in a rational and healthy manner to the diversity that thousands of years of the history of our continent has bestowed upon us – a matter of not merely tolerating difference but of actively respecting it and even honoring it, a matter of realistically acknowledging that each of our countries is not a nation but that it needs to be nurtured into a 'nation by consent'. Instead of saying, as our rulers are used to saying, that some European imperialist came and gave us this or that country as it is, and that that is final, we need all, rulers, politicians, common citizens, to begin to speak a new and different language about our political existence as countries and peoples in the modern world. We have done all the worst things we can do to force the peoples and groups in each of our countries together, and that is not working. Now, we urgently need to nurture a healthy respect for the diversity that we have, and to explore it to give ourselves peace, order, stability, and a bigger and better share in the beauties of the world.

And, finally, one other such country is India in Asia.[2] As would be remembered, the far northern provinces of this country broke off at independence and became the new countries of Pakistan and Bangladesh. Even after that, India is still the world's largest country in territory and the second largest in population (second to China). It is a land of great diversity - the home of some 2000 ethnic groups or nationalities, and of a wide range of geographical and topographic variations. Naturally, because of this country's enormous size and complexity, countless studies have been done on various aspects of the development of its federation, but the aspect that is of interest to us here is the history of the structuring of the federation. In the early making of the Indian federal constitution, especially in the immediate light of secession of the far northern provinces from the country at independence, the initial priority concern of India's founding fathers was to insure the federation against the possibility of disintegration. As a result, the idea of using ethnic or linguistic basis for the organization of the states of the federation was rejected by the founding fathers. To the contrary, they asserted that the country was made into a federation only for the sake of administrative convenience, but must be thought of as a country of one people. As a result, not much weight was given to ethnic, religious and other kinds of diversity in designing the structure of the federation. But soon afterwards, popular demands arose for the recognition of the country's ethnic and linguistic pattern for restructuring the federation. As that kind of demand gathered momentum, most of India's leading statesmen opposed it. In fact, India's first Prime Minister, Pandit Nehru, threatened to resign rather than accept it – out of fear that it would lead to the breaking up of India. But these leaders were serious democrats, willing in the end to accept whatever the majority of their countrymen wanted for their country. As a result, by 1953, the use of linguistic basis for reorganizing the states had won the day – and even Nehru embraced it. And so, India's first states to be organized on linguistic basis came into existence in that year.

In 1956, a States Reorganization Commission was set up to consider the whole problem and make recommendations. Following its recommendations, the process of linguistic organization of states advanced rapidly, and was broadly completed by the end of the 1960's. Naturally, this has meant that the states differ widely in territorial size and in population. For the development of modern India, this incorporation of cultural identities into political and administrative units was a very major step. And then the strength that this step imparted to the Indian Union was further reinforced by another step – namely, the devolution of power from the federal center to the states. The process of devolution resulted in the following list of "exclusive" powers for the states: public order; police; education; local government; roads and transport; agriculture; land and land revenue; forests; fisheries; industry and trade (limited); state Public Service Commissions; and Courts (except the Supreme Court of India).It also laid down another list of subjects, known as the Concurrent List, on which the states and the center can make laws (provided the two do not clash). This list includes criminal laws and their administration; economic and social planning; commercial and industrial monopolies; shipping and navigation on the inland waterways; drugs; ports; courts and civil procedures. In the matter of fiscal devolution, that is the allocation of resources from the center to the states, Indians have progressively resolved this over the years by setting up commissions to review the situation. Each such commission recommended more and more devolution of resources to the states. As a result of the recommendation by a 1988 commission, the share of the states was raised to 85% and the share of the Union was set at 15% - apart from the fact that each state can legislate and raise taxes of its own.

By thus being politically realistic, and by responding constructively to their country's cultural diversity, India's political leaders have generally guided their country along the paths of stability and progress. According to S.D. Muni, the "elaborate structure of power devolution has combined with the linguistic basis of federal unity to facilitate the management of cultural diversity in India and help mitigate pulls towards separatism and disintegration". Muni adds that both at the central and state levels, Indians are dedicated to "a consciously followed approach to preserve and promote the cultural specificities of diverse groups", and that that "has helped such groups identify with the national mainstream" And Indians have generally strengthened the political life of their country by consciously remaining loyal to the integrity of their democratic institutions and to democratic politics.

For a country as vast and as diverse as this, India has had a commendably stable and peaceful political life. That is not to say that India has not had its own political troubles. She has had her ethnic and religious conflicts too; but the general tenor of her political life has been one of responsible leadership, love of country and people, respect for the uniqueness of each national or linguistic group, stability and progress. Most of India's ethnic conflicts are usually between particular ethnic groups and the Union – quite often as if there were no contradictions or differences between individual ethnic groups. In the contest between the states and the Union government, the issue usually is about the sharing of economic resources or decision-making power, and it is quite common for groups of states, (that is different ethnic groups) to join together and form coalitions in order to strengthen their bargaining power against the Union. India deserves its worldwide reputation and respect as "the world's largest democracy". Its economy has been one of the fastest growing in the world since the last quarter of the 20th century.

India has a lot in common with the countries of Black Africa. Like them, it is a Third World country, a former British colony, and a land of copious ethnic and cultural diversity. In the challenging task of nation building, African political leaders and rulers can change the history of their continent around by learning seriously from the Indian experiences and responses.

Restructuring

Africa, then, needs to alter its political course, learn from others, and realistically and constructively provide for its ethnic and other types of diversity. But how this will spell out will differ from situation to situation on our continent. In many situations, new federations will emerge, or old federations will restructure, each constituting each of its ethnic nations, large or small, into a state, with devolution of powers and resources that would empower each state to manage its own unique affairs, and to mobilize the strengths of its culture and ethics for orderly governance, leadership and progress, in a democratic society and

264

country. In some situations, in deference to reality, and without rancor, the agreement might even emerge to disengage some ethnic nations to go and try a country of their own, separate from the countries to which they have belonged. In other situations, the agreement might emerge that a group of contiguous small ethnic nations could band together and create a negotiated new country – outside the larger country to which they have all belonged. In yet other situations, the agreement might arise to readjust borders, or even to amalgamate neighboring countries, in order to reunite particular ethnic nations. It all depends on what the people, through discourse and in sincere good will for the future of their peoples, arrive at.

The objection might be raised that some of the possible options mentioned in the above paragraph are excessive in their thrusts. But it is important to note the point that nothing that is mentioned in that paragraph is, as an idea or proposal or demand, unknown or strange on the African continent today. For quite some time, the call for "restructuring" has grown louder and louder in many countries of Sub-Saharan Africa. The desire or call to restructure is behind the shouts of "ebyaffe, ebyaffe – kingdoms, kingdoms" that President Museveni of Uganda complains of hearing in many parts of his country. It is the factor behind the slowly growing movement, largely unnoticed in the world, of peaceful contacts and customary interactions of certain split peoples across existing country borders in parts of Africa (a movement particularly noticeable in recent years across the border that runs through the homeland of the Yoruba nation of southwestern Nigeria and Benin Republic).

In Nigeria, the call to restructure is very loud indeed, and grows louder all the time. Hardly does a day pass without its appearing in the Nigerian news media, and from persons of various ethnic origins. For some Nigerians, restructuring means the re-making of the Nigerian federation so that each of its peoples, or groups of closely related peoples, should (by choice) constitute a state and have its own state constitution, and enjoy the constitutional freedom to manage much of its affairs – in a federation with a federal government considerably weaker in powers and resource control than hitherto, and under constitutional arrangements that guarantee a much larger share of Nigeria's resources to the states – generally very similar to the structure of the Indian Union. Most foreigners looking at Nigeria on the surface believe that Nigeria has done well with its federation by progressively creating more and more states, until she now has thirty-six states. In fact, Nigeria has virtually ceased being a federation. As earlier pointed out, the act of creating more states, plus other factors, has been exploited to arrogate more and more powers and resources to the federal government, until the country has become more like a unitary state. Moreover, employing its powers to satisfy its chosen geo-political objectives in the country, the group that has controlled federal power for most of the years since independence has sometimes created states that answer to its geo-political desire only – for instance, a given number of states as between the North and the South, such that the North will always have more states than the South. At the same time, it has seized on local demands for states to split up the larger nationalities, mostly in the misguided belief that thus fragmenting and weakening such peoples weakens them and strengthens Nigeria's federal centre. Hence the growing demands for the restructuring of the federation – to create states along ethnic lines, and to considerably enhance the power of each nation to structure and manage itself according to its native culture and needs, and to allocate considerably more of Nigeria's resources to Nigeria's component nations and states.

For some other Nigerians, restructuring means that at least some of the peoples of Nigeria should be free to separate from Nigeria and form new countries – some of which would be ethnically homogenous, and some of which would be countries formed by negotiation among contiguous and related peoples – new countries where, unlike in Nigeria, mutually agreed laws and rules would be respected and thus have a chance to confer the blessings of order and stability. The spirit behind the current generation of 'separation' or 'secession' proposals is considerably different from the hurt, fear and anger that exploded into the Eastern Nigerian, or Biafran, secession attempt in 1967. No doubt, Nigeria's pattern of interactions among its peoples is such as regularly and profoundly generates animosity and resentment and even bloody conflicts – even more so today. But the latest language and temper of separation or secession bear more the mark of sober and constructive concern for the peaceful development and progress of Nigerian (and African) peoples in the modern world – a sober and constructive desire that very substantial peoples like the Yoruba or Igbo or Hausa-Fulani should be allowed to separate and use their innate capabilities to achieve speedy progress in the world (as the Japanese have done in Asia), free from the maelstrom and the stinkpot that Nigeria has become, unhampered by the usual acrimonies and conflicts so powerful and so disruptive in Nigeria. All of these calls for restructuring offer Nigeria the chance yet again to resolve, in one direction or other, its very tangled problems – in a peaceful manner.

An additional brief note is necessary concerning the subject of "secession". In most parts of Africa, governments, and supposedly "patriotic" citizens, used to react to secession as a taboo – as a horror that must not be mentioned. Many still do. But that is changing considerably. More and more people in most countries are now conceding that it is better to let the subject be openly ventilated than to shut it up. In a 2002 speech, the veteran Nigerian nationalist, Chief Anthony Enahoro, dwelt a little on the subject: Given Nigeria's traumatic experience with the sudden declaration of secession by the Eastern Region of Nigeria in 1967, and the terrible civil war that it provoked, as well as various emerging movements for secession in parts of Nigeria, he said,[3].

"I suggest that the following question is pertinent: Should the constitution allow for the ultimate change of secession? In the past, this issue has been treated as a taboo topic but the absence of thought and debate on the matter is a poor substitute for judgment. Obasanjo has helpfully opened discussion on it in his book "This Animal Called Man", *wherein he stated that any future constitution of Nigeria must provide for a right of secession. This is but a recognition of the reality that, short of brute force, the only way that different nationalities can be kept together in the long term is by their will to stay together. Our expectation is that in the new Union of Nigeria in which all nationalities are treated fairly, no nationality will have cause to want to secede. It is nevertheless prudent that provision should be made for this possibility, however remote it may seem at present. The peace and stability of the*

departing nationality, no less than the peace and stability of the surviving members of the Union, would require that a pre-agreed peaceful procedure should be followed (by any nationality seeking to secede)."

In short then, the realization has grown, and is growing, that, in any multi-nation African country (even in the better governed ones), the desire of some nationalities to secede and become separate countries on their own is a constant possibility. And more and more people are accepting that it is better to be realistic about this matter and provide constitutional and peaceful ways for secession. That General Olusegun Obasanjo, of all Nigerians, did once accept this realistic attitude to the question might surprise a lot of people. He is much better known for his expressed commitment to Nigeria's survival intact as a country. However, he wrote the comments here quoted of him in 1998, the year before he won the presidential election that ushered in his eight-year presidency of Nigeria. Up to that point, his experience in Nigerian affairs had been as a leading military officer in the terrible war to suppress Biafran secession, and his brief time as Head of the Military Government after the assassination of his boss, Gen. Murtala Mohammed, in an attempted military coup. The leaders of the attempted military coup in which Gen. Murtala Mohammed was killed announced expressly that one of their most important goals was to cut off from Nigeria certain nationalities who, in their opinion, were obstacles to the smooth running of Nigeria. (The unsuccessful coup makers got so far as to read an announcement on national radio, stating that a major objective of their coup was to exclude from Nigeria the Hausa-Fulani states of Northern Nigeria, because, in their view, the political and religious postures of those states made Nigeria unworkable). Then, in the course of the late 1990s, in response to the violently repressive dictatorship of General Sanni Abacha, many Nigerian peoples were openly talking about secession from Nigeria. Obasanjo's Yoruba nation came under enormous repression, forcing large numbers of the Yoruba elite to flee abroad for dear life, and forcing important Yoruba leaders to begin openly to consider Yoruba secession from Nigeria. Obasanjo himself (even though he never associated openly or secretly with the desires of his Yoruba nation) became one of the worst victims of the Abacha repression, landing in prison and almost losing his life there. In the light of these experiences, Obasanjo apparently had become realistic enough by 1998 to accept that it is better to provide for a constitutionally ordered and peaceful exit for any nationality that wants to secede, rather than having to go repeatedly into bitter and destructive wars, fight clandestine plots, and live with violence and fear.

In the circumstances of Africa today, the great obstacles to rational and consensus-driven restructuring and transformation are the attitudes, ambitions and delusions that have been generated and nurtured by our colonial and post-colonial history – the desire in some peoples or groups to control and even dominate others, the concept of the ruler or leader as a "strong man" or as banner of a particular ethnic group, the belief in the inevitability of conflict between peoples that are different (that what is at variance is necessarily at enmity), the consequent subliminal fears of nation by nation in each of our countries, the concept of politics as a business by which the politician may be enriched, and, above all, the unexamined, uncritical, loyalty to things as they are (no matter how bad and destructive they are), resulting in a nebulous and ultimately destructive urge to hold on to what we have and refuse to consider what we can have. Moreover, progress cannot be made if the political elite approach this matter of transformation while still sticking to and invoking the established traditions of polarization and rivalry and hostility. What the situation calls for, therefore, is a great continent-wide struggle to promote a new spirit of realistic approach to the obvious facts of Black Africa's existence, as well as a new passion for unfettered progress towards prosperity in Africa.

Expanded Role for the African Union

As should already be obvious, a very important statement by this author is that we Africans in each of our countries are, and should be, sovereign over all matters that affect our countries. All the paths mentioned above as possibilities towards restructuring and transformation on the continent are matters entirely for the citizens and peoples of each country to decide on and effect. For the first fifty years of our independence as countries in the world, the persons who have led our countries have arrogated to themselves the right and power to choose and decide all things for the people. Even in the one thing in which they have found it politically incorrect in the world not to appear to seek their people's mandate – namely, the choice of rulers through elections – they have usually manipulated the voting, pushed the people's voice aside, and chosen themselves. Even worse, the ones who are trained to employ the state's military power in order to enforce the state's will have come forth again and again to seize the state and rule, and then to cancel the institution of elections for as long as they wish. In the confusions, conflicts and violence that have thus engulfed each country, our people have been diverted from tackling in an orderly manner the big challenges that confront Africa in the modern world – challenges such as the molding of meaningful relationships among the diverse peoples and cultures in each country in order to live in some stability and peace, such as carefully choosing our own ways of taking advantage of the development resources increasingly available in our world in order gradually to rise out of poverty, and such as adroitly charting our paths through the intricacies of a world economy and international relations in order to give us better chances and respectability in the world. At independence, each of our countries started from extremely warped and precarious foundations. We have not given ourselves the chance to maneuver our way out of those foundations to success, prosperity and perhaps even power in the world. The call of this book is that we should stop, look carefully at where and how we stand, and, as a continent (the most backward of all the continents of the earth), decide and take steps to conquer our weaknesses and to move in deliberately more orderly ways towards prosperity, power and influence in our world. We can do this.

Yes, the heart of the struggle has to be in the political life of each country. But, to facilitate and give needed push to the struggle, we are fortunate to have the new proactive Pan-African spirit as it has been given form in the new African Union. The new African Union package for intervening in African countries in situations of war crimes, genocide and serious abuses of human rights, is a great step forward. The very ambitious provisions of the African Union for economic cooperation and collaboration for prosperity on the African continent are also a great step forward. And so, too, to a great extent, are the AU provisions for good governance in African counties. But even in the few years since the creation of the African Union, experience has shown, as previously pointed out above, that it is easier for the AU to state and provide for the maintenance of good governance than to get it done. It is one thing for an African ruler to come to African Union meetings and make great speeches, and vote for the most noble human and peoples' rights provisions; it is another thing entirely for him to go home to his country and begin to carry out what those speeches and provisions demand and promise. As a result, African governments continue to rig elections, African military leaders continue to overthrow governments and constitutions, African rulers and politicians continue to amass huge unearned wealth from stealing public money, African governments continue to use the powers of state to suppress and repress political oppositions, to shut down news media establishments and incarcerate journalists, to disrupt and marginalize some nationalities, and even to empower and facilitate *jihads* against some of their citizen groups.

In the context of all these, some of the AU's governance interventions have produced ridiculous outcomes. For instance, when President Gnassingbe Eyadema of Togo died in February 2005, his son, Faure Gnassingbe, pushed aside the Togo constitution and had himself sworn in as successor. Adjudging that to be a military coup, the AU called for restoration of the constitution and threatened to suspend Togo. To avoid that fate, Faure Gnassingbe organized an election three months later and, by all accounts, heavily rigged it – and that proved sufficient to make the AU withdraw the threat of suspension! In the August of 2005 also, a military coup in Mauritania led to AU suspension of that country. In response, the military rulers organized an election in 2007, an election that was generally assessed to be free and fair. The AU rescinded Mauritania's suspension, but then in August 2008, another coup toppled the elected government – causing yet another suspension of Mauritania by the AU. Happenings such as these make the AU's actions look ridiculous.

A different sort of weakness is that some African countries are too powerful, in terms of Africa and the African Union, to be touched by the AU, even when manifestly guilty of poor governance. Thus, when the Nigerian government was widely and vociferously accused of rigging elections in 2007 and of virtually levying war against some of its own citizens, the AU could not raise a finger – because the AU could not afford a Nigerian backlash. More or less the same scenario ensued when the AU encountered a resolute and defiant Mugabe in Zimbabwe in 2008. In such circumstances, the much touted Peer Review System for African rulers in the context of the AU can hardly be anything other than cosmetic.

Moreover, in the matter of intervention for good governance, the AU cannot avoid questions about the legitimacy and integrity of its actions – as long as it must employ the services of countries where good governance does not exist to enforce requirements of good governance in some other countries. The March 2010 call by President Mouamar Gadhafi of Libya, until shortly before then Chairman of the African Union, that Nigeria should consider breaking up into smaller countries in order to end the religious and inter-ethnic conflicts and blood-letting in Nigeria, was not unreasonable in the circumstance; but it was also not unreasonable that Gadhafi too should be asked, at that same time, to bring his many decades of one-man rule in Libya to an end and institute measures towards an open participatory democracy there. An old African proverb says, "When I point my finger at my neighbor, there are three pointing back at me". In the prevailing nature and character of governance and politics in virtually all African countries, no African ruler commands the moral authority to urge political change in any other African country, or even to oversee developments in any other African country.

In July 2013, a very significant piece of this truth sprang clearly onto the African stage – when the African Union appointed former President Obasanjo of Nigeria to lead a 60-man team of African observers to the coming election in Zimbabwe. A Zimbabwean organization known as the Pan African Forum which claims to defend Africa at all costs, instantly responded to reject Obasanjo's appointment. The spokesman for the group, Dr. David Nyekorach-Matsanga, charged that Obasanjo was unfit for the task because of his sordid record of election rigging in his own country Nigeria, and because of his poor leadership of African interventions in many African countries.[4]

In short, for the African Union to become an effective and truly respected agency in the fight for good governance, open governmental and political processes, accountability, and fully participatory democracy in Africa, and for it to be a champion of the transformation and restructuring urgently needed by Africa, it needs to modify its strategy. In addition to what it has already taken on, it needs to promote a mighty movement of political change. One of the outstanding positives in the African situation, since the beginning of the 21st century, is the African Union – the hopeful fact that the African Union, in spite of its frailties, is generally well regarded in Africa (and the world) and is looked up to with much expectoration by Africans – in contrast to its predecessor, the OAU. This, for Africa, is a very significant political capital. The African Union should employ that political capital to champion political transformation and change in Africa. What the African Union needs to do is to launch a movement of political review, dialogue and restructuring all over Africa. One way it might approach this is to declare a Decade of Political Transformation in Africa – an all-pervading movement of discussion and reconsideration of the ways in which we have received and handled our countries and our relationships in each of our countries, with the clear objective of producing a consensus-driven willingness and readiness to dialogue, and to restructure, in ways that can produce stability and peaceful progress towards prosperity in Africa. In consonance with the established practices and methodology of the African Union, this may mean that an AU body or agency be created and vested with the charter, the powers, and the resources for this mission.

The directions and modalities of the response to, and handling of, the movement's mission will, of course, vary from country to country, according to the conditions and wishes of the people of each country. In some countries, the mode might be national conferences under whatever name. In some others, the mode might be similar to Nelson Mandela's South African format of open dialogues, voluntary disclosures, bond-building, and nation-building. In yet others, it might be a grand mixture of various approaches. Whichever mode a country might choose or evolve, the important thing is that it must all be in the context of openness, freedom, mutual respect, restraint, and mutual avoidance of discord – all enveloped in the hope and resolve that Africa can, and will, change, and become abidingly peaceful and stable, progressive and prosperous.

How the International Community can Help

To carry out a program of this magnitude and depth, requiring immeasurable creativity, persistence, sensitivity and statesmanship, Africa will need the understanding, empathy, and very active support, of the international community. Unfortunately, any crystallization of such new input by the international community into the African situation faces obstacles posed by some strong and entrenched attitudes among many of the world's most influential persons and agencies, African and non-African. For instance, while African leaders have steadily and commendably put together the ambitious African Union structures on their continent, they have, unfortunately, sent some unwholesome messages to the international community. They have commonly said that the non-African world cannot comprehend the realities of the African situation, and that it is the exclusive responsibility of Africa to deal with conflicts on its own continent. President Olusegun Obasanjo, president of Nigeria (and therefore ruler of about one-fourth of all Black Africans) from 1999 to 2007, and chairman of the African Union for some of that time, repeatedly told the world that only Africans themselves could solve African political problems, that only Africans themselves could understand, and that non-Africans' perceptions of African situations were, of necessity, inaccurate. Where genocide seemed an incontrovertible fact and many governments of the rest of the world proclaimed it as such (as in Darfur), Obasanjo insisted that there was no genocide, that genocide was a product of the West's inaccurate perceptions. Obasanjo's contemporary as President of the Union of South Africa, Thabo Mbeki, emphatically proclaimed the same. During an official visit to the United States president (President Bush) in June 2005, Mbeki went to great lengths to silence any suggestion that non-African governments should send troops to help bring genocide to an end in Darfur – or even to peace-keeping interventions anywhere in Africa.

274

He stated:

> *"It's critically important that the African continent should deal with these conflict situations on the continent. And that includes Darfur. . . . We have not asked for anybody outside of the African continent to deploy troops in Darfur. It's an African responsibility, and we can do it."*[5]

Although any African will easily recognize that these African leaders were motivated by African pride and African desire to show self-reliance, there can be no real objective doubt that their attitudes stood to do much harm to Africa's interests. In the first place, since few Africans were likely to agree with their position on this matter, they were, in effect, creating a situation whereby conflicting voices of Africa would be projected in the world. And, as it happened, such a conflict of African voices was projected. In a press conference in 2006 with the United States Secretary of State, Condoleezza Rice, the Foreign Minister of Senegal, Cheikh Tidiane Gadio, completely contradicted Obasanjo and Mbeki. Gadio declared that the situation in Darfur was "totally unacceptable". When Secretary Rice made the statement that her country had been working hard on the Darfur situation and had averted "some of the humanitarian disaster that was forecast", Gadio, obviously unable to restrain himself, virtually exploded,

> *"Madam Secretary, you know you have to deal with the facts on the ground - - - Those militias, they are still very active - - - killing people, burning villages, raping women".* [6]

Even though Gadio's country, Senegal, had committed to sending its troops to join the African Union forces in Darfur, Gadio still bluntly asserted that the African Union alone could not do the peace-keeping task necessary in Darfur. Senegal, he said, was

> *"totally dissatisfied with the fact that the African Union . . . has asked the international community to allow it to be an African solution to an African problem.- - - The U.N. Security Council, the European Union, the African Union, the United States, we should*

275

all come together in a new way to deal with the suffering of the people of Darfur - - - We have to do something."

Secondly, and perhaps more importantly, the predominant AU posture that African conflicts should be left to African solutions alone had, for years, the unfortunate consequence of absolving the leading powers of the world of their responsibility to humanity on the African continent. Since the terrible developments in Somalia, during which international peace-keeping forces found themselves fatally entangled in conflicts with the Somali warlords, the United States and Western European countries have been reluctant to send troops to African trouble spots. In the circumstance, nothing could be more welcome to them than an Africa that tells the world, "These are African problems, and we should be left to handle them all on our own". Both the United States and NATO had no doubt that genocide was going on in Darfur. During one trip to Africa, the American Secretary of State, Condoleezza Rice, affirmed without mincing words, "By our accounts, it was and is genocide". Both the United States and NATO also knew that obstructions in the UN Security Council (notably by China) would arise to limit and slow down the requisite amount of United Nations response, and that the government of Sudan would resist any intervention. The situation was identical to what had happened repeatedly in the Yugoslav conflicts – when Russia (in support of Serbia) had resisted action by the UN Security Council, but the United States and NATO had sidestepped the United Nations to act in the interest of humanity. But in the case of Darfur, there was the sharp contrast that both the United States and NATO did not want to commit their troops. They devoted most of their effort to sending relief supplies to the troubled Sudan, even though such relief had no way of stopping the continuing destruction and killings in the villages. In addition to that, they offered equipment and training assistance to the fragile African Union forces there, even though the whole world was aware that the African Union forces in Darfur could not have the troop strength, or the logistical strength, to stop the genocide, or to keep going for as long as necessary. The United States and NATO therefore found themselves in a morally awful spot – and, unfortunately for humanity in the circumstance, the African Union's posture of "African solutions for African problems" made it possible for them to keep in that awful spot with some salve to their conscience for a long time, while large numbers of defenseless villagers were being daily killed in Darfur. .

NATO and United States authorities were able to sustain this moral position also because the ordinary citizens of the Western world simply did not understand what was happening in Darfur and what Western governments and authorities were really engaged in there. Most of the Western media, as well as Western governments, kept before the eyes of Americans and Europeans the picture that there was "conflict' going on in Darfur. Yes, there were conflicts going on there. And such conflicts consisted of Sudan's government armies fighting against local militias in wars that had been going on in that country since the 1950s. These were wars in which the government of the country, controlled by Muslim Arabs of its northern provinces, had been employing unrestrained military pressure to suppress mostly Christian Black African peoples of southern Sudan in order to continue to keep them as marginalized provinces of Sudan. Those were the conflicts in all of southern Sudan, including Darfur. Genocide in Darfur was a relatively new development, starting in 2003. It consisted, as earlier stated, of special Arab militias, formed, armed, and supported by the Sudan government, and given freedom to go on their own all over Darfur, to surprise peaceful villages, destroy all assets of village life (houses, water wells, crops, livestock, etc.), kill the villagers, and rape and kill the women, etc. What was on-going here did not have the elements of "conflict" between armed opponents. It was deliberate, systematic, and unrelenting effort at genocide, at brutally wiping out whole peoples through mass killings of peaceful, unarmed and defenseless villagers. It was a lot worse than the world saw in the course of the disintegration of Yugoslavia – in, for instance, Kosovo.

Sudan's other situations that qualify as "conflicts" might admit of the traditional ways of dealing with conflicts – third-party interventions, negotiations, ceasefires, treaties, mutual demobilizations, etc. In the genocide in Darfur, the situation was totally different. It was a situation that called on mankind to make the statement that, no matter what resistance might be mounted in United Nations counsels or by governments or regional organizations, no defenseless people, among the peoples of the earth, shall be fair game for deliberate and systematic mass killing by another people, for any reason whatsoever.

In a *Washington Post* article that this author regards as one of the best things ever written in the Western media on the Darfur crisis and the African political troubles in general, Susan Rice called on the United States, NATO, and Africa, to change their postures with regards to the Darfur situation, and urgently embark on doing the morally compelling thing there. "Since African governments alone cannot quickly muster the troops needed to halt the killing in Darfur", she wrote, the rest of the international community must act urgently. Those who were well informed about Darfur (especially the International Crisis Group (ICG), an independent nongovernmental organization), had estimated that NATO needed to send at least 12,000 to 15,000 troops, with at least a small United States contingent, ready to remain in Darfur as the African Union also increased its force there to 12,000. Predictably, Sudan would vigorously oppose the coming of such a strong force, and China would try to use its Security Council veto at the U.N. to back Sudan. But NATO and the U.S. must not allow themselves to be stopped from this urgent "responsibility to protect" defenseless human life. Just as they had side-stepped Serbian opposition backed by Russian U.N. veto and gone to protect life in Kosovo, so must they now side-step U.N. consent and go to protect life in Darfur – since African lives were not of less value than European lives. They must not also regard the Darfur situation as an African regional affair to be left for Africa alone to handle – the responsibility to protect innocent civilians facing genocide was by no means a regional issue. Hopefully, the

African Union would be able to handle situations like Darfur fully someday, but that was still in the future. Finally, the world must not continue to confuse the notions of "conflict" and "genocide" in Darfur. What was going on in Darfur was not a conflict between two forces but genocide, the massive killing of innocent, defenseless, villagers. In Africa, the world failed to stop genocide in Rwanda; it must not fail in Darfur.

That was a wonderful statement concerning the specific case of Darfur. "But the same human moral imperative that applied to the crimes in Darfur", concluded Susan Rice, should also apply to many other situations in Africa – "situations in which some stronger peoples, some incensed peoples prepared for aggression, or even some governments, target particular people groups more or less for extermination. In such cases, the world cannot, and should not, lose time to act in defense of defenseless human life".[7]

It needs to be added that, with regards to Africa's political turmoil in general, the view of many African leaders that African situations cannot be understood or helped by the rest of the world is false, and the insistence that Africans alone should be left to deal with Africa's political instability is a threat to humanity on the African continent. For Africa to achieve the type and level of political transformation that can sustain stability, peace, and progress on the continent, Africa will need the support and help of the rest of the world, and Africa will need consciously to open up to such help and support.

Former Colonial Rulers:

Furthermore, given the history of the African situation, any serious step towards political restructuring and transformation in Africa runs the risk of resistance from certain influential forces in the world outside of Africa. Of such resistance, perhaps the most tenacious category would very probably emanate from some of the former imperial rulers of African countries, who are still concerned about continued preservation and protection of their interests in their former African possessions, and still defensive of the structures that they emplaced to serve such purposes. For instance, in the case of Nigeria, any careful observer would easily find that, among the very large mass of Nigerian intelligentsia who believe and desire that their country should change peacefully and become democratic and progressive, the fear that the former imperial overlord of Nigeria, Britain, would never allow any serious change to the political structure installed at independence is a very frustrating and debilitating feeling. Nigeria was Britain's most precious and most prestigious possession in Africa, and since independence it has become even more desirable on account of the development of its great petroleum wealth. However, its political and moral life dismays the world, and its poor security condition increasingly makes it an emerging base for Islamic extremism and international terrorism. Most Nigerians reject these trends and desire change but, having no answer to the very solid culture of corruption and election fraud, they have essentially no chance of getting the change in the present political condition of their country. No informed Nigerian doubts that Britain holds a key to the possibility of positive and constructive dialogue, peaceful political change, restructuring, and transformation, in this country.

It is important to the interests of Nigeria, Britain, Africa, and indeed the world, that Britain should turn its considerable influence in Nigeria in the direction of promoting the progress of democratic politics, and the elimination of hidden and corrupt manipulations in the management of Nigeria's public affairs. A Nigeria of openly democratic politics, accountable governance, and respect for human rights and the dignity of life has a great chance of becoming, economically and politically, a very influential country in the world, and a partner that can considerably promote Britain's interests and enhance Britain's worldwide influence.

In some former French possessions too, French presence, even including French military presence, is still real, even five decades after independence. In such countries, the French have, from time to time, intervened in the political conflicts. Even as recently as January 2013, the Republic of Mali owed to French military intervention the relief of its northern provinces from the hold of radical Islamic terrorism. In a general quest for stability and transformation through dialogue in Africa, French support and

280

assistance can go a long way to strengthen local and African Union initiatives. Even other former European overlords that have had much less visibility in their former African possessions still command considerable capability to assist the cause of transformation also.

Towards EU-Africa Partnership[8]

In short, the European founders and first rulers of the countries of Africa are all in a position to assist Africans to choose, embark on, and seriously pursue, the quest for political change, transformation and stability in Africa. A lot is made today of the growing economic influence of China in Africa, but the truth really is that, no matter how large China might come to loom in the economies of Africa, she stands not much of a chance of acquiring the kinds of influence that Europe has, and will have for a long time to come, in Africa. For Africa, Europe is not merely a memory of colonialism, or merely a matter of the economy. Christian civilization, the very roots of education, immortal European names in the making of the earliest schools and churches all over Black Africa, the heritage of European languages, the impact of European cultures on the general modern development of African cultures, even the simple logic of geography, plus the almost inevitable suspicion of China's strangeness and China's ways, all these and more destine Africa to be closer to Europe than to a country like China. For instance, China may appear to be strengthening her relationship with some African rulers by using her power in the United Nations to shield and support some authoritarian African governments and some of Africa's human rights abuses, but she is also increasingly thereby strengthening suspicions and fears of her intentions among the African intelligentsia and common people in general. An unambiguous European rejection of poor governance, corruption and human rights abuses in an Africa that Europe learns to treat as a partner might still antagonize some African governments and rulers today, but the generality of the African intelligentsia and common people will value it nevertheless as important to the improvement of the quality of life on their continent.

The great obstacle to the growth of Europe-Africa partnership has been the pattern of European perception of, and attitudes to, their former African possessions. For the most part, Europe continues to view Africa, not as a continent that can become an equal partner in progress in the world, but as a continent to be manipulated for the satisfaction of European interests. In the circumstance, Africans cannot easily get rid of the suspicions and fears of the attitudes that Europe brought out of colonialism, even though the force of history inclines Africa to be much closer to Europe than to any other part of the world. For the relationship of Europe and Africa to develop for the mutual benefit of both, and for Europe to be able to have full beneficial influence on the political evolution of Africa, Europe must rise beyond the "culture of colonialism" in its approaches to Africa.

Some signs, still very shaky, that Europe may be starting to change along such lines have appeared since the beginning of the present century. These consist of the movement of EU-Africa summits that was inaugurated in the year 2000. Following the creation of the European Union, Euro-African relations continued to witness, as before, European economic aid to Africa, but practically no political dialogue between the two continents. Africa was experiencing some of its worst political turmoil and human rights abuses in these years, but concerning such issues, the EU was focused almost exclusively on eastern Europe where the Soviet empire had just collapsed. But the EU could not continue like this with respect to Africa. For one thing, the massive Chinese entry to the African scene in these years could not be long ignored. China seemed about to replace Europe as Africa's top foreign investor and trade partner. And then the massive growth of international, Islamic fundamentalist, terrorism, the Al Qaida terrorist attacks on American targets in Africa, (soon to be followed by the unprecedented terrorist attacks by Al Qaida on American soil on September 11, 2001) demanded that Europe must pay stronger attention to its southern neighbor.

In the light of all these, some African and European countries convened a summit in 2000 in Cairo, capital city of Egypt, intended to be the first of many summits. A second summit scheduled for 2003 could not be held because of the Zimbabwe situation - especially because Britain vetoed the sitting of the EU with Robert Mugabe of Zimbabwe whose land distribution policies were generating serious human rights concerns, especially as they affected Zimbabwean white farmers. At last, in 2007, Portugal, which then held the presidency of the European Union, championed the convening of the second summit. "It's important to reaffirm human rights values", said Portuguese Foreign Minister Luis Filipe Marques Amado, "but it's also necessary not to break off Africa-EU dialogue. - - - It's against Europe's interest to cut off dialogue with an entire continent , which is also Europe's nearest neighbor". Many other European voices added that Europe needed "a strategic partnership with Africa"; the EU needed to shake off the out-of-date images of Africa as the seeker of aid, and of Europe as the donor traditionally dictating political terms as conditions for the granting of economic aid. Europe and Africa should advance to a responsible adult relationship of "equal partners" based on mutual respect and political dialogue. Gomes Cravinho, an economist of Portuguese-Angolan descent, wrote:

"Emphasizing aid, to the detriment of political dialogue, promotes or sustains a relationship that is postcolonial in nature - - - we are developing a joint European-African strategy, which incorporates concerns from both sides. So far, we have focused on 'our money' and what 'you have to do' to spend it, a relationship that takes no account of sovereign states and their particular needs, and reduces African interlocutors to merely technical agents".

Africa responded warmly. During a visit to Lisbon in December 2006, Alfa Konare of Mali, then president of the AU Commission, voiced the sentiments of the generality of African leaders. "Relations with Europe" he said, "are fundamental to Africa, and we are sufficiently adult to know how to choose our allies".

In the end, in December 2007, the second summit was held in Lisbon, capital of Portugal. Most African and European governments were represented - some 27 from Europe and 25 from Africa. There were also observers from the African Union, the African Commission, the European Parliament, the European Commission, the Council of Europe, and the United Nations. Of the leading members of the European Union, Britain boycotted the summit – still in protest against the presence of Mugabe.

Since the end of the summit, it has been criticized in some quarters for various particulars. First, it has been criticized for doing virtually nothing about human rights. Apart from carpeting both Mugabe of Zimbabwe and Al Bashir of Sudan for their poor human rights records, the summit did nothing about human rights. And that was not an accident; it was deliberate policy. The view taken by the summit's Portuguese hosts was that Europe and Africa should focus first on creating a partnership tradition, and that dialogue on the important issue of human rights would have its right time later. Nor were the European governments alone in focusing on strategic interests at the summit; African governments wanted to focus on strategic interests too. A spokesman for the Union of South Africa, Foreign Ministry Deputy Director Gert Grobler, said, "South Africa and Africa would want this summit to focus on the substance of expanding the strategic partnership between the continents – that must be the key focus".

The summit has been somewhat criticized too for failing to deal with the question of corruption in African governments. But this, obviously, was a difficult and delicate matter. In the opinion of some leading Africans, a discussion of corruption could not be limited to Africa but needed to include participations in corruption by both Africa and Europe. The Guinea-Bissau economist, Carlos Lopes, pointed out, before the summit, that there was no sense in discussing corruption in Africa alone, since "there is no corrupt people without others who corrupt them. Big international contracts have shown that corruption in Africa is, to a large extent, generated by (European and other) suppliers and speculators". Many leading Europeans too readily admitted that corruption in Africa was, ultimately, dependent on European banks that receive and help to launder the stolen money from Africa. Closely related to the issue of corruption is also the issue of political conflicts in Africa. The summit also skipped this.

Finally, in terms of failings, the summit did not exactly produce the much heralded "partnership of equals". One development which showed up towards the close of the summit was to demonstrate that a partnership of equals had not exactly been born. In the last stages of the summit, the European Union side strongly urged the African countries to sign to Economic Partnership Agreements (EPAs) that had been under negotiation long before the summit. The background to this is that as far back as 2002, the EU had proposed these EPA agreements to African and other third world countries, their most important proposal being reciprocal opening of markets between the EU market and these poorer markets. The African countries had been resisting, because of fears that the reciprocal market opening demanded by the EU would not only cut into their national revenues, but would also give powerful European companies unlimited access to African markets and kill the weaker African companies. For the Africans, the sudden and emphatic demands of the EU side on this old subject was a surprising and unwelcome step, a sort of return by Europe to its traditional posture of controlling donor. With their economic bargaining position considerably strengthened by their growing economic relations with China, the Africans felt more confident to turn down the EPA drafts. Senegalese President, Abdoulaye Wade, responded, "We are not talking any more about EPAs - - - we are going to meet to see what we can put in place of the EPAs". When some of the weaker African countries were then privately prevailed upon to sign up, some other African leaders warned that Europe should not take the unhelpful step of returning to the old game of dividing Africa against Africa.

In spite of all its failings, however, the 2007 summit was a considerably important step forward in terms of a Euro-African partnership. It did not, it is worth repeating, exactly produce a partnership of equals, but it sprouted many small pointers towards a future of fruitful partnership between the European Union and Africa. Even the mere gathering of most African governments with most European governments in Lisbon was itself a major sign of change. This is so especially because, of the former European colonial powers in Africa, Portugal had been the most hated in Africa in the years of the independence decade. As would be remembered, while all other colonial powers had been granting independence to their African possessions, Portugal had proclaimed the strange position that the Portuguese African possessions were actual provinces of Portugal and were therefore not eligible for independence. As a result, the Portuguese possessions had become the scenes of the most destructive independence wars on the African continent, a fact that had then focused the bitterness of all of Africa on Portugal. It was therefore a very significant sign of a coming revolution in relationships that Africa was willing by 2007 to view Portugal as an emerging partner. This in itself was a very big success.

Furthermore, even though the summit did not deal with important issues such as human rights, conflicts in Africa, and corruption, it did lay out a procedural norm as well as an agenda for the summit system. In the words of Luis Amado, Portuguese Foreign Minister, the idea of the summit system was to identify the problems that members of the partnership were facing and to tackle such problems in a multilateral manner, since the problems were not limited to any one country. The summit system would operate through programs of action for stated periods, so that progress on each program of action could be assessed at the end of its period. Accordingly, the first period was identified as the years 2008 to 2010, and the programs of action for that period were listed as follows, with the provision that progress on each of them would be assessed in the subsequent summit to be held in 2010:

1. Peace and security
2. Democratic governance and human rights
3. Trade and regional integration
4. Mobility and employment
5. Energy
6. Science
7. The information society and space
8. Climate Change and Migration.

All told, therefore, the 2007 summit, and the whole Euro-African summit system that it was represented as beginning, were a significant step along positive directions in the evolution of relations between the European Union and Africa. Apparently, because of the problems generated by the worldwide recession which started in 2008, the summit slated for 2010 has not been able to hold. But there is no reason to believe that the summit system has fizzled out. Hopefully, what we now have is no more than another delay, similar to the kind of delay that held off the summit scheduled for 2003 until 2007. If the summit system resumes again and continues to develop, it can influence not only Africa's economic, political and social development, but, particularly importantly, it can promote transformations in African governance, human rights record, and democratic politics. And it can strengthen the economies of both Europe and Africa. This is not only in the interest of either Europe or Africa; it is in the interest of both. And both need to continue to put effort into it.

Towards US-Africa Partnership

The United States of America is, obviously, one of the biggest potential sources of understanding and help to transformation in Africa. A natural link between America and Black Africa exists in the fact that some 22% of America is made up of persons of Black African origin – not just recent immigrants, but folks who were in this country from its inception, and who have been integral to all its struggles, pains and successes. In the development of African nationalism in the years after the Second World War, the example of, and hope in, America, and general knowledge of America's opposition to colonial empires, were encouraging factors. Educated Africans generally embraced America as the author of the Declaration, at the end of the First World War, of the right of all peoples to live and rule themselves in freedom. Some of the foremost Black African nationalists (like Kwameh Nkrumah of Ghana and Nnamdi Azikiwe of Nigeria) were among the earliest African persons to come as students for higher education in America in the 20th century. Some of them, while students in America, had some experience of Black American politics and journalism. And the American Declaration of Independence provided some of the source of their freedom rhetoric later in the African struggle against colonialism.

Unfortunately, the coming of the Cold War in the years after the Second World War, plus America's lack of direct knowledge about Africa, molded America's policy in such a way that America came to be perceived in much of Africa as another "colonial power" bringing its enormous power and influence to reinforce European colonialism and neo-colonialism on the African continent. In particular, as would be remembered, Portugal, unlike the rest of Europe, insisted that its African colonies were not colonies but provinces of Portugal and therefore not eligible for independence, and the peoples of the Portuguese colonies had to take up arms to fight for their independence. Rather than employ its influence in Europe to turn Portugal away from this course of conflict, the United States became a major supporter of Portugal in its needless wars in Africa – and the peoples of the Portuguese colonies found themselves confronting American weapons and American influence.

Moreover, as country after country in Africa became independent, they were ruled by leaders with little or no knowledge of world politics, and no experience in the nuances of international relations. In that general atmosphere, no other power in the world had the kind of opportunity that America had to help the newly independent countries define the world. But America's Cold War stance in Africa created the circumstance whereby some of the more radically nationalistic leaders of newly independent African countries were identified by America's policy makers as allies of America's Cold War enemies, and therefore as America's enemies. Unfortunately, as it turned out, some of the inexperienced leaders of the new African countries came to imagine that salvation in the struggle against neo-colonialism and its American support belonged in seeking counter-support from the communist powers. In Africa in general, it thus was difficult for a lot of informed Africans to recognize, or accord deserved appreciation to, aspects of American policies that were helpful to Africa. For instance, America's influence was considerably effective in pushing apartheid South Africa gradually towards change, and President John Kennedy's Peace Corps program was a welcome source of help to development in many African countries; but these tended to be beclouded by prevalent suspicions and fears of neo-colonialism. Even so, to show how much expectation Africans had for change in American policies towards Africa, most informed Africans perceived President Kennedy as the beginning of such change, and that made President Kennedy very popular all over Black Africa. In short, rather than harvest America's large potential wealth of Black African goodwill in Africa, American policy makers in the Cold War tended generally to go in search of, and to find, enemies on the continent. The records will show some day how many leaders of new African countries who knew nothing about communism or the nuances of the clouded international terrain were firmly identified by American officials as communists or collaborators of the Soviet Union, and were treated as such.

Even in subsequent years, in the years after the Cold War, because America still must rely heavily on information recycled from former Cold War allies (former colonial powers in Africa), America continued to pursue towards Africa policies that did not address African situations meaningfully. In the three-month period of genocide in Rwanda, in the years of genocide in Darfur, in the disasters and revolt in the Niger Delta in Nigeria, in the collapse of order in Liberia and in Liberia's neighbors, in the more or less steady growth of Islamic terrorism in some parts of Africa, America long seemed to lack clear policy directions. Even in the area of business, American government policy makers had generally tended to defer to their perceptions of British or French "areas of interest" in tropical Africa, thereby considerably limiting the scope and success of American private businesses in the region.

In these circumstances, elements desirous of democratic governance and accountable leadership all over Africa remained painfully unsure how to touch America. And as a result of all these, there exists the negative perception, common among substantial parts of the African intellectual and political elite, that America's policy towards Africa is impossible to grasp. This includes feelings that America seems to regard Black African lives as less valuable than White European lives, and that America seems content to validate and re-use outmoded post-colonial European policies in Africa rather than develop well informed policies of its own. It also includes feelings that where its economic and strategic interests seem to be touched, as well as in uncertain and borderline situations, America would give its support to even the most authoritarian, the most corrupt, and the most repressive African regimes and groups, and employ its enormous influence against even the most promising democratic potentials in Africa, and against manifestly democratic elements in any African country.

Of course, those who feel these things about America are aware of, and grateful for, American economic aid in Africa and the usually reliable American relief to Africans in various types of disaster. It is just that they cannot accept that aid and relief should be substitutes for appropriate policy directions towards their suffering continent.

289

Even much more importantly, most African intellectuals and politicians who feel these ways about American policies towards the Black African sub-continent commonly derive the intensity of their feelings from their basic perception of America's place in our world. Obviously, America is not just the greatest country in our world today; it is the greatest country in the known history of the world. No other country in human history has ever been as important to its generation of the human race as America is to our modern world. And that is not merely because America is the world's greatest economic and military power, but because America seriously holds and cherishes human values that are absolutely crucial to the quality and dignity of human life. America is exceptional, and exceptionally important to our world, because of its respect for, and defense of, human freedom, and because of its sincere efforts at inclusiveness in its own land. That is not to ignore the history of slavery and segregation in the American past, or even of survivals of racism in contemporary America. But over and above these, there is easily recognizable a uniquely American loyalty to the principles of human rights and human freedom, and a dependable progress of the American society in issues of human rights and freedom.

In the Reagan years in the 1980s, America advocated a policy of "constructive engagement" with apartheid South Africa – in the belief that if the world kept doing business and interacting with apartheid South Africa, the captains of apartheid would gradually give up their extreme racist philosophies and ways. We Africans were very skeptical about that, of course; what we wanted was that the world should isolate apartheid in every way, and thereby destroy apartheid. In Black African elite circles, there was generated much discussion of American policies towards Africa as a result of this development. And that usually led informed Africans to ventilate their opinions of America itself. I took part in many of such discussions – in the leadership of the political party of which I was one of the national leaders and which I represented in the Nigerian Senate, in the Senate Foreign Relations Committee of which I was Vice-Chairman, in the Nigerian Anti-apartheid Movement, in a World Conference on Actions against Apartheid which I attended in London as a Nigerian representative, and in some of our universities.

Our typical response in these forums was that a policy of constructive engagement with apartheid would be retrogressive, and would even strengthen apartheid – and that the American government was seriously wrong in assuming that the leaders of apartheid, and the white society of apartheid South Africa, were like Americans who could be influenced gradually to yield up traditional racist positions. The opinion was frequently expressed that, unlike white South Africans, Americans were a people whose country was consciously founded on principles of human freedom, who tended, on the whole, to defer to those principles as enshrined by their founding fathers in their constitution, and who were able, even if only slowly, to move forward in accepting an open and inclusive society. In contrast, white South Africa was not, we believed, a society in which a Martin Luther King Jnr. could arise or have an impact. And white South African institutions did not, and could not, have the kind of integrity possessed by such American institutions as the American federal government and its agencies, or the United States Supreme Court – all of which could be relied upon, if it came to the crunch, to uphold the American constitution and its provisions for the constitutional rights of all. That was how most of us saw America. For most of us, America was the moral leader of the human race in our times; there might arise other powers as great as, or even greater than, America economically and militarily, but there probably would never be another country as dedicated as America to the principles and demands of human freedom – and we believed that the makers of American policy were grossly mistaken by equating a country like white South Africa with America.

Naturally, people who tend to perceive America in these terms cannot but feel strongly about the fact that America continues to view Black Africa through spectacles fashioned by European colonial agents of an earlier time and different circumstances. They cannot but feel strongly about the fact that American policy makers tend to employ towards Black Africa policies that were evolved by Europeans in a time of Europe's arrogant power in Africa. America was not a colonial power in Africa; America is known to have at least subtly disapproved of colonial empires by the middle of the 20th century – and it is wrong that American policy makers should borrow, concerning Africa, attitudes and policies from European imperialist traditions.

However, some very positive factors have gradually entered into the scene of American-African relations in more recent times. One is that a lot of Africans have been migrating to America in recent decades. Until the 1950s, while Africans lived under European colonialism, virtually all of African emigration, consisting mostly of African students, was to Europe. Since the 1960s, more and more of African emigrants, students and others, have chosen America as their destination. By the beginning of the 21st century, probably as many African emigrants have been heading to America as to Europe. And, according to various surveys, African immigrants to America are usually well educated men and women – very commonly college graduates, or High School diploma holders eager to take advantage of American college education. Some surveys by the United States Census Bureau have it that Nigerian immigrants are the most educated national group of immigrants in contemporary American history.

Another is the election of a man of Black African origins, Barak Obama, as president of America. Most informed people in Black Africa celebrated the coming of the Obama presidency as probable beginnings of a radical transformation in the relationship between Black Africa and America. One incalculable positive in the situation is that President Obama occupies the position to speak to Africa in a way that no other leader of a non-African country can possibly do. Of all the leaders of the great powers of our world, only President Obama can look Africa in the eyes and voice uncomfortable truths – without fearing to be regarded as domineering or patronizing. Some of the fruits of that positive showed up in the Obama speech to Africa during his stop in Accra, Ghana, on his first visit to Black Africa as president. Here are some gems from that wonderfully futuristic speech: [9]

> "The 21st century will be shaped by what happens not just in Rome or Moscow or Washington, but by what happens in Accra, as well. This is the simple truth of a time when the boundaries between people are overwhelmed by our connections. Your prosperity can expand America's prosperity. Your health and security can contribute to the world's

health and security. And the strength of your democracy can help advance human rights for people everywhere. So I do not see the countries and peoples of Africa as a world apart; I see Africa as a fundamental part of our interconnected world, as partners with America on behalf of the future we want for all of our children. That partnership must be grounded in mutual responsibility and mutual respect. And that is what I want to speak with you about today.

We must start from the simple premise that Africa's future is up to Africans. I say this knowing full well the tragic past that has sometimes haunted this part of the world. After all, I have the blood of Africa within me, and my family's own story encompasses both the tragedies and triumphs of the larger African story. Some of you know my grandfather was a cook for the British in Kenya, and though he was a respected elder in his village, his employers called him "boy" for much of his life. He was on the periphery of Kenya's liberation struggles, but he was still imprisoned briefly during repressive times. In his life, colonialism wasn't simply the creation of unnatural borders or unfair terms of trade – it was something experienced personally, day after day, year after year.

My father grew up herding goats in a tiny village, an impossible distance away from the American universities where he would come to get an education. He came of age at a moment of extraordinary promise for Africa. The struggles of his own father's generation were giving birth to new nations, beginning right here in Ghana. Africans were educating and asserting themselves in new ways, and history was on the move. But despite the progress that has been made – and there has been considerable progress in many parts of Africa – we also know that much of that promise has yet to be fulfilled. Countries like Kenya had a per capita economy larger than South Korea's when I was born. They have badly been outpaced. Disease and conflict have ravaged parts of the African continent.

In many places, the hope of my father's generation gave way to cynicism, even despair. Now, it's easy to point fingers and to pin the blame of these problems on others. Yes, a colonial map that made little sense helped to breed conflict. The West has often approached Africa as a patron or a source of resources rather than a partner. But the West is not responsible for the destruction of the Zimbabwean economy over the last decade, or wars in which children are enlisted as combatants. In my father's life, it was partly tribalism and patronage and nepotism in an independent Kenya that for a long stretch derailed his career, and we know that this kind of corruption is still a daily fact of life for far too many. Now, we know that's also not the whole story. Here in Ghana, you show us a face of Africa that is too often overlooked by a world that sees only tragedy or a need for charity. The people of Ghana have worked hard to put democracy on a firmer footing, with repeated peaceful transfers of power even in the wake of closely contested elections. And by the way, can I say that for that the minority deserves as much credit as the majority. And with improved governance and an emerging civil society, Ghana's economy has shown impressive rates of growth. This progress may lack the drama of 20th century liberation struggles, but make no mistake: It will ultimately be more significant. For just as it is important to emerge from the control of other nations, it is even more important to build one's own nation. So I believe that this moment is just as promising for Ghana and for Africa as the moment when my father came of age and new nations were being born. This is a new moment of great promise. Only this time, we've learned that it will not be giants like Nkrumah and Kenyatta who will *determine Africa's future. Instead, it will be you – the men and women in Ghana's parliament – (applause) – the people you represent. It will be the young people brimming with talent and energy and hope who can claim the future that so many in previous generations never realized.*

Now, to realize that promise, we must first recognize the fundamental truth that you have given life to in Ghana: Development depends on good governance. That is the ingredient which has been missing in far too many places, for far too long. That's the change that can unlock Africa's potential. And that is a responsibility that can only be met by Africans.

As for America and the West, our commitment must be measured by more than just the dollars we spend. I've pledged substantial increases in our foreign assistance, which is in Africa's interests and America's interests. But the true sign of success is not whether we are a source of perpetual aid that helps people scrape by – it's whether we are partners in building the capacity for transformational change."

In short, history has produced an American leader who is able to stand strongly on his feet, look Africa in the eyes, and speak to Africa in powerfully new terms. The vast majority of Africans who have agonized helplessly about the terrible conditions of their continent widely celebrated as brother and ally an American president who is able to say authentically to Africa that the poor governance, the corruption, the discriminations, the constantly rigged elections, the repression, and the consequent poverty in African countries, have denied the vast masses of Africans of the fruits of national independence, have bred cynicism and despair, and made Africa to fall far back, even among the Third World, in the struggle for progress and prosperity. For a lot of Africans it was refreshingly new to listen to President Obama as he told Africa in his Accra speech that the irrational structures and boundaries foisted on Africa by European imperialism create terrible difficulties, no doubt, but that the failure to rise beyond these and achieve progress and prosperity belongs to Africans themselves. He told Africa that America would offer aid as always, but that America is more committed to seeing Africa transform itself and become a partner with America in the quest for order, peace, freedom, progress and prosperity. Africa's new struggle for open and participatory politics, for order and stability, and for progress and victory over poverty, is, he says, more important, though less dramatic, than the anti-imperialist wars of the mid-20th century, and the warriors who must fight it and win it are the ordinary people and the youths of Africa, appropriately invested in and empowered by their countries.

By looking Africans in the eyes and speaking to Africa in these terms, President Obama has, hopefully, inaugurated a new American tradition of candor – of family candor – in America's dealings with Africa. And no other force in the world commands as much capacity as this to help Africa towards political change, transformation and stability – and towards progress and prosperity.

Towards Fuller Dimensions of Pan-Africanism

Many Africans also hope that the coming of the Obama presidency, and President Obama's "family" approach to Africa, will inaugurate yet another immensely valuable asset for Africa's change, transformation, and progress – namely, a heightened and proactive attention by the African-American political elite to homeland Africa. Since the independence of African countries, African-American contacts with, and impact on, Africa have tended to be distant, episodic and peripheral. And that is a big departure from the early 20th century Pan-African passion among people of African descent in the United States and the rest of the New World. In fact the philosophy of Pan-Africanism, the idea that people of African descent in all parts of the world have common interests and needs and a common struggle, was originated by people of African descent in the New World in the late 19th century. In the hands of African-Americans and black West Indians like Edward W. Blyden, W.E.B. Du Bois, Marcus Garvey, Sylvester Williams, and others, a Pan-African Movement emerged, holding its first international conference in 1900 and further conferences in 1919, 1921, 1923, 1927, and 1929. All these conferences, held in various European cities, were the work of

African-Americans and persons from the West Indies, and were attended mostly by them. It was gradually that the conferences began to have some Africans from homeland Africa, mostly African students studying abroad, especially in America and Britain. Because of the Great Depression and the Second World War, the conferences were not resumed until 1945 – by which time the number of Africans attending became quite large, most of them students abroad, some of them already beginning to emerge as the nationalist leaders of their countries in Africa. In the years after 1945, the nationalist struggle for independence gradually gathered momentum in Africa, and its leaders invoked the Pan-African spirit to attempt to coordinate their scattered nationalist struggles on the continent. In the circumstance, the Pan-African Movement gradually became an exclusive African affair. By the time that many African countries became independent , and the founding of the Organization of African Unity by these independent countries in 1963, Pan-Africanism had become exclusively and entirely an African movement.

Thus, though Pan-Africanism originally envisaged a convergence of homeland Africans and Diaspora Africans, such a convergence never materialized in any political sense – and the result has been that the two have gone their different ways, consumed in their different types of political struggle. On the whole, the African Diaspora in the United States has done quite well – with their shining victories in the civil rights struggles, and the emergence of the Obama generation of Black American political leaders, all in the context of an America whose innate receptiveness to change and openness has risen to new heights. As for the African political elite in homeland Africa, they won independence for the wobbly and incoherent countries that European imperialism created for Africans, but have proved inept at understanding the peculiar problems inherent in such countries – not to talk of meaningfully tackling the problems. Lacking the right orientation, the African political elite have lacked the perspicacity required in the circumstances of their new countries, and have moved from step to step that tend to turn the problems into conflicts, poverty, the denial of opportunities and of human dignity, and horrendous human suffering.

That is why the Obama factor can become an invaluable asset for Africa and Africans. Following on the Obama lead, the considerably influential Black American political elite, and the political elite of the African Diaspora in the rest of the New World, can bring enormous influence to bear upon the quality of governance in Africa, upon African elections, upon the development of democracy, upon corruption in Africa, upon African responses to the requirements of human freedom and human rights, and ultimately upon African perceptions of, and responses to, the types of countries that European imperialism bequeathed to Africa. Africa has in America a very solid body of influential Black American men and women who, like President Obama, can look Africa in the eyes, and with authentic family candor and genuine concern, tell Africa the truth, and urge a change of course in Africa. One institutional measure that would be helpful now is the original Pan-African Movement revived, to bring the African-American political elite and the African political elites together, in the overall interest of the Black man, and the prospects and image of the Black man in the world.

Needless to say, the most important requirement in this situation would be that Africa should recognize its assets and consciously seek to include and involve them in the greatly needed struggle for change and transformation on the African continent. The conception of Pan-Africanism as an exclusive bonding philosophy of African governments is grossly inadequate. It is true that the Constitutive Act of the AU declares that the AU shall "invite and encourage the full participation of the African Diaspora as an important part of our Continent, in the building of the African Union", and that the African Diaspora has been defined as "consisting of people of African origin living outside the continent, irrespective of their citizenship and nationality and who are willing to contribute to the development of the continent and the building of the African Union". But all that the African Union has done in this regard since its foundation in 2002 has been to issue invitations, on its websites, to the general African public and the African Diaspora for comments and suggestions on some of the AU's debates and plans – especially the issue of an African Union government. That can hardly be described as rallying the forces – which is what Africa needs in the present circumstances. The

African Union needs to set up a body that is rich in expertise and in Diaspora content, to study the question how the Diaspora can be effectively involved, "in full participation - - - in the building of the African Union - - - in the development of the African continent". The questions before this body should include how to construct a Pan-African Movement and African Union that actively include the African Diaspora, and how, through these, the African Diaspora can become a regular functional player in the affairs of Africa and the African Union, and an effective contributor to the building of the new African society, democratic political traditions, and material progress. Part of the new Pan-African strategy should consist of various specialized Pan-African associations – of journalists, of lawyers, of jurists, of college students, of college professors, of engineers, of scientists, of university women, of businessmen and entrepreneurs, of lawmakers, etc. – each of which brings its own angle to the Pan-African and African enterprise.

Towards Asia's Contributions to African Transformation

Relations between Africa and Asia have grown considerably in recent years, mostly generated by the fact that Africa has become a major source of the world's energy supply. Leading the way towards Africa in Asia in recent times have been the People's Republic of China, India and Japan.

From the 1990s, China gradually became a major trade and investment partner to many African countries. The magnitude of China's clout in Africa was particularly exhibited in a China-Africa summit in Beijing in November 2006, attended by fifty African heads of state. For now, the feelings of most Africans about the growing influence of China in Africa are ambivalent. The growing partnership in investment and commerce are seen as, at last, a welcome liberalization of the international dimensions of Africa's economic life. But there are also questions as to whether the aggressive penetration by China could be the beginning of a new type of economic imperialism on the African continent. However, even in spite of this ambivalence, China has acquired a presence that can impact political developments in Africa. And the probability is that that influence will grow bigger, even though it is unlikely, at least for a long time in the future, to rival seriously the influence of the West.

For now also, China's stature in Africa is somewhat compromised from the perception among the African intelligentsia that China is so focused on her economic gains in Africa as to be willing to ignore, or even support, serious human rights violations – as she did in a country like Sudan. The recent partition of Sudan into two separate countries has removed much of China's need to support Sudan against the world and against much of African opinion. Even so, as resistance to corrupt and repressive governance grows in Africa, China is certain to need to adjust its over-all posture in Africa towards strengthening good governance and support for human rights. The pressure on China to do that is sure to grow in Africa. Moreover, Black African people, increasingly in battle against human rights abuses on their own continent, are closely watching China's human rights records at home in China as well as the growing record of China's responses to human rights issues on the world stage. If China were to become more positively responsive to the demands of human rights generally, China can acquire more influence in African affairs and become a contributor to restructuring and transformation in Africa.

Japan and India can also become important contributors to transformation on the African continent. As a commercial and investment partner of Africa in modern times, Japan is considerably older than China. And many Africans would love to see Japan play more proactive roles in helping transformation, change and progress on their continent. India, of the most powerful countries of Asia, is, geographically, Africa's closest neighbor. India is also, historically, the closest to Africa. From quite early times, trade and other interactions with India across the Indian Ocean played very significant roles in the making of the civilizations of both the coast and interior of East Africa. As the modern Indian economy has grown since independence, the historic traditions of contact have inevitably drawn India and Africa closer economically. Moreover, as a former British colony and home of great ethnic diversity, India has very strong similarities with African countries. In these regards, India and Africa have a lot to learn from each other. In short, therefore, the chances of a modern Afro-Indian partnership are very strong – and the benefits of such partnership, for both, are potentially great.

Towards Africa's Strong Role in the International Justice System

Finally, it is essential to Africa's healthy development, and to Africa's appropriate place in the world, that Africa operate as a full member of the international community. Therefore, the African Union's denunciation of the International Criminal Court over its warrant of arrest for the president of Sudan for alleged war crimes and human rights violations in Darfur was a serious misstep by the African Union. Watchfulness over Africa's independence is essential, but the African Union's building of a wall of immunity around Sudan's officials, in spite of all that the world and Africa knew about happenings in Darfur at that point, does not seem plausible as an act in defense of Africa's independence. Rather, it looks like a message by African rulers that they will stand by any African ruler even in the worst cases of human rights abuse – a damaging negation of the declaration in the Constitutive Act of the African Union that the AU will responsibly defend human and peoples' rights on the continent.

The posture of Africa's rulers towards the International Criminal Court has since grown even more hostile. Following the ICC's indictment of some leading Kenyan politicians for human rights violations in the 2007-8 Kenyan massacres, the rulers of Kenya responded by tagging the ICC as a neo-colonialist institution biased against Africans. By the end of 2014, the AU had taken the position that the ICC was disproportionately pointed against Africans, that the ICC needed to be reviewed to make it fairer, and that charges against Africans pending before the court be meanwhile dropped.

All of these call for very careful handling by the AU, otherwise they could rob the AU of credibility and send the alarming message that Africa demands some specially inferior place in the world. Of course, it is crucial that the international criminal justice system should have fairness and integrity. For that reason, the AU, having taken the position it has now taken, will need to take serious steps towards getting the ICC reviewed, and not risk appearing merely to be protecting African rulers by shutting the ICC out of Africa. Africa's vital interests in the world demand that Africa's rulers and representatives dutifully present their principals (the African people) as full and responsible stake holders in the world's order and in the integrity of the international organizations, agencies and institutions that serve the interests of a world that is progressively becoming conscious of the common interests and duties of the human race.

Without doubt, one of the most important developments in our world in the decades since the end of the Cold War is the emergence and growth of the doctrine that mankind has a "Responsibility to Protect" its members. Like the rest of mankind, (in fact, perhaps more than other human groups today), the people of Africa need that the emerging international justice system, with the International Criminal Court at its core, should mature as a universally respected servant of our world in the protection of the dignity of human life – a source of fear for all the powerful who might be tempted to abuse the dignity of man, or to take human life with impunity. Africa also needs that the justice system being constructed within the African Union's "responsibility-to-protect" and justice machinery be a highly respected piece in the emerging international justice system, and not develop or appear to be a device for cordoning off and protecting powerful evil doers on the African continent. Africa also has the same caliber of high stakes in the many agencies and organizations that are emerging and growing in our world for the fight against corruption, for the tracing and recovery of resources fraudulently appropriated by powerful officials and hidden beyond their countries, for the care of displaced persons and refugees, for watching over the conduct of governments and powerful public officials, police and judicial systems, in their handling of the weak and vulnerable members of the human race. And Africa needs that Africa's governments and the African Union constitute major parts, and major support, of the kinds of fight that these many bodies and agencies have taken on in our world.

In summary, full and fully responsible and respectable membership of, and responsiveness to, the international community and its evolving justice system, are critical to Africa's transformation – to the fulfillment of Africa's great needs of good governance, open and participatory democracy, politics of

302

inclusiveness and consensus, accountability in the management of public affairs, and respect for human rights and for the dignity of human life.

Of vital national interests of all

Africa is the world's second largest continent, and the home of over 15% of the population of the world. In terms of new investment and development, Africa is one of the largest areas of new opportunities in our world. A politically stable and peacefully growing Africa is potentially a big asset to the vital national interests of most countries and regions of the world.

The world's economies need that the navigational channels of the seas in the Gulf of Guinea in West Africa, the seas off the coasts of west-central Africa, the routes around the Cape of Good Hope, and the seas around the Horn of Africa, be open and peaceful for commerce, and for the movement of energy to feed the economies of most parts of the earth. The spasmodic troubles with oil production and movement in the Nigerian Niger Delta, the political threats to oil production in Cabinda in Angola and in disputed territories between Sudan and South Sudan, the chaos-induced and poverty-driven piracy in the waters off the Horn of Africa, etc., all these frequently cause enormous losses to the world's economies and depress the quality of life for people of countless countries.

The danger of Islamic fundamentalist terrorism is growing in Africa – particularly in places like Somalia, countries of the African Mediterranean coast (the Maghreb), and countries of the interior of West Africa (the broad grassland, Sahel and desert territories comprising Mauritania, Mali, Burkina Fasso, Niger, Chad, Northern Nigeria and Northern Cameroons). A sort of introductory international shot from the Northern Nigerian terrorist brew reached the United States on Christmas Day 2009, when a well-educated Nigerian youth from a respectable Northern Nigerian Muslim family flew with explosives strapped to his underpants on a large commercial aircraft, with the intention of blowing up the aircraft and its tens of passengers over the city of Detroit. The Nigerian youth was reported to have been   recruited by Al-Qaida in Yemen – a report that should raise the fear that some of the literate and more exposed of the Islamic terrorist elements of Northern Nigeria may already be attracting attention for recruitment among the most capable international terrorist organizations. About the same time, Al Shabaab, the Somali terrorist organization and affiliate of Al Qaida, showed signs of growing capability to operate in other parts of East Africa beyond Somalia. Moreover, Al Shabaab and the radical Islamic movements of Northern Nigeria also appeared to be groping towards collaboration – as evidenced in growing indications that Al Shabaab was, at some point, seeking to extend its activities to helping the Islamic terrorist organizations in Northern Nigeria to improve on their terrorist capacity, for a major jihad in Nigeria. Subsequently, Al Shabaab has suffered some significant setbacks in its Somalia base at the hands of the forces of the African Union. But, meanwhile, the danger has grown that Al Qaida is becoming an even more active player on the African continent generally – through various regional affiliates, copy-cat groups, and splinter groups. All available evidence indicates that Al-Qaida in the Islamic Maghreb (AQIM) has grown quite considerably, especially in post-Gadhafi Libya. AQIM and another al-Qaida affiliate, Ansar al-Sharia, are the leading suspects in the attack on the United States consulate in Benghazi on September 11, 2012, which resulted in the assassination of the American ambassador to Libya and three other American officials.

Besides, AQIM, as we said in an earlier chapter, did not only establish a linkage with the insurrection in the northern provinces of the Republic of Mali in West Africa, it took possession of that insurrection. French forces intervened very effectively in northern Mali in 2013 and dislodged the terrorists from their main bases. But the terrorists, commanding formidable arsenals of sophisticated weaponry as well as large amounts of funds, have proved much better organized and much stronger than the international community first thought. Consequently, what all concerned non-Muslims and moderate Muslims of West Africa have increasingly feared in recent decades has now happened, as the terrorists dislodged from northern Mali have scattered into other countries of the Western Sudan and Sahel (especially to Northern Nigeria, Chad, and Northern Cameroon) and reinforced terrorist presences there.

In Nigeria in particular, these developments have galvanized the culture of Islamic jihadism historically inherent in much of Muslim Northern Nigeria, and have ultimately produced Boko Haram, undoubtedly the most capable, most violent and most destructive Islamic fundamentalist terrorist group that Sub-Saharan Africa has seen. By the end of 2014, Boko Haram had succeeded in overrunning much of Nigeria's three Northeastern states (Bornu, Adamawa and Yobe), controlling there a large territory over which it claimed to have established a "caliphate". In the states of the Nigerian Northwest, where radical Islam has traditionally enjoyed considerable resonance, and where Sharia systems were established in about 2001 in defiance of the rest of Nigeria, Boko Haram has been quite free to strike at will. More or less the same is true of the states of the broad Nigerian Middle Belt, where Muslim and non-Muslim peoples are interspersed in an intricate jigsaw, and where inter-ethnic and religious conflicts have grown more and more virulent in recent decades. Located in this region, Nigeria's capital city of Abuja has proved repeatedly vulnerable to Boko Haram's attacks. Even in the states of the Nigerian South (all the way to the Atlantic coast), the threat of Boko Haram had become very real by the end of 2014. Nigerian military authorities acknowledged by then that Boko Haram cells existed in some Southern cities – including Lagos, Nigeria's great port and business capital. A bomb explosion in the Apapa port of Lagos in 2014 was believed to be Boko Haram's work And there were some fears in Nigeria too by the end of 2014 that the powerful successor of Al Qaida in Iraq and Syria, ISIS, might have started to have contacts with Boko Haram. Furthermore, by late 2014, Boko Haram was seriously expanding its terrorism from Nigeria to neighboring countries – Cameroon, Niger and Chad – and beginning to look like a regional threat rather than merely a Nigerian problem.

During the first quarter of 2015, the armed forces of Cameroon, Chad and Niger (especially Chad) began work with the Nigerian armed forces to respond to Boko Haram. That produced considerable effect; but then other developments arose to make Boko Haram an even greater threat than before. In the last months of 2014, some militant groups in Libya had pledged allegiance to the formidable terrorist group, ISIS, and that had immediately established ISIS as major force in the Maghreb – thus enormously heightening the threat of terrorism over the territories of the Sahara Desert and the West African Sahel and Sudan. Not surprisingly, Boko Haram, experiencing some serious pressure from Chadian forces, followed suit early in 2015 and pledged allegiance to ISIS. Thus, suddenly, ISIS became a major player in the expansion of terrorism on the African continent, in a   broad spread of territory extending from North Africa to the Sahara Desert, the West African Sahel and Sudan, and most of the countries of the West Africa.

If international terrorism succeeds in establishing firm roots in these lands – comprising most of the Moghreb and many countries of West Africa (Mali, Mauritania, Senegal, Burkina Faso, Niger, Nigeria, Chad, Cameroon) –that would be a source of very major danger to all of Africa, and even to the world. The combined spread of desert territories here, altogether constituting one of the largest and most arid deserts in the world, if it became a home to Islamic terrorism, could threaten the world with terrorist danger far and wide and be extremely difficult to tackle.

Finally, an unrestrained descent of Sub-Saharan Africa into political and public immorality and brigandage, endemic electoral fraud, rejection of accountability in public leadership, corruption and robbery as culture of public stewardship, in a continent of shattered cultures, ethical rootlessness and material hopelessness – all these could pose very serious danger to the global village that our world has become. It could mean that much of the younger generation of Black Africa might grow up steeped and entrapped in a dangerous quagmire – a threat to law, order and values in society and in business on a worldwide scale. Of such youth threats, the beginnings are already with us – in, for instance, the sophisticated international fraud networks based among some well-educated youths of Nigeria (known as "419" in their country) that have succeeded in defrauding many people in various parts of the world of substantial amounts of money, the drug-trafficking networks among the same groups, the remarkably efficient pirate gangs based among some youths of Somalia on the Horn of Africa, the sprawling camps of radical Islamic youths in various locations in Northern Nigeria and the Sahel, camps from which these youths rampage, burn, destroy and kill on a large scale.

The challenge of Africa is therefore not a challenge for Africa only; it is a challenge for the whole world – a challenge that touches the vital interests of most countries in our world. It is a fight that Africa must win. It is a fight that the world must help Africa to win. It is a fight that Africa can win. And, above all, this book is dedicated to the very confident hope that it is a fight that Africa will win.

Conclusion

The critical imperative in the Black African situation is that influential African leaders and rulers should realize that the political paths they have been treading in the name of "nation building" since independence are, to put it flatly, wrong. Given the type of countries we have, we have only two options for nation building in the political sense. One is to try and force the various nations in each of our countries together, to pursue overt and aggressive integrationist policies, all aimed at suppressing the uniqueness of the nations in each country and, over time, hoping to achieve a homogenous national society. In various ways and guises, this is the option every one of our multi-nation countries has been pursuing. It has been worse than futile; and it has generated complex conflicts, brought terrible pains into the lives of our people generally, and vitiated efforts at economic and social growth. The other option is to accept and embrace the uniqueness of each nation in each of our multi-nation countries, give it constitutional freedom to manage much of its own unique affairs in its own way, so that it may make its own kind of contributions to the country to which it belongs. Sincerely and conscientiously pursued, this path can greatly reduce conflict, or even eliminate conflict in many cases, generate openly democratic political systems, and curtail (or even eliminate) corruption – and generally lead to success.

This latter direction is the direction to which the rest of the world should concentrate most of their political help to the countries of Black Africa. It is only in the context of a sincere acceptance of, and respect for, the uniqueness of each nation in every one of these countries that democracy can flourish and socio-economic progress can advance. In the months before the Nigerian national elections of 2007, the United States and some other influential countries and international agencies sent "pre-election assessment" observers to Nigeria to observe the arrangements being made for free and fair elections in the country. And then, during the elections, international observers from the world's leading democracies, from African agencies, from international agencies of the wider world, and from some of the world's leading news media, descended on Nigeria, very copiously and visibly covering the electoral processes in all parts of Nigeria. Yet, all those efforts did not restrain the authorities of Nigeria from going on to run the most blatantly rigged election in Nigeria's history. The urge to "unite" Nigeria and make all parts of it conform to a submissive integration into a "Nigeria national society" or, as it is commonly called in Nigeria, a "Nigerian mainstream", is a very powerful motivator of policy and politics among some very influential Nigerians. For such influential Nigerian political leaders, therefore, deference to the opinions of the world about "democracy" or about "free and fair elections" is flatly unacceptable, being seen as an obstacle to the goals sought. In the context of all these, the call of the wider world for "democracy" in Africa is a futile exercise. The world's richest donor counties often warn that their aids to African countries will be linked to serious efforts at moving towards democracy. United States Ambassador Thomas R. Pickering spoke for his country (and, in effect, for all rich donor countries) when he said at the United Nations on October 28, 1991:

"Reforms to governance are essential, both for sustainable economic growth and political stability. - - - The bottom line of good governance is democracy itself. It is not our role to decide who governs any country, but we will use our influence to encourage governments to let their people make that decision for themselves. In sum, we will help those who move towards democracy". [10]

That was 1991. This is 2015, and the need to repeat that warning again and again since 1991has been increasingly more pressing – as is obvious in parts of President Obama's speech in Accra, Ghana, quoted a few pages earlier. The world needs to shift its efforts into encouraging and supporting programs of transformation in each African country, based on a sincere respect for the ethnic national diversity of each country and the uniqueness of each of the nations in each country. This is what the Guinea-Bissau economist, Carlos Lopes, meant when he suggested that Africans need to give more priority to the concept of "tolerance" of group differences, than to the concept of democracy. It is also what Elliot P. Skinner meant when he wrote: "African countries will continue to be racked by conflicts unless leaders agree about how to govern their multi-faceted nation-states and how to distribute their economic resources equitably. Without compromise that would ensure "ethnic justice", neither so-called "liberal democracy" nor any other species of government will succeed in Africa".[11]

It is not true that recognizing, respecting, and constitutionally empowering the nations in a country will necessarily lead to the breaking up of the country. The Indian Union, with more ethno-linguistic groups than any African country, is proof that such a fear is mostly an empty fear.

From this point in Africa's history, the future of Sub-Saharan African countries seems to point in the direction of either of two distinct probabilities. First, those countries which seriously abandon the methods of governance learnt under colonialism, which rationally examine and respond to structures bequeathed by European colonialism, which adopt methods based on respecting and constitutionally empowering their component nations, and which conscientiously allow their various nations' cultures the scope to work out those nations' paths and contributions to progress and prosperity – countries which operate in these ways are likely to give themselves the better chance to manage their differences and difficulties in a peaceful and orderly manner, and to achieve political stability, socio-economic progress, and prosperity in the world. From such countries, even if any nation seeks to separate in order to start a new country of its own, the exit is likely to be managed in such a way as to ensure the welfare of the nation that departs and of the ones that remain together behind. In sharp contrast, those countries that continue to hold on to the colonial authoritarian styles of holding their peoples together by any type of constitutional or political devices, are likely to continue to experience instability and conflicts, and to continue to lag behind in the human struggle for the better life. And from such countries, nations seeking to separate and start their own countries are likely to be many; secessionist attempts are likely to be frequent; and each secessionist attempt will be very likely to generate conflicts, violence, and serious hurt and destabilization of all concerned.

CHAPTER TEN

Further On The National Question

We must now conclude with a short final statement specifically on the nations or nationalities that we Black peoples created and nurtured in our long history, and that we entered into the modern world with – the nations that now constitute the component parts of our modern countries. We will attempt a restatement of some of the most important conclusions already arrived at in the earlier chapters, but now giving focused consideration to what the proper place of our nations should be in the history of our modern countries and our sub-continent.

I live with the profound and unwavering hope that Black Africa will revive and find its true self and voice in this modern world. I believe that that hope, and the resolve to make it a fulfillment, is the God-ordained duty of every offspring or descendant of the Black people of the world. The past five centuries have tended to exhibit one-sidedly, to emphasize, and to compound, Black Africa's weakness among the peoples of the world; the next five can reverse that trend and highlight Black Africa in the advance guard of the world's march in transformation and progress. The natural capacity is there; the perception of the best and most fruitful road to the goal is the all-important need.

It is, obviously, in sensible and constructive solutions to the "national question" that Black Africa will find more peaceful political development than hitherto, avoid violent upheavals and violent revolutions, and fulfill its destiny. Our intellectuals are not incorrect in their opinions that the political difficulties and conflicts in Sub-Saharan Africa are not caused only by what most call the "ethnic" factor and some the "national" factor. Essentially, the crux of such arguments is that it is many realities – and not just the ethnic or national factor *per se* – that have generated our conflicts. There is much truth in that, as some earlier chapters of this book have amply shown. But, as some chapters of this book have also amply shown, the ethnic or national factor has been crucial in almost every case. It is the basic and critical potential upon which all other factors have fed, in every Black African

311

political conflict situation, to ignite and expand conflicts. In our conflict situations, the ethnic or national factor is the common determinant, for most people, of the group to fight for and the group to fight against. It is almost invariably the effective tool for mobilization, the source of the most powerful battle cry. Even in a case like the conflicts in Rwanda and Burundi where the opponents are not easily identifiable as different ethnic, linguistic or religious groups or nations, a perception of themselves as different ethnic groups has been the most powerful factor, the fixer of the battle lines, in the conflicts. The ethnic or national factor is the base of such conflict-generating behavior as attempts at ethnic domination, ethnic rivalries over scarce or dwindling resources, ethnic and regional contests over state-disbursed assets or opportunities. Even most of the disruptive or hostile manipulations of Black African countries by external forces feed on the patterns of inter-ethnic relations in each country. And in those of our countries where religion has played big roles in conflicts, the religion has usually sharpened the differences between nationalities, or followed and reinforced the lines of ethnic or national division and conflict.

Some of us think that admitting the ethnic or national factor as a factor in our political conflicts tends to paint us, Black Africans, as primitive or backward. But Black Africa is by no means unique in having the ethnic or national factor as a very important factor in the politics of countries or in political conflicts. On the contrary, on virtually all continents, as shown in an earlier chapter, multi-nation or multi-ethnic countries are being shaken by ethnic or national ambitions, or being broken or plunged into conflicts. The universal truth is that, at certain stages in the history of our world, human ethno-linguistic groups, or nations, crystallized and developed, and each human is a member of one such a group or nation in our world today. And each ethnic group or nation, large or small, wants to hold to its territory, to sustain and develop its culture, and, as much as possible, to control its own life and destiny, and have its pride respected. There is nothing primitive or backward in that.

In our recent history in Black Africa, our nations or nationalities went through a brief experience during which people from another continent and other cultural backgrounds came and created multi-nation countries in our land – and did it in ways that planted the seeds of discord and conflicts. Our problems of today spring from the sad fact that, after the creators and first managers of such countries left us to manage our own affairs, we did not, in any of the new countries, ask ourselves the question whether what they had given us was how we really want to live. In every country, the few literate persons who came to hold the powers of state simply, thoughtlessly, went on to assume that their duty was to hold tightly intact their new country, and to subdue the peoples or nations in their new country - in the name of "nation building". In some countries, numerically or politically stronger groups resolved to themselves that they must rule (that they have been destined to rule) and control the lives of all other nations in their country. Even though massive bloodletting, wars, massive human displacements, refugee camps, and ferociously barbarous deprivation, resulted from such nation-building follies, and even though some initial development gains, as at the time of independence, were thus destroyed in many countries, we still would not look to see whether changes were needed and what changes we could make. In fact, among some Black African politicians, there has been a tendency to justify these follies by denying the authenticity, the rights, or even the existence, of the nations in their countries. It is this pattern of political leadership and governance that ought to be seen as primitive and backward – representing, as it does, a stiff-necked refusal to look honestly at facts, to acknowledge truths, and to defer to realities. Various nations of ours can live peacefully in a country and prosper together – if the leaders and masses of those nations would invest serious commitment and dedication into the attainment of such harmony.

The national question should also be viewed from another angle. Many of Black Africa's indigenous nations, large or small, are a much more dynamic and much more potent force than our modern rulers, since independence, have been ready to recognize and allow for. For instance, in the three Regions of Nigeria of the 1950s, the three large peoples (the Yoruba of the Western Region, the Igbo of the Eastern and the Hausa-Fulani of the Northern) each led its Region to impressive achievements in development and progress. In the years since the mid-1960s, as most powers and assets in the Nigerian federation have been increasingly appropriated to the federal government (to the detriment of the various parts of Nigeria), the kind of achievement orientation and push characteristic of the Regions of the 1950s has disappeared from Nigeria.

The dynamism and potency is also observable from a negative angle. For instance, the rebellion by the Tiv people against the Northern Region in the 1950s mightily tested Nigeria's strength; so did the Yoruba revolt of late 1965 against the fraudulently imposed Regional government and the supporting federal government; so has the Ijaw insurgency since independence against the Nigerian federation; and so did the thirty-month civil war sparked by the attempt of the Igbo people to liberate themselves from repression, violence and insecurity in Nigeria. Such pictures are true also in every one of the countries of Black Africa. Since independence, successive governments of Uganda have burnt their fingers in repressive acts against the Baganda people. The first government of independent Ghana, fervently supported by some young nationalist zealots, seemed to want the nationalities in their country to disappear for a united Ghana to appear. Those nationalities are still there - if anything, growing stronger, and each finding their place in Ghana's recent advance in success and prosperity. The list goes on and on.

Given some little room and some modicum of freedom to employ its inner strength, each of our nations, large or small, commands the ability to be a strong agency of development and progress, in the context of its multi-nation country. Rather than thoughtfully allow that little room and freedom, the rulers of every one of our countries since independence have all tended to view the many nations in their countries as nuisances, and as obstacles to development, progress and "nation-building" – obstacles that need to be subdued, in order to clear the road for development and progress or, in some countries, in order to clear the road for unclouded control of power by a nation aspiring to be dominant over the other nations in its country. In the process, we have, in virtually every country, used the power of government for a venture of subverting, dividing and weakening our nations. In every nationality assaulted in this way by the rulers of the country to which it belongs, the success of the assault has been usually ephemeral, usually breaking the said nationality into two – a small part that yields to, and collaborates with, the assaulting force, and a larger and stronger part that is left embittered and defensive. Thus, our rulers have been converting assets that ought to be the sources of our strength in the modern world into disoriented forces that promote our weakness. To succeed, each of our countries needs the strength and loyalty of its component nations. Leaders of Black Africa have universally failed to recognize that – and have universally believed and acted the opposite.

There is another angle to the national question. In his statement quoted in an earlier chapter, Alfred Ilenre, Secretary-General of the Ethnic Minority and Indigenous Rights Organization of Africa (EMIROAF), wrote:

"The absence of a cultural base has created an atmosphere for interlopers and rustics in politics to manipulate the political space to their advantage".

In probably all Black African countries, many perceptive citizens are strongly convinced that a lot of the corruption being perpetrated in the affairs of their country are possible only in the distant corridors of their country's central government - and would be impossible in the management of the affairs of their own nationality. In short, many politicians of contemporary Africa handle the affairs of their countries in ways they would not, and could not, treat the management of their own native nation. The distant arena of their country's politics and leadership makes it easy for many politicians to hide away to perpetrate moral atrocities. Leading and serving at home among their own people, they would not ever think of doing much of what they have been doing in public life. Moreover, many of these politicians would not have the credentials and character qualifications that their nation would demand for leadership positions in its affairs. Those politicians who rule over their own people and still perpetrate crude and thoughtless governance there are always those who are corruptly anchored to the distant central government of their multi-nation country. In short, the general silencing of the nationalities, and their essential exclusion from the affairs of the countries to which they belong, are major parts of the roots of rampant corruption and lack of dignity in the public life of Black African countries. One good way to reduce, or even eliminate, corruption is to situate more of the politics and public business of each country at the level of its nationalities.

Starting from this premise, the demand for more roles for the nationalities has been growing all over Black Africa. It is largely the support base for the demand for a National Sovereignty Conference. In many countries, it is usually the foundation for the growing demands for national restructuring. Restructuring means, for a lot of people, that the nationalities should become the basis for the delimitation of states in our federations (as is done in India), that a process of devolution should give the states more powers and more resources, that in fact the states (or nationalities) should control their own natural resources, and that the central government should become considerably weaker and smaller. In this way, for instance, the Nigerian federation would become a union of Nigerian peoples or nations. Commonly, the people in power, unable to respond to these views and demands in any meaningful way, simply try to silence them by force, or by not answering at all while simply continuing with their authoritarian styles of nation building and their corruption.

There is yet this other facet to the national question. It is almost impossible to find a Black African country whose leading citizens have adhered loyally to the true character, essence, and practice of democratic, participatory, elective, politics. As earlier pointed out in an earlier chapter, a major part of the reason for this is to be found in the ways in which the colonial rulers introduced and managed the supposedly democratic politics in African countries in the last years of colonial rule. By introducing crookedness and favoritism into the electoral process in order to achieve the outcomes that they had predetermined, the colonial administrators nurtured the cynical belief and attitude that the democratic processes of party formation and election campaigns were just a superficial tradition, and that the actual choosing of rulers was a hidden function of the power of government or of some dominant group. But another important reason has been that no nation in any of our countries has had the freedom or opportunity to find its own kind of harmonization between its indigenous political culture and the culture of "democratic" politics introduced by former colonial rulers. That kind of harmonization has been impossible in the context of the multi-nation countries

316

created by colonialism. Therefore, attachment of leading citizens, out of conviction, to the democratic political system has never happened in most of Black Africa. This is a major root of the almost universal electoral manipulations, and the blatant rigging of elections, in our countries. It is also a big factor in the resistance of some of our incumbent rulers to giving up power after they have manifestly lost elections. Quite commonly, our elections are employed for obtaining undemocratic outcomes. And the costs of losing power, or being out of power, are simply too heavy and too painful in Black Africa. For sustainable changes to occur in this important aspect of our modern political life, we would need to find ways to enroll the inherent strengths of our indigenous nations.

In summary, we certainly have European colonialism to blame for a lot of our problems, but we have our own rulers and leaders since independence to blame for a great deal more. By any calculation of earthly possibilities, at independence Nigeria (Black Africa's most populous and richest country) was a country poised for greatness in the world, a land of considerable promise and hope. But Nigeria's rulers have made the very worst imaginable out of their country. We will always be able to say that the British gave Nigeria a wobbly or even crooked constitutional and political foundation to grow from, but are we going to say that we were not humans enough to make, after independence, the adjustments that would have increased our chances of success as a country? Nigeria's Hausa-Fulani rulers wanted to crush the Yoruba and Igbo, because the outstanding strengths of those two nations were seen as threats to "nation building" and as obstacles to undisputed dominance by the nationality which the British had put in charge at independence. We have succeeded quite well in confusing and disorienting those two major nationalities, and thereby done irreparable damage to the overall prospects of Nigeria, and turned Nigeria, in the eyes of the world, into a huge and inscrutable monstrosity. Is all this still the fault of the British?

Questions similar to these hang over virtually every country of Black Africa. What did France have to do with Laurent Gbagbo's disruption of the Ivory Coast in the last months of 2010? Which former colonial power is orchestrating Mugabe's disruption of Zimbabwe – or rigged elections in Kenya – or tutors every

317

regime in Uganda to keep trying to weaken and disestablish the Buganda nation and its kingdom? Which former colonial powers are teaching our rulers all over Black Africa today to rob our countries and treat our people with disrespect and even brutality? After our men and women have gone to school in other lands and returned home to become leading citizens in our countries, which former colonial powers then tutors them to forget all the beauties of political and economic life that they saw and enjoyed in those other lands? It used to be quite pleasant to use Nigeria's foremost international airport, Murtala Mohammed Airport, and a breeze to drive the great highway connecting the port city of Lagos to the city of Ibadan in the immediate interior. Today, the great airport is in tatters and the highway is a death trap. Did the British do that? Is it the British that have reigned over the steady destruction of the economic life of the peoples of the Niger Delta since the late 1960s?

Millions of such questions demand to be asked. And unless we Black Africans begin seriously to attend to such thoughts, it may be a long long time, and after a whole lot more of poverty, conflicts, pogroms, coups,   mass revolts, refugee camps, and complicated revolutions spilling seas of blood, before Black Africa will find a sensible, productive and respectable path through the modern world.

Questions Concerning Our Identity and Future

We have tried in various ways to address important issues relating to the political difficulties confronting the peoples of Black Africa in our times, and to examine ways by which we might seek and find solutions – all with the objective of heading off further, and more cataclysmic, conflicts in our sub-continent, and of opening doors to a better future for ourselves as a section of the human race. We are today the poorest part of the world, and our countries are, on the whole, the least stable and most troubled countries in the world. We absorb a disproportionate share of international peace-keeping efforts on the earth, and our land holds a disproportionate share of the earth's violently displaced persons, refugees and refugee camps. Compared with much of the rest of the world, the picture of our part of the world looks very bleak indeed.

The political and economic problems that we thus face are big and tough, and our conquest of them will mostly determine how we, the peoples of Black Africa, will come to stand and fare among the peoples of the world. However, there are other orders of problems confronting us - problems which we now hardly even perceive or acknowledge, problems whose resolution too is crucially important to our place in the future of the world. I refer to the questions called for concerning our cultural integrity and identity among all peoples.

On the apex of this order of problems, over-arching them all, is the problem of language. In common with all sections of the human race, we have our indigenous languages, products of our long history. But as a result of our brief colonial experience under European overlords, we have become peculiar in the world as peoples who must not speak our own languages, but must speak the languages of former colonial rulers, for all the most important functions of human communication in the world. Within our countries, we employ these European languages for all functions of administration (even at the most intimate local levels of government), we employ them for teaching our children in our schools and colleges, we employ them to communicate all the details of our modern commerce, businesses, transactions, and contracts, we employ them for all the higher needs of communication in our politics and in our systems of justice, and in all the arenas of international contact and concourse. In all international agencies, and all international functions, representatives of our various countries must employ the languages of Europe to communicate with one another and with the rest of the world.

It is very difficult for our policy makers to change this language situation. Since every one of our countries consists of many nations and indigenous languages, no other solution has, in the eyes of most of our rulers, seemed applicable to the language problem in each country – other than the continued use of the foreign language of the colonial experience, and the relegating of our indigenous languages to irrelevance. Such attitudes and policies can easily be made to seem reasonable when it is pointed

319

out that some attempts made in some countries to promote some common language or languages (such as Nigeria's attempt to promote emphasis on four main languages – English, Hausa, Yoruba and Igbo) appeared to threaten the relegation of the languages of many smaller peoples to insignificance, thereby provoking widespread political resistance.

Yet, for many and very important reasons, change must happen in this matter. Though most Africans would readily admit that it is difficult to change our language situation, yet, certainly, most would lean strongly to the opinion that the spectacle of Black African leaders communicating with the world only through the agency of European languages ought not to remain permanent in the world.

Moreover, in increasing numbers of Black African countries, the natural cultural barriers to mastery of the European foreign language, and the inevitable ambivalence in the attitudes of many people to the colonialist's language after independence, are already together causing manifest deterioration in the mastery and quality of the foreign language, in both speech and writing. Increasingly, for instance, the English language spoken and written by many members of the highest literate elite in many Anglophone countries of our subcontinent is quite difficult to recognize as the English language of well-educated people. Meanwhile, many Black African languages too are deteriorating, both in speech and in writing. Since the foreign colonial language, though increasingly poorly spoken, poorly written, and poorly taught, is nevertheless the language of all important things, the language of the high job and the job place, the language of promotion and elevation, it is becoming a very common practice for our educated families to teach only it to their children, and to shield their children from exposure to their native languages. In Nigeria's cities, for instance, it is quite common for families to put up notices in their homes, warning residents and visitors alike that the speaking of Yoruba or Igbo (or "vernacular") is not welcome – the belief being that, in this way, children will be able to master the English language needed for elevation in the Nigerian administrative, political or economic system. Also, it is not uncommon these days for our governments to downgrade the provisions for the teaching of native languages in our schools.

It used to be, in British West Africa in general, that the earliest years of school education (kindergarten, nursery, pre-primary) were conducted in the local indigenous language, and that English was then gradually introduced and taught from the later classes. The men and women who were raised in this way generally grew up to have a strong grounding in language, and to become some of the best writers of the English language in the world – as well as very good speakers and writers of their own native languages. Now, in Black Africa, African children are losing out at both ends. The European foreign language that is being thoughtlessly pushed upon them is getting poorer in quality, and they are losing any measurable grounding in their own native languages. For the careful observer, it is not difficult to see that, among many African peoples, more and more of the young cannot sustain a good conversation in their native languages, and cannot write their native languages at all. Thus, all over Black Africa, educated Africans are becoming culturally deprived and culturally stunted elites that are steadily losing grasp of the foreign languages which they hug as status symbols and rapidly losing their own native languages as well.

Happily, some of our countries are now making some welcome amends in this important matter of language. A few have adopted some indigenous language or languages as official language, in addition to the language of the former colonial rulers – a progressive step now commonly adopted by multi-nation countries worldwide to protect their languages. Of our countries, the Union of South Africa holds the lead here, for adopting eleven languages as official languages – Afrikaans (the sole official language under the apartheid regime), English, Zulu, Sotho, Ndebele, Northern Sotho, Swazi, Tswana, Tsonga, Venda, and Xhosa. In the world at large, more and more multi-nation countries are adopting a plurality of official languages. India, for instance, has adopted twenty-two. In contrast, most Black African countries have preferred to keep the language of their former colonizers as sole official language, thereby leaving their indigenous languages unprotected. Many African countries have no language policy at all. What all these mean is that many Black African peoples are gradually, imperceptibly, becoming peoples without a strong or stable language heritage.

Language is the most important tool for transmitting a culture. One of contemporary Africa's frontline intellectuals, Tiyambe Zeleza, puts it better. Language, he says:

"is the carrier of a people's culture; it embodies their system of ethics and aesthetics, and it is a medium for producing and consuming knowledge, a granary of their memories and imaginations."[1]

When a language declines, its culture declines also. Language is also very closely associated with its people's identity. The languages of Black Africa are threatened with decline today, and many even with extinction. This is so because, for a language to grow in the changing circumstances of the world, its people, its primary speakers, must keep using it. No matter how large a people or nation may be in population, if they gradually cease using their language, it will gradually decline – and the decline, if unrestrained, can lead to its extinction. There is therefore no foundation to the feeling that one often finds among, say, the large Igbo or Yoruba of Nigeria, that their language can never become extinct. Any language can become extinct – if its people stop speaking and writing it and stop teaching it to their children for some generations. In fact, both the Igbo and Yoruba languages (the languages of two of Black Africa's largest nations) are already variously classified in serious studies as "endangered" or "seriously endangered" – on a scale from 'potentially endangered', 'endangered', 'seriously endangered', to 'extinct'. What this means is that both of these languages are rapidly declining and may become extinct – because the elite of the Yoruba and Igbo (two peoples who are perhaps the most progressive in education in Black Africa) have been increasingly taking the unfortunate and destructive decision that their children be taught English only. In response to some publication including the Igbo language among languages that may become extinct in about fifty years, a senior Nigerian official, Chukwuemeka Wogu (then Federal Nigerian Minister of Labor and Productivity, himself an Igbo), lamented in a July 2010 public speech:

"Until the shocking revelation that the Igbo language may go into extinction in the next 50 years, most of us had thought that the Igbo language enjoyed a high level of scholarship- - -. The

Igbo language may be becoming extinct because the Igbo family stopped speaking to their children in their mother tongue".[2].

Precisely the same things that Minister Wogu says about the Igbo language are also true of the Yoruba language.[3] While many first-rate scholars are studying the Yoruba and Igbo languages in universities all over the world, the native speakers of both languages in Nigeria are increasingly giving up their own languages for some inferior and deteriorating quality of the English language. Some sections of the Yoruba and Igbo elite are already sounding the alarm, but their alarm is not loud enough, and their two languages face the danger of what some scholars have termed "language death".

African languages, whether of the larger or smaller African nations, can decline – and can become extinct. According to linguists, some African languages now extinct were still being spoken as recently as 1938. And many African languages are already going through the process towards extinction. Most linguists tell us that the incidence of decline of languages is accelerating in the world, due to the fact that many peoples of the world are using their own languages less and less and adopting other peoples' more influential languages more and more – and that Sub-Saharan Africa is one of the regions where the phenomenon is most pronounced in the world. Black Africa is thus being bled and denuded culturally, though imperceptibly. And this ought to be a matter of profound concern – to Africans themselves, and also to the rest of mankind.[4]

In totality, therefore, our modern countries, the political heritages of only a brief period of European colonialism in our recent history, are steadily becoming graveyards of our ancient nations and indigenous cultures. And this needs not be so. Nothing that these countries can give is likely to be a sufficient and satisfactory trade-off for the loss of our indigenous cultural heritages. To take advantage of, and benefit from, the growing development assets of our world, we do not need that our sub-continent should turn into a series of cultural graveyards. In fact, as we are already seeing, a people uprooted from their own culture, a people without firm moorings in a culture of their own, are unlikely to be able to benefit seriously from the technologies and other development assets that the modern world offers to all.

Overview

The lessons available to us from our history as independent countries so far, and from the modern history of the rest of the world, are many and rich. First, our indigenous nations are far too potent for us to push successfully down and subdue in order to "build" the countries that we recently received from our brief foreign rule. Efforts in that direction have shown no signs of success anywhere, and patently have no chance of succeeding. All we have had, and all we are likely to continue to have, from such efforts are disruptions, anger, conflicts, and turmoil. While such troubles last, none of our countries can develop or progress, no matter the strength of its economic resource base. In the midst of such troubles, no country in our sub-continent can possibly make a success of any kind of constitution. Moreover, in the hands of an elite divorced from their cultures and cultural mores, and owing no allegiance to any ethos in which they and the masses of their people are used to having confidence, disruptive forces like corruption, unrestrained greed for power and wealth, disrespect for rules and laws, all have a fertile ground in which to fester and diversify. And the totality of the effects of all these factors, if unchecked, will be to generate a new wave of political turmoil far much more devastating than Black Africa has seen since independence.

The loyalties, discipline, and aspirations of group well-being that our indigenous nations in Black Africa can contribute to our development and progress are inestimable. It is such national assets that built the foundations of the prosperity and power of the then small nations of Europe (the English, the Spanish, the Scotts, the Dutch, etc.) at the beginning of modern times. And it is such that built the strong foundation of the nation of Japan as a modern nation in the late 19th century, and that is now building strong foundations for various nations in Asia. Though a country of diverse immigrants, the United States of America somehow, uniquely, found ways to generate and mobilize such assets of group strength – essentially by sincerely holding out the new country as a land of opportunity for all its immigrants of diverse origins – and thereby grew its own type of "nation". That is the root of America's exceptionality. The task confronting us in Black Africa has its own uniqueness too. Most of the nations we inherited from our indigenous history are small, but each, nevertheless, has its own strength. Our task is to find ways to mobilize those strengths for the overall strength of our new countries – not to try and subdue or to destroy them. That is the only viable road to true strength, development and progress for Black Africa.

It is important to repeat what has been said again and again in earlier chapters of this book – namely, that the ways in which the task will be carried out will necessarily vary from place to place on our sub-continent. Three things are generally crucially important in the task. The first is that we must, for a change, learn to listen respectfully and hear clearly what our indigenous nations, large or small, are saying, and have the political courage to dare unique approaches to nation building. Most probably, we will still have most of the countries that we now have, but each country will be different – in the sense of being an entity built on a mutually brokered agreement by all its nations, and run on decent respect for the terms of such agreement.

The second important thing is that we must be prepared to accept that some of our nations might desire to venture separate countries of their own, carved out of the countries to which they now belong. In cases where such a request is voiced, we must command the political courage to listen to it and consider it respectfully, and be prepared to defer to it, on the basis of pre-agreed rules and procedures.

And the third important thing is the need for agreement mutually arrived at and conscientiously respected by all the nationalities in any of our countries. This is in fact the critical point of departure from the character of the multi-nation countries that European colonialism bequeathed to us. Without such an agreement mutually created and mutually conscientiously respected, any multi-nation countries that we may have, whether by preserving our countries of today or by creating new and smaller multi-nation countries anywhere on our subcontinent, will have essentially no chance of succeeding. Without it, even the most carefully demarcated multi-nation country, the most enthusiastically welcomed by its component nationalities, will, as Hizkias Assefa has said in the particular case of the Horn of

Africa, resemble the former country or countries from which it was excised. As long as such countries are

"not completely ethnically homogeneous they will be faced again by an "ethnic" or "minority" problem or a "nationalities question," just like their predecessors. The problem of "ethnic conflict" then starts all over again"[5].

It needs to be added that even in any of our countries that may have the fortunate starting base of ethnic homogeneity, it will still be crucially important that powerful rules, cultural norms, societal and educational principles and practices, and exalted institutions, that emphasize respect for the rules and laws be instituted and conscientiously accorded preeminence. It will be unwise for even our ethnically most homogenous countries to assume or imagine that the political attributes and behavior of a whole century of capricious, irrational and corrupt leaderships will vanish on their own.

POSTSCRIPT

I believe this is it. I believe this is what I have heard from Black Africa all my life. I have been continuously favored from early in life with the privilege of learning about and hearing Black Africa – first as a child raised by the traditional elite of a proud Black African people with a great history and great traditions; then as a student of an African college of one of the greatest universities of the Western world, learning a whole lot of new things about Black Africa's history, while also skipping from country to country in student conferences in Black Africa's tropical lands; then as a university professor seeking deeper knowledge about Black Africa, teaching it to students at various levels of the university system, and traveling Black Africa to see, to belong, to learn and to teach; and then as an elected public official of Nigeria, Black Africa's most populous and richest country, interacting with public officials from all over Africa. Finally, in the past twenty-five years, I have had the privilege of standing on a hilltop at a distance to observe Black Africa at some remove from the events, and to listen to, absorb and ponder, its voice and its echoes. I believe that I have reflected faithfully here what I have heard the voice of Black Africa saying – namely, that Black Africa wants to order its political life and affairs somewhat differently from the paths charted by the architects of its brief European colonial experience, and wants to benefit a lot more from the assets of its own cultures, history and peculiarities. Big changes, transformations, redirections, revolutions, will almost certainly come in most parts of Black Africa – peacefully if possible, or by any other means as the mounting urge finds expression. I have written this book in the strong desire, and the fervent hope, that it can and will all come peacefully.

To borrow words from the most illustrious descendant of Black Africa in our times, President Obama: Yes, we can do it. We can embark on, and push through with, the changes now – and not wait until we are engulfed in further and bigger turmoil.

Barack Obama was a young man without a rich or influential family to lean on when he dared to venture into striving for change. Against all odds, he became the president of the world's most powerful country, the United States of America – and proved that when one strikes out with dedication, determination and hope, nothing is impossible. In the course of that struggle, he gave to the youths of his Black African root a great gift – the magic of the explosive affirmation: "Yes we can". Then, a few months after he became president of America, he stood on the soil of Africa, in Accra, Ghana, and added yet more power to that gift: "This is a new moment of great promise" he said. "Only this time - - - it will not be giants like Nkrumah and Kenyatta who will determine Africa's future. Instead, it will be you – the men and women - - - the young people brimming with talent and energy and hope, who can claim the future that so many in previous generations never realized".

That is the historic challenge to the youths of Black Africa of our time. Happily, those youths are up to it. They are the most literate generation of Black African youths in history – the most educated, the most travelled in the world, the most copiously interconnected with youths of other lands, the most knowledgeable about trends in the wide world. The task before them is daunting. They must deal rationally and courageously with the realities of the countries bequeathed to their peoples by the European colonial experience, and they must accomplish changes that will enable their societies to advance strongly into stability, order, progress and prosperity in the world. They can do it – and they must rise up, step forward, and do it. It is a duty they owe themselves, their peoples, their progeny, and their world.

NOTES

ONE
A Plague On All Our Houses?

1. Because conflicts and wars have been prevalent and persistent in post-independence Africa, the study of such conflicts and wars has tended to occupy center stage in contemporary African studies. The literature on the subject is therefore large and constantly expanding. For a general picture, see French, Howard W: *A Continent for the Taking: The Tragedy & Hope of Africa,* Alfred Knopf, 2004; Reader, John: *Africa: A Biography of a Continent,* Alfred Knopf, 1998; Davidson, Basil: *The Black Man's Burden,* James Curry, 1992; William, S. ed: *Ethnicity in Modern Africa,* Boulder Colorado, Lynne Rienner. 1979; Chazan, N. et al: *Politics and Society in Contemporary Africa,* London, Macmillan, 1988;

2. Akintoye, S.A.: *Emergent African States: Topics in 20th Century African History,* London, Longmans, 1973, 78-115; Nnoli, Okwudiba, Ed: *Ethnic Conflicts in Africa,* Dakar, Senegal, CODESTRIA BOOKS, 1998.

3. Biaya, T.K: "Ethnicity and the State in Zaire", in Okwudiba Nnoli, Ibid, 327-350; C. Young and V. Turner: *The Rise & Decline of the Zairean State,* Wisconsin, 1985.

4. Markakis, J: "Ethnic Conflicts in Ethiopia and Sudan", paper presented at UNRISD Workshop on *Ethnic Conflict and Development,* Dubrovsnik, Yugoslavia, 1991; Iyob, Ruth and Khadiagala, Gilbert: *Sudan: The Elusive Quest for Peace,* Boulder, CO, Lynne Rienner, 2006; Khalid, Mansour: *War and Peace in Sudan: A Tale of Two Countries,* New York, Kegan Paul, 2003; Totten, Samuel and Markusen, Eric, eds: *Genocide in Darfur: Investigating the Atrocities in the Sudan,* NY, Routledge, 2006.

5. Akintoye, *Emergent African States,* op. cit, 132-145; Okwudiba Nnoli: *Ethnic Politics in Nigeria,* Ibadan, Vintage Publishers, 1989; Ihonvbere, J.O. and Falola, T: "Hegemony, Neo-colonialism and Political Instability in Contemporary Nigeria", *African Review,* 2, 2, 1984;

Oyeweso, Siyan: *Perspectives on the Nigerian Civil War*, Lagos, OAP Publications, 1992.

6. Denis Amoussou-Yeye: "Inter-ethnic Relations and Socio-Political Dynamics in Benin", In Okwudiba Nnoli: *Ethnic Conflicts in Africa*, op cit, 379-399.

7. Quoted in Dominic Kofi Agyeman: "Ethnic Conflicts and Politics in Ghana", in Nnoli, Ibid. 183-204.

8. Kiwanuka, Semakula: *Amin and the Tragedy of Uganda*, Munchen, Weltforum Verlag, 1979; Sempangi, F.K: *A Distant Grief: The Real Story Behind the martyrdom of Christians in Uganda*, Glendale, CA, G.L. Reagal Books, 1979.

9. Lemarchand, R: *Burundi*, Cambridge, Cambridge University Press, 1994; Genocide Watch: *Case Study: Genocide in Rwanda, 1994*.

TWO
Deepening Plague

1. Hashim, Alice V: *The Fallen State: Dissonance, Dictatorship & Death in Somalia*, Lanham, MD, Univ. Press of America, 1997.

2. Akpan, M.B: "Black Imperialism: Americo-Liberian Rule Over the African Peoples of Liberia, 1841-1964", *Canadian Journal of African Studies*, Vll, 2, 1973; Boley, G.E.S: *Liberia: The Rise and Fall of the First Republic*, London, St. Martin, 1985.

3. Marshall-Fratani, Ruth: "The War of Who-is-Who: Autochthony, Nationalism & Citizenship in the Ivoirian Crisis", *African Studies Review*, 49, 2, 9-43, 2006.

4. International Crisis Group, op.cit

5. Genocide Watch: *Case Study: Rwanda*, op cit; Melvern, Linda: *A People Betrayed: The Role of the West in Rwanda's Genocide*, New York, Zed Books, 2000.

6. Wrong, Michela: I*n the Footsteps of Mr. Kurtz: Living on the Brink of Disaster in Mobutu's Congo*, Harper Collins, 2001; Nest, Michael: *The Democratic Republic of Congo: Economic Dimensions of War & Peace*, Boulder, CO, Lynne Rienner, 2006.

7. Amanza, O: *Museveni's March from Guerrilla to Statesman*, Kampala, Fountain publishers, 1998.

8. Lonsdale, John: *The Conquest State, 1895-1904,* p.11, quoted in Oyugi, W.O: "Ethnic Politics in Kenya", in Nnoli: *Ethnic Conflicts in Africa*, 287-309.

9. Oyugi, W.O: "Ethnic Conflicts in Kenya", Ibid.

10. Guimaraes, Fernando: *The Origins of the Angolan Civil War: Foreign Intervention & Domestic Political Conflict*, Palgrave Macmillan, 2001.

11. Mandaza, I., ed: *Zimbabwe*: *Political Economy of Transition, 1980-86*, Dakar, CODESTRIA, 1986; Sithole, M: "Managing Ethnic Conflicts in Zimbabwe", in Nnoli; *Ethnic Conflicts in Africa*, 351-378; Breytenbach, W.J.: "Ethnic Factors in the Rhodesia Power Struggle", *Bulletin of the Africa Institute*, 1977.

THREE
Emerging Possibilities Killed

1. Wadim Schreiner: "Forgotten Wars: Coverage of wars and conflicts in Africa in international TV news programs", *Media Tenor*, August 2003.

2.   Perham, Margery, 1951, quoted in Akintoye, S.A: "Nigerian Pioneers in the Recording & Studying of African & Black History", in Toyin Falola & Adam Padock: *Emergent Themes & Methods in African Studies,* Trenton, N.J., Africa World Press, 2009.

3. See Akintoye, S. Adebanji: *A History of the Yoruba People*, Dakar, Senegal, Amalion Publishing, 2010; Lugard, Sir Frederick: *The Dual Mandate in British Tropical Africa*, London, Blackwood & Son, 1922.

4. Clapperton, Captain Hugh: *Journal of a Second Expedition into the Interior of Africa from the Bight of Benin to Succattoo*, London, John Murray, 1829.

5. Clarke, William H: *Travels & Explorations in Yorubaland, 1854-58*, ed. by J. Atanda, Ibadan, Ibadan University Press, 1972.

6. Last, D.M: *The Sokoto Caliphate*, Longmans, 1971.

7. Fartua, Ahmed Ibn: *Kanem Wars of Idris Alooma*, Translated from the Arabic by H.R.Palmer. , published in his *Sudanese Memoirs*, Lagos, 1938.

8. Egharevba, J.U: *A Short History of Benin*, Ibadan, Ibadan University Press, 1960.

9. Falola, T. ed: *Igbo History & Society: Essays of Adiele Afigbo*, Trenton, NJ, Africa World Press, 2005.

10. Akinjogbin, I.A: *Dahomey & its Neighbors, 1708-1818*, Cambridge, Cambridge University Press, 1967.

11. Ajayi, J.F.A & Crowder, M. eds: *History of West Africa*, Vols. 1 & 2, London, Longman; Davidson, Basil: *The Black Man's Burden*, James Curry, 1992.

12. Ajayi & Crowder, eds: *History of West Africa*, Ibid.

13. Hochschild, Adam: *King Leopold's Ghost*, NY, Houghton Mifflin, 1999.

14. Semujanga, Josias: *Origins of Rwandan Genocide*, Amherst, NY, Humanity Books.

15. Oyugi, Walter: "Ethnic Politics in Kenya", & Mpangala, G: ""Inter-ethnic Relations in Tanzania", chapters in Nnoli, Okwudiba, ed: *Ethnic Conflicts in Africa*, CODESRIA, Dakar, 1998.

16. Sithole, Masipula: "Managing Ethnic Conflicts in Zimbabwe", in Nnoli: *Ethnic Conflicts*, Ibid.

17. Quoted in Garvey, Marcus: "Moshoeshoe: Basuto King, Warrior & Statesman, 1791-1870".

18. The Alaketu of Ketu, Benin Republic: Interview in the Alaketu's Palace, Ketu, 2010.

FOUR
Kneading Troubles Into Countries

1. Perham, Margery, 1951, quoted in Akintoye, S.A: "Nigerian Pioneers in the Recording & Studying of African & Black History", in Toyin Falola: *Emergent Themes & Methods in African Studies,* Trenton, NJ, Africa World Press, 2009, op. cit.

2. Lugard, Sir Frederick: *The Dual Mandate in British Tropical Africa*, op. cit.

3. Dowden, Richard: *Africa: Altered States, Ordinary Miracles*, Public Affairs, NY, 2008, 450.

4. According to the Kenyan scholar, Ali Mazrui, Jomo Kenyatta was a boy when Kenya became a country under the British, and he survived British rule by 15 years.

5. Quoted in Itse Sagay: "Nigeria: Federalism, the Constitution and Resource Control", Lecture delivered at the Fourth Sensitization Program of the Ibori Vanguard, at the Lagoon Restaurant, Lagos.

6. Smith, Harry: *Blue Collar Lawman,* on line, 1987; Ajayi, Sir Olaniwun: *Nigeria: Africa's, Failed Asset*, Bookcraft, 2009; Mario de Queiroz: "Africa-Europe: Goodbye Rhetoric, Hello Political Dialogue", *IPA*, Lisbon, March 16, 2007; "From a Strategy for Africa to an EU-Africa Strategic Partnership", IPA, Dec. 6, 2007.

FIVE
Factors In Our Conflicts

1. For some recent accounts of the economic experience of post-colonial Africa, see Meredith, Martin: *The Fate of Africa: From Hopes of Freedom to the Heart of Despair*, Public Affairs, New York, NY, 2005; Calderisi, Robert: *The Trouble with Africa: Why Foreign Aid Isn't Working*, Palgrave Macmillan, New York, NY, 2006.

2. Genocide Watch: *Case Study: Genocide in Rwanda,* op. cit.

3. Maathai, Wangari: *Challenge for Africa,* Arrow Books, 2010.

4. Dowden, Richard: *Africa*, op. cit.

5. See Prah, Kwesi: "Towards a Strategic Goepolitic Vision of Afro-Arab Relations", Paper Submitted to the African Union Experts' Meeting on Strategic Geopolitic Vision of Afro-Arab Relations, Addis Ababa, May 11-12, 2004.

SIX
Quests For Solutions

1. All quoted in Afigbo, Adiele: "The Idea of Igbo Nationality and its Enemies", in Falola, Toyin, ed: *Igbo History and Society: The Essays of Adiele Afigbo*, Trenton, NJ, Africa World Press, 2005, 425-445.
2. For details, see *The Constitutive Act of the African Union*, 2002.
3. *The Parrot*, Oct. 12, 1960.
4. By Malam Bala Garuba in *West African Pilot*, December 30, 1964.
5. *African Report,* May 30, 2007.
6. Gowon, Yakubu: Paper presented at Seminar of the Arewa Consultative Forum, Kaduna, 2009.
7. President Yoweri Museveni, Busoga, Uganda, February 2009.

SEVEN
Trends In Our World

1. Scully, Gerald: "Multiculturalism and Economic Growth", Policy Report No. 196 for the National Center for Policy Analysis, Dallas, Texas.
2. Lampe, Stephen: *Building Future Societies*, Millennium Press, 1994.
3. Yujiro Hayami & Yoshihisa Godo: *Development Economics: From the Poverty to the Wealth of Nations*, third ed, OUP, 2004.
4. Scully, Gerald: "Multiculturalism & Economic Growth", op. cit.
5. In the interview with *AFRICAN ABROAD, USA*, Oyeyemi said:

> *"If you look at the top 25 countries with the highest indices for human development according to the United Nations in 2010, there are certain things that are common to them. Through a research I conducted very recently, I found out that 80% of them have their population belonging to a single ethnic group with at least about 60% majority. 70% of the 80% have over 80% of their population belonging to one single ethnic group. In this same group of countries, 88% of them have a single religion as being dominant at*

the range of about 70% and above. Among these countries, 72% of them have a single dominant language. The data also reflected that 84% of all these countries have at least two of these three all-important variables: Ethnicity, Language and Religion in majority."

EIGHT
Coming Challenges

1. For instance, in Nigeria, most people are surprised that the small peoples of the Niger Delta have been able to put up such a strong revolt against Nigeria's federal power and sustain it for decades.
2. Alfred Ilenre (Secretary-General, Ethnic Minority & Indigenous Rights Organization of Africa – EMIROAF): "The Bane of Uncompleted Decolonization", *The Guardian*, April 11, 2010
3. Bishop Emmanuel B. Gbonigi: Press Conference, Ibadan, 2010.
4. "Biafra Message", Biafra Foundation Website, 2010.
5. Oodua Foundation Website, 2010.
6. Quoted in Adebanwi: "The Yoruba Vision", Paper presented at the Yoruba Retreat, Ibadan, Nigeria, Oct. 26-29, 2007.
7. Ibid.
8. Ibid.
9. Dowden, Richard: *Africa: Altered States, Ordinary Miracles*, 439-485.
10. Enahoro, Chief Tony: "The National Question: Towards a New Constitutional Order", Guest Lecture at the Yoruba Tennis Club, Lagos, July 2, 2002.
11. Soyinka, Wole, quoted in article by Ilenre, *The Guardian*, April, 11, 2010.
12. *The News Magazine*, Jan.14. 2010, quoted in Ilenre: Ibid.
13. 15. Bolaji Akinyemi, Interview , Dec. 19, 2010.
14. Moses Kalanzi: "Why Buganda should not be sacrificed for the Stability of Uganda", Forgotten Diaries. Internet, Feb. 20, 2010.

15. See the Scottish National Party's publication *Choosing Scotland's Future: A National Conversation – Independence and Responsibility in the Modern World,* 2011.
16. For some literature on African traditional modes of governance, see Hanson, Holly Elisabeth: *Landed Obligation: The Practice of Power in Buganda,* Heinemann, 2003; Crowder, Michael & Ikime, Obaro: *West African Chiefs, Their Changing Role under Colonialism and Independence,* Ife University Press, Ile-Ife, 1970.
17. For details, see Smith, Harry: *Blue Collar Lawman,* on line, 1987; Ajayi, Sir Olaniwun: *Nigeria: Africa's Failed Asset,* Ibadan, Bookcraft, 2009.

NINE
Way Forward

1. A selection from Ali Mazrui's writings on the subject. "Conflict in Africa: An
    Overview", in Alfred Nnema & Paul T. Zeleza, eds: *The Roots of African Conflicts: The Causes and Costs,* James Currey, Oxford, UK, 2008; "The Genesis of Conflict Around
    Africa", in *Somali Watch,* Jan. 28, 2001; "An African Half Century", *Guardian,* 7 Dec. 2010.
2. Muni, S.D: "Ethnic Conflict, Federalism and Democracy in India", in Kumar Rupesinghe & Valery A. Tishkov, eds: *Ethnicity and Power in the Contemporary World,* United Nations University Press, Tokyo, NY, Paris, 1996.
3. Enahoro, Chief Anthony: "The National Question: Towards a New Constitutional Order", Guest Lecture at Yoruba Tennis Club, Lagos, July 2, 2002.
4. African World Media, July 15, 2013.
5. Rice, Susan E: "Why Darfur Can't be Left to Africa", *The Washington Post,* Aug. 07, 2005.
6. Rice, Susan E, Ibid
7. Rice, Susan E, Ibid.

8. Mario de Queiroz: "Africa-Europe: Goodbye Rhetoric, Hello Political Dialogue", *IPA*, Lisbon, Mar. 16, 2007; "From a Strategy for Africa to an EU-Africa Strategic Partnership", *Europa*, May 16, 2008; Mario de Quieroz: "EU-Africa: Dodging the Human Rights Issue", *IPA*, Dec. 6, 2007.

9. President Obama's Speech in Accra, Ghana, July 11, 2009

10. UNO, Africa Day Devoted to Debt Relief.

11. Skinner, Elliot P: "African Political Cultures and the Problems of Government", *African Studies Quarterly*, vol. 2, issue 3, 1998.

TEN
Further On The National Question

1. Zeleza, Paul T: *The Inventions of African Identities and Languages: The Discursive and Developmental Implications,* Selected Proceedings of the 36th Conference on African Linguistics, pp.14-26, 2006, Somerville, MA: Cascadilla Proceedings Project.

2. Speech by Minister Chukwuemeka Wogu at the Second International Conference on the Extinction of the Igbo Language, Oweri, Nigeria, July 20, 2010, in Report by Ngozi Sams: "Igbo Language May Go Extinct", July 20, 2010.

3. Fabunmi, F.A. & Salawu, A: "Is Yoruba an Endangered Language?", in *Nordic Journal of African Studies, 14, 3, 2005, 391-408.*

4.Wurm, S.A: *Atlas of World Languages in Danger of Disappearing*, UNESCO Publishing, 2001; Ndhlovu, Finex: "Language and African Development: Theoretical Reflections on the Place of Languages in African Studies", *Nordic Journal of African Studies*, 17, 2, 2008, 137-151; Bamgbose, A: *Linguistics in a Developing Country*: University of Ibadan Inaugural Lecture, Ibadan University Press, Ibadan, 1973.

5.. Assefa, Hizkias: "Ethnic Conflict in the Horn of Africa", in Rupesinghe & Tishkov, eds: *Ethnicity & Power in the Contemporary World,* UNU Press, 1996.